Liberty Theatres of the
United States Army,
1917–1919

Liberty Theatres of the United States Army, 1917–1919

WELDON B. DURHAM

McFarland & Company, Inc., Publishers
Jefferson, North Carolina, and London

LIBRARY OF CONGRESS CATALOGUING-IN-PUBLICATION DATA

Durham, Weldon B.
 Liberty theatres of the United States Army,
1917–1919 / Weldon B. Durham.
      p.   cm.
 Includes bibliographical references and index.

 ISBN-13: 978-0-7864-2539-6
 ISBN-10: 0-7864-2539-3
 (softcover : 50# alkaline paper) ∞

  1. Liberty theaters. 2. World War, 1914–1918 — Theater
and the war. 3. World War, 1914–1918 — United States.
4. Soldiers — United States — Social life and customs — 20th
century. 5. United States. Commission on Training Camp
Activities. I. Title.
D639.E8D87 2006
940.4'7 — dc22   2006015610

British Library cataloguing data are available

©2006 Weldon B. Durham. All rights reserved

*No part of this book may be reproduced or transmitted in any form
or by any means, electronic or mechanical, including photocopying
or recording, or by any information storage and retrieval system,
without permission in writing from the publisher.*

Cover photograph: Lobby and Box Office, Liberty Theatre, Camp
Grant, Illinois (National Archives, photo no. 165-ww-565b-26)

Manufactured in the United States of America

McFarland & Company, Inc., Publishers
  Box 611, Jefferson, North Carolina 28640
    www.mcfarlandpub.com

To David Schaal

Acknowledgments

I'm most grateful to John E. Taylor and Ed Coffee of the Modern Military Branch, Military Archives Division, National Archives, for their knowledgeable and patient assistance. Edwin R. Flatequal and Edward Anthony of the Washington National Records Center, Suitland, Maryland, did much to aim me toward the right warehouse bay and to make getting in and out of the facility as easy as possible. John Slonaker of the U.S. Army Military History Research Collection, Carlisle Barracks, Pennsylvania, and Col. Charles R. Spittler, chief of the Army's Special Services Division, allowed generous access to information about army entertainment services.

Oscar Brownstein, Patti Gillespie, Orville Hitchcock, and Alexander Kern read an early draft of this book and made many constructive comments. I'm also grateful to Stephen M. Archer and Larry D. Clark, colleagues at the University of Missouri–Columbia, for their assistance and counsel. Don Wilmeth also made invaluable suggestions regarding the scope of the book and the location of archival resources I had overlooked.

Lynn Rossy's persistent asking of the question, "Isn't that book done yet?" has many times gently goaded me back to the keyboard. She far surpasses the highest standard of spousal support.

Finally, I dedicate this book to David Schaal, a mentor and friend for the past forty years. David has lavished upon me the support and praise a writer needs to get past expressive blocks. His warm, unqualified acceptance has been a steady anchor in my life and in my career.

Table of Contents

Acknowledgments — vi
Introduction — 1

1. The American Theatre and the U.S. Army on the Threshold of Modernity — 9
2. Old Soldiers — 23
3. Camp Life Reforms in World War I — 29
4. The Purpose and Form of the Commission on Training Camp Activities — 36
5. Commercial Theatres or Government Theatres? — 48
6. Mobilizing the Commercial Theatre — 53
7. Tents, Theatres and More Theatres — 66
8. Money Matters — 84
9. Discord — 96
10. The Iron Hand — 101
11. The Tightened Rein — 108
12. Camp Shows —
    Tent Chautauqua — 116
    Musical Comedy, Tabloid Musical Revues and Burlesque — 119
    Comedies and Melodramas — 127

	Response to Touring Musicals, Comedies and Dramas	133
	Minstrel, Speciality and Concert Performers	137
	Motion Pictures	138
	Vaudeville	145
	Stock Companies	148
	Soldier Shows	150
13.	The Federal Government and the Entertainment Industry	156
14.	Demobilization and Army Theatre Since World War I	159
15.	Amateurs and Professionals: Conscience and Commerce	171
Appendix A. Liberty Theatre Openings and Closings		177
Appendix B. Liberty Theatre Expenses		180
Appendix C. Gross Receipts and Estimates of Attendance		182
Appendix D. Average Weekly Receipts of Liberty Theatres		185
Notes		189
Bibliography		205
Index		213

Introduction

In the winter of 1917-18 the United States' war-making machinery groaned and knocked under the stress of massive mobilization. Finished war goods were in short supply and the national rail system struggled to move raw materials, weapons, equipment and troops to designated locations. Devastating winter storms buried half the country under an icy blanket and coal for heating was limited to a miserly ration. In the middle of this turmoil and these feverish preparations to send a million or more soldiers to France, the U.S. War Department built and opened the first of 42 Liberty Theatres in nearly as many training and debarkation camps.

The Liberty Theatres have been little more than a footnote in histories of the home front in the Great War. Most commonly those footnotes have suggested inaccurate assessments of this project of the War Department's Commission on Training Camp Activities (CTCA) because historians have relied upon the soaring rhetoric of the wartime pamphlets proclaiming CTCA's goals in building and operating the theatres without looking closely at how the theatres were actually managed and what the managers actually put on the camp stages and movie screens. Nancy K. Bristow adroitly analyzes the CTCA's proclamations and sets them in the vivifying context of the broader progressive mission of constructing new ideals of masculinity and femininity. She rightly notes that founding declarations of intent suggest that the camp theatres would function to paternalistically control the troops and instill urban, middle-class values. But Bristow takes as accomplished fact what the CTCA said it would do. The CTCA told the public it would carefully examine plays and movies before they were shown in the camps so they would be morally uplifting.[1] But the CTCA's earnest avowals were little more than public relations ploys. Examining attractions before they appeared in the camps proved unworkable and screening committees were disbanded when they proved to be ineffective.

Bristow and Ronald Schaeffer also emphasize the CTCA's police efforts to suppress prostitution and the use of alcohol while minimizing their attempts to divert the attention of soldiers toward positive, constructive recreational programs such as the Liberty Theatres.[2] This book shifts the focus of history onto the CTCA's use of live theatre and movies as positive forms of social control, Indeed, the CTCA expended far more effort on diversion than on policing and vowed at the time that they believed constructive forms of recreation would be more effective than police work in shaping camp life around new ideals. This book explains why and how these theatres were built and run and discloses an enormous gap between what the CTCA promised and what was delivered to the camps. It also points out the significant legacy of the theatres and other recreational initiatives of the War Department and of the civilian service organizations, such as the Young Men's Christian Association, also supporting welfare and recreation projects in the army camps.

The United States' entry into the European war signaled this nation's readiness to assume unprecedented geopolitical responsibilities. The mobilization for war, the combat experiences that followed, and the precarious peace that emerged after November 1918 rapidly accelerated profound changes in the relationship of American society with its military establishment. This account of the Liberty Theatre project is a glass magnifying the remarkable alterations in military life wrought by a government acutely sensitive to its responsibilities to 4 million citizens it was conscripting and to their families and heirs. A modern military emerged from America's experiences in World War I to take its place in a society that has since become heavily militarized.

The story of the Liberty Theatres is also the story of the American theatre in an era when the theatre's function and organization as a cultural institution was undergoing radical changes. The business of producing and distributing commercial entertainment was in the era of World War I rapidly adopting a corporate model of organization and operation and abandoning the model of the independent impresario and the temporary business partnership. For 15 years two powerful and aggressive companies had battled for control of the legitimate theatre in America through acquiring theatres and winning exclusive contracts with popular stars and prolific and successful producers. In 1917, a few powerful businessmen maintained control of theatres, producers, writers, and performers with threats and abuse, onerous contracts only they could break with impunity, civil suits, lockouts, and blacklists. By 1917, motion pictures had made deep inroads into the theatre's economic base of audiences, theatres, actors and writers.

The theatrical touring circuits outside of New York had been vital to the process of extracting profits from productions validated by Broadway exposure and then sold in cheapened versions all over the country. Those circuits were falling apart and America's commercial theatre establishment was in financial crisis as the war began.

At the same time, a diverse noncommercial theatre, really without precedent in the U.S., was emerging in the form of art theatres in major cities, community theatres and play-reading groups in cities large and small, and amateur theatres on college campuses. European forms of realism and symbolism were altering the conventions of playwriting, while the motives and practices of acting ensembles such as the Moscow Art Theatre were revolutionizing American acting. A new non-painterly stagecraft born in the visionary experiments of the Swiss director and teacher Adolphe Appia and the English director and writer Gordon Craig was undercutting the dominance of the picture-frame stage. A modernist American theatre challenged the cultural supremacy of an old theatre redolent of dead or dying 19th-century values and procedures. This account of the Liberty Theatre venture provides a window looking out upon the fractional field of American theatre in a period of sweeping change brought about by the new technology of motion pictures, by incorporation as a way of managing business assets, by nearly revolutionary changes in the production and consumption of theatrical entertainment, and by the changing attitudes about entertainment and the use of leisure. Cultural reformation immediately before, during and after World War I altered the social function and status of all forms of entertainment, including theatre.

Liberty Theatres of the United States Army traces relations between the CTCA's idealistic leaders, the head of the CTCA, and the theatrical producers, managers, and performers forming the hands that finally delivered the goods the leaders idealistically envisioned. In doing so it represents the theatre and the entertainment industry of which it is a part at a time when it was moving from the margins to the core of American culture. The Commission on Training Camp Activities institutionalized legitimate theatre, vaudeville, motion pictures, and amateur theatricals as a vital part of the mobilization effort in World War I. The CTCA linked the entertainment industry, then undergoing revolutionary changes brought on by new management methods, new technology and the changing tastes of new audiences, with a rapidly modernizing army being refashioned to sustain the nation's new position in global politics and in the global economy.

Thus one sees in the pages of this book the outlines of two institutions undergoing far-reaching transformations. The CTCA masterminds who conceived the theatre project were clear about what they wanted to accomplish. However, they thought they could depend on an existing entertainment establishment, properly managed and disciplined, to achieve those goals. The field of entertainment was itself a complicated bureaucracy, and when the realization of the CTCA's reform vision required that establishment to innovate and reform itself, the CTCA encountered heavy resistance. In fact, the resistance was so intractable that the reformers frequently had to concede and conform to the ways of the entertainment business. They set out to oppose the values of popular entertainment but their theatres were ultimately co-opted by mass-market entertainment products. The story of the Liberty Theatres thus replicates in miniature the structure of the reform process that begins with idealistic hopes and devolves into tentative half-measures, and it highlights the difficulties endemic in managed, engineered, or administered social change.

* * *

The course of researching and writing this book has illuminated for me the many ways I have personally encountered the sweeping legacy of the Liberty Theatres, of the CTCA's other recreational initiatives, and of American society's evolving attitudes and actions toward its military veterans. In November 1951, my family—Dad, Mom and brother Larry—drove to California to visit my brother Bob at the Long Beach Naval Hospital. One of the most memorable events of the trip was meeting Eddie Cantor, heir to the entertainment throne once held by Al Jolson, who was appearing at the hospital as a volunteer for the USO. This experience at age 12 put me in close touch with an offspring of the Liberty Theatres, the camp and hospital shows of the United Service Organizations Inc.

The auditorium was partly a gymnasium, partly a theatre and partly a lounge with room for patients in wheelchairs and on gurneys. Cantor was there with an accompanist on the piano and he performed for about an hour at midmorning for fewer than 20 patients. He had magnificently large, white teeth and shining dark eyes and the blackest hair I'd ever seen. He was very relaxed and cordial, joking and singing, not from a stage but as he strolled from patient to patient, taking a hand here, sitting on the corner of a gurney there. He shook my hand and he spoke briefly with my little brother, Larry, who had eyes almost as large and hair almost as black as his. Then he was gone. I don't remember applause but I do remember his brisk, businesslike exit down the hall toward his waiting car. He didn't do a show. He just touched everyone and sang to them and talked to them and then he left. He was doing what hundreds of performers had done in Liberty Theatres, YMCA huts, and military hospitals in World War I. And what hundreds more had done in permanent and improvised performance venues around the globe in World War II.

A few years later I was a 20-year-old seaman recruit at the Naval Training Station in San Diego, spending a Sunday afternoon in the base library (a CTCA legacy), taking comfort I didn't at the time fully recognize from simply handling books. My attachment to books led me to volunteer to establish the ship's library (another CTCA legacy, although I didn't know that at the time) on an icebreaker during lengthy tours of the Arctic and the Antarctic.

At Pearl Harbor, Hawaii, where the navy sent me next (recompense for months of ice-bound service aboard the U.S.S. *Burton Island*) I became an habitué of the Submarine Base library and gymnasium and a basketball coach at a teen club serving families in military housing around the naval station. Movies at an outdoor theatre in a crater behind the Pacific Fleet headquarters cost a dime and equipment for hours of lunch-break volleyball was free. Three years later, now a college junior at San Jose State University, I won a role in the chorus of a college musical by shamelessly swiping and using a goofy grin I'd seen on the face of a performer in a USO troupe from the University of Oregon touring a musical through the Pacific region. The Vietnam-era G.I. Bill supported my graduate education in Iowa, and, more recently, the U.S. Department of Veterans Affairs awarded me compensation for hearing loss suffered while I was in the service. The perquisites I have encountered exist as a result of reforms in military life and federal responsibility for the welfare of veterans put in place in World War I and its aftermath. And my experiences have been far from unique, for they have also been the experiences of millions of servicemen and women

* * *

Records of the Commission on Training Camp Activities, located in the National Archives, as well as records of the Construction Division of the Office of the Quartermaster General of the U.S. Army, located at the Federal Records Center, Suitland, Maryland, are primary sources for this history of the Liberty Theatres. Government documents such as the *Annual Report* of the U.S. War Department, and the *Report of the Military Entertainment Committee of the War Department* provided some corroboration of statements of purpose and an overview of the achievements of the venture. Newspapers published in the camps and preserved by the Library of Congress have been examined, as have microfilm copies of newspapers from cities near the training camps. The trade journals of the entertainment industry further illuminate conditions in the industry and the industry's view of the camp theatres. CTCA and Quartermaster papers reveal the purposes and organization of the camp theatre venture and they describe the buildings, their equipment and operations, as well as the titles of some of the attractions (plays, movies, concerts, vaudeville shows and soldier shows) presented in them. Further details about the attractions have been recovered from standard theatre history sources. Papers in the Shubert Archives, New York City, provide valuable insights into the personality and professional style of Marc Klaw, who was the CTCA's first theatrical booking agent. These details, highlighted against a background of information about recreational programs in military training camps and regular army garrisons before, during, and since World War I, afford a glimpse of the significance of the Liberty Theatres as a crossing of the paths of an emerging modern U.S. Army and an emerging modern American theatre.

The book begins with an effort to place both the American theatre and the U.S. Army in the proper context at a time of sweeping changes. This first chapter surveys an array of societal forces converging in the construction and operation of the camp theatres. There follows an account of how various forms of amusement and recreation, especially theatre, have been abiding on the margins of military culture since British troops occupied major colonial cities and the Continental army camped in sites as inhospitable as Valley Forge, Pennsylvania. Two succeeding chapters discuss the political, social, and strategic motives for reforming military camp life as the American army mobilized for combat in France. The genesis and makeup of the War Department's Commission on Training Camp Activities is also clarified to reveal the interests and competencies of the persons selected to serve on the CTCA. Two chapters on the initially wary relationship between military camp commanders, the CTCA, and America's commercial entertainment establishment reveal how the predispositions of the generals, key CTCA operatives and key business leaders in the American theatre slowed and disabled the camp theatre project in its earliest days.

Five chapters are devoted to accounting for how live entertainment and motion pictures were brought to the camps, how the theatre buildings were designed and constructed, and how money was raised to operate them. The CTCA haltingly attempted to improve the efficiency of their management of the camp theatre project. Dissension marked early relations between those in the CTCA from the field of recreation and those in the field of commercial entertainment. New leadership emerged in December 1917. Several resignations and reassignments in early 1918 swept aside the dissenters and paved the way for greater management coherency.

Chapter 12 offers an examination of each of the several kinds of entertainment brought to the training camp stages and vividly illustrates how operatives steeped in the ethos of the status quo can refract the light of reform ideals. The number, size and locations of the camp theatres meant that virtually all available entertainment resources, except the first rank of the biggest stars in the newest, most popular shows, were drawn upon to keep the camp stages filled. Accordingly, this account of the camp theatres offers a rather unique snapshot of the kind and quality of entertainment ordinarily available outside the country's major theatre centers in 1917–1919.

The drama of the army training camp theatres of World War I has a lengthy denouement, because, after 20 years of dormancy, the concepts and practices of the CTCA were revived, revised, and deployed in World War II. Moreover, in constantly changing forms they continue to be a part of the military experience to this day. That history is briefly sketched in chapter 13, while conclusions and reflections on the significance of key events in the history of the army camp theatres and of the whole venture are offered in the final chapter.

1

The American Theatre and the U.S. Army on the Threshold of Modernity

In January 1918, a few months into America's direct involvement in the European war, President Woodrow Wilson's War Department was amassing a force that included the Regular Army, made up mostly of volunteers; the National Army, made up of draftees; and the National Guard, a military reserve controlled by the individual states but equipped and called into service by the federal government. The Regular Army was being trained in service facilities already in existence, such as Fort Sheridan, Indiana. The National Army was being mobilized in 16 new camps scattered around the country, and the National Guard was being brought into fighting trim in another 16 new camps. Building these camps and cantonments was a construction feat second only to the making of the Panama Canal, and it was accomplished in just three months.

In 1914 the Regular Army numbered just over 90,000, and only about a third of those were prepared to engage in the European war. Preparedness measures in the next three years raised army strength to just under 400,000. Then came a massive conscription campaign and in the 19 months before the armistice the United States Army, as the combined federal force came to be known, grew to just under 4 million. Over 1.5 million of these soldiers eventually stood to fight alongside exhausted, occasionally mutinous British and French soldiers in the hundreds of miles of twisting trenches stretching from the English Channel to the Swiss frontier; they faced an exhausted and starving German army dug in to the clay and rock of northern France.

The scope and form of this massive mobilization was unprecedented in American history and it radically altered the institution of the U.S. military. The U.S. Army became in 1917–19 the modern political instrument it has shown itself to be in World War II and the Cold War that continued for another 44 years, in Korea and Vietnam, and in the Middle East. At the end of the 19th century, the Regular Army had an academy-trained, professional officer corps, but the ranks of the enlisted were scorned as indigent wastrels, and the military was seen as a haven for the lawless and violent. The army of 1900 was also strategically marginalized through commitment to garrison duty, border protection, and coastal defense, but in 1917 it began to emerge as a formidable feature of the nation's political and cultural life and an awe-inspiring weapon abetting the nation's growing geopolitical and imperial interests. The nation needed forces capable of conducting industrialized warfare on an intercontinental scale and the Wilson administration created just such an instrument of modern realpolitik. Mobilization for total war and the creation of a new military for a new age of geopolitical responsibility necessitated the forging of links between the military and the nation's industries—agriculture, manufacturing, and transportation—and so was born the military-industrial complex that has become a dominant political and economic force.

The Wilson administration's idea of a modern military included heavy dependence on citizen-soldiers, patriotic men and women who would pass quickly and efficiently from civilian life through military training and into deployment, and then, when the conflict was over, return to their civilian lives, unharmed (except as through combat) and infused with a heightened sense of national pride and community spirit. Wilson took a step toward realizing his idea of a new military by opening the mobilization camps to faith-based social welfare organizations. He took the precaution of appointing trusted civilian aides to oversee their work and to close training camps and their environs to prostitutes and alcohol, then thought to be root causes of military delinquency. He also endorsed efforts to civilize life in the training camps and in bivouacs of the American Expeditionary Force in France so that service in the war would leave soldiers unscarred by their military experience; indeed, their lives would be spiritually, mentally and emotionally enriched.[1] What form did these civilizing efforts take? A snapshot of a wintry day and evening in one of the new training camps will expose one of those initiatives.

* * *

Everything about Camp Sherman, Ohio, was new and raw. It had been hurriedly hammered into being from July to September 1917 in quickly cleared level fields a couple of miles north of the village of Chillicothe. On

September 5 the camp began receiving young men freshly drafted from Ohio, western Pennsylvania and West Virginia. When their training was completed, the green soldiers became part of the 83rd Division, an element of a "National Army."[2]

By January 10, 1918, almost 33,000 soldiers occupied this precisely patterned city of over 1,300 unpainted new buildings. Winter bit hard into southern Ohio, sending waves of blizzards across the upper Midwest. At Camp Sherman still-falling snow and moaning winds muffled and distorted the sounds of drill commands issued to formations of shivering soldiers weaving two by two through deep trenches of drifted icy whiteness. Winter-weight uniforms had not yet been delivered, so soldiers bundled against the cold as best they could without greatcoats and proper headgear. Bitterly cold drafts whistled through the raw pine siding of the hastily constructed barracks buildings in the temporary camp, chilled the food in the steel trays in the mess halls, and bit at the feet of clerks curled up in front of typewriters in offices. The laundry was warm down to a worker's waist, but spilled water froze in minutes on the concrete floor. Only the bakery was toasty and snug. Winds whispered through cracks in the deformed siding on latrines. Comfort was not to be found.

Two feet of snow blanketed the camp and the narrow roads to Chillicothe. The railroad spur linking the camp to Columbus, 35 miles to the north, was the only way in or out. Icy winds kept the daytime temperatures near zero. More and worse was on the way as a deep low rolled out of the central Gulf into the path of a high pressure cell tracking into the Ohio Valley from the Pacific Northwest. Gale force winds, heavy snows and arctic cold lay ahead.[3]

Nevertheless Thursday's training went ahead mostly as scheduled. At four o'clock the men were free from military duties until the call to Retreat, the final assembly of the day, at 5:45. In the interim, gear had to be cleaned and stowed, machinery serviced, and horses groomed and bedded down. Those who quickly finished these tasks had a brief time to rest, smoke, and talk. Barracks buildings, each providing beds and lockers for 60 men, bustled as soldiers warmed themselves and prepared for Retreat and for the evening meal. Additionally, service buildings manned by soldiers assigned to the Division Exchange Officer or by representatives of the Young Men's Christian Association, the Knights of Columbus, the Jewish Welfare Board, and the Salvation Army also welcomed men looking for a respite from barracks life. Here they could find a place to sit and relax or read a newspaper or magazine or play a board game. Some joined singing groups lead by civilian musicians assigned to the camp. A few found their way to a library, planned by the American Library Association, staffed by civilian volunteers and supplied with donated books. Beneath the blanket of snow and ice were

Liberty Theatre, Camp Sherman, Ohio. The men pictured not identified. Billboards announce coming attractions, including *Hans und Fritz*, a tabloid musical based on a long-running comic strip by Rudolph Dirks. *Hans und Fritz* was produced by Gus Hill, a director of the Columbia Amusement Company, the dominant producer of burlesque. The show toured camps from late February through April 1918. Stagehouse bracing is visible at far left, and the angle of the incline of the auditorium floor is evident from the positions of the exit doors (courtesy National Archives, photo no. 165-ww-565b-35).

areas cleared for playing fields. NCOs promised boxing instruction and competitions and calisthenics when weather permitted.

Company commanders made a few final announcements at Retreat, including the news that the camp theatre would open at 7 p.m. in Section F on Elyria Street between Cleveland Avenue and Cincinnati Avenue, and that the first of the long-promised musical shows would be offered. The "Liberty Theatre," as it proclaimed itself on its facade, had been open unofficially since December 3, so it was no stranger to the soldiers— many had gone there to see movies offered by the Division Exchange Officer.

The play announced for this evening on billboards around the theatre was *Flora Bella*. Few in the camp had heard of the Viennese-styled operetta written by German-born Felix Doermann, then revised and adapted by British dramatist Cosmo Hamilton and American actress Dorothy Donnelly. John Cort had produced it at the Casino Theatre in New York just over a year earlier. Viennese operetta, characterized by its reliance on danceable waltzes given elaborate orchestrations, and by romantic tales involving handsome soldiers who court feisty, playful heroines in fashionable homes and elegant palaces, had been in vogue on the American stage for almost 30 years. However, ill feelings toward Austria and Germany put a temporary end to the vogue in 1914. Hamilton and Donnelly had heavily Americanized their adaptation and had shifted the locale to Russia, an ally of the Western powers in the European war, the side heavily favored in public opinion at the time. It ran 112 performances, just enough for it to be called a hit by those marketing a cheapened version of the show mounted in Chicago for a regional tour. It is highly unlikely that anyone in the audience at Camp Sherman recognized the names of any of the members of the small company playing one-night stands across mid–America.

And the ticket prices, at 25 cents and 50 cents, about half what the soldier could expect to pay at a civilian theatre, made the soldiers wince. Each private's meager monthly paycheck of about $36 was already ravaged by the time he received it. Almost all were buying war bonds or thrift stamps, and each soldier's war insurance premium took a healthy $8 bite each month. Some were compelled by law and by their own consciences to contribute at least $15 to the support of a family.[4] After these inroads, a private had only a few dollars to buy smokes, treats, toilet articles and a fare or two into Chillicothe. Still, the thought of seeing some lively dancing girls and hearing a few jokes and songs, especially in the soldier's own theatre, seemed enough to break down resistance. That evening, despite the high price of a ticket, the dubious appeal of the show, and the penetrating winds and threatening snows, over 2,000 soldiers lined up at the camp theatre entrance.

The building was huge — one of the largest in the camp — seating just over 2,200 on one floor. Those paying 25 cents sat in side sections and at the rear of the house where sight lines were poor and where one could hear little except the loudest musical numbers. Those who paid 50 cents sat in the more desirable center section. All perched on long wooden benches. Legroom was ample, but the benches and their backs were hard, unpainted planks. The floor, too, was bare, unfinished wood, so the shuffling of the 4,000 boots added to the din created by the battering winds and the regimental band playing popular and patriotic songs from the theatre orchestra pit.

As promised, the new manager of the Liberty Theatre, a "real" theatre man sent out from Washington, addressed the crowd, as did the camp commander. Frank Lea had only a few words — mainly promises to supply the men with the best entertainment available. The general briefly emphasized the need for recreation and diversion as a complement to the hard work of preparing to win a war. These preliminaries aside, the soldiers were ready for the main attraction. The regimental band, now under the direction of the theatrical company's musical director, stepped fretfully into the unexplored territory of the show's score — a collection of tunes by the French composer Francis Cuvillier, with English lyrics by Percy Waxman — which critics had tossed off as pleasant but unremarkable. Soon the curtain parted to reveal the generalized elaborate interior, a part of the camp theatre's stock of scenery. The freshly painted but otherwise old-fashioned setting was supposed to represent the country house of a minor nobleman in Czarist Russia, but the only quality it projected was a vague sense of tinseled opulence. The soldiers had to imagine the Russian décor designed by the renowned Austrian artist Joseph Urban that had been the highlight of *Flora Bella*, according to the New York critics. The libretto, in all respects typical French farce, concerned a vital but restless young nobleman and his oddly prudish wife. The soldiers who paid enough attention to follow the plot learned that the nobleman's wife is a former cabaret dancer, a fact she is bent on concealing from her husband. He discovers a photograph of an alluring woman in dancing tights who strongly resembles his demure bride, but she exhibits far more sexual fire. He takes his discovery to his father-in-law, a penniless cad who has lived for years off his daughter's cabaret earnings. The old man tells his son-in-law that the picture shows his wife's twin, a woman the young nobleman has never met. In a trice, the husband is off to Petrograd to meet his scintillating sister-in-law. Meantime, the wife also has been persuaded to return to Petrograd to dance one more show to help her old dance master. Incredibly enough, the excited husband sees the show, falls in love with the dancer and so rekindles his waning affection for his wife.[5] The story, one of many similar ones offered by Cosmo Hamilton in dozens of novels, plays and musicals, helped earn the author the soubriquet of "the evangelist of sex contentment."[6]

Had there been a soldier in the crowd with sophisticated tastes in musical comedy, he surely would have thought the evening unremarkable at best. The brilliant solo voices, the vivacious dancers, the animated actors needed to invigorate the stuffy conventions of *Flora Bella* were not to be found in this road company. Those with little experience of metropolitan, middle-class theatre must have been equally disappointed if not indeed baffled by the marital troubles of a philandering Russian nobleman and his deceitful spouse. Those sharing the convictions of most of small-town and rural America might have been offended by the spectacle and the story. Still more, perhaps the majority of the men in attendance, experiencing little sex contentment at that time, might have been delighted that the chorus girls in the second act's cabaret scene were indeed right there, on a stage, to be sure, but only a short walk from those miserably cold, lonely barracks and parade grounds.

1. The Threshold of Modernity   15

At the final curtain, the players rushed to the tiny dressing rooms backstage, changed, packed, and made their icy way to the siding where their railcar waited to shuttle them back to Chillicothe. The company manager was there to rush them aboard, regretting more deeply every minute that he hadn't ended the performance early and returned to Chillicothe where they stood some chance of avoiding a costly travel delay. Even as the second act curtain had been going up, he and Frank Lea had totaled and split the box office receipts, 70 percent for the company and 30 percent for the theatre. The receipts came to a respectable $1,068, despite low-priced tickets (50 cents), bad weather and sparse advertising. The company manager's share allowed him to pay his expenses and deposit a small profit to the producer. A weather delay would be costly, perhaps even disastrous for the producers, because they operated on such a narrow profit margin.

Frank Lea viewed his share as a fine start for his camp theatre. He paid no rent, the utilities were free, and the soldier help was inexpensive. His overhead was less than 20 percent for the evening, including a stipend for the band and a small wage to the soldiers who helped in the box office and backstage. When he was able to get to Chillicothe, he'd be able to make a comforting deposit in the theatre's bank account.

Snow silenced the grinding wheels of the touring company's railroad car as it slowly shunted toward Chillicothe. Choking drifts closed streets, walkways, and roads in the blacked-out camp. Outside the windows of the car nothing moved except the whirling whiteness and the whining wind. In silent barracks the exhausted men burrowed deeper into their rough blankets and tried to shut out the cold seeping through the flimsy walls.

The *Flora Bella* company reached Chillicothe, but they missed their next few dates as the worst blizzard in anyone's memory halted all transport and most industry throughout the upper Midwest and the Ohio Valley. The next two days, soldiers at Camp Sherman endured some of the most dangerous circumstances they would know this side of the Atlantic. Temperatures reached minus 15 degrees and winds of nearly 50 miles per hour heaved up mountains of snow. The Liberty Theatre was deserted until near the end of the next week.

* * *

The Liberty Theatre at Camp Sherman was the first of 42 camp theatres established and operated in U.S. Army training camps throughout the United States in the next 13 months, and its first days are emblematic of the history of the entire project. The War Department's Commission on Training Camp Activities built the theatres from appropriated funds, but their operations were financed, with the exception of the local managers' salaries, out of box office receipts. Given this arrangement, the Camp Sherman experience on January 10 seemed to promise a bright, profitable future for the project. A near capacity audience gathered despite cruel weather conditions and reached into shallow pockets for admissions that paid for the talent and left the theatre with a small profit as a hedge against less prosperous evenings. Additionally, a scheme for providing free admission was already underway. If it worked one of the most mettlesome problems facing the camp theatres—the poverty of the soldiers—would be solved.

Frank Lea could have genuinely believed that his portion of the vast War Department experiment in improving the quality of camp life was launched into months of vital, popular, and profitable service. Camp Sherman's Liberty Theatre remained in near-continuous service until July 6, 1919, closing only during the worst weeks of the influenza epidemic in October 1918. During its 73 week history, soldiers saw seven to nine attractions each week. Touring professional shows such as *Flora Bella* made up less than a third of the calendar; motion pictures, vaudeville, and amateur talent, including soldier shows, made up the bulk of the theatre's offerings. The population of Camp Sherman varied from 16,000 to 32,000, and wide swings from week to week were common. Yet in all that time the theatre's 2,228 seats were filled to only about 36 percent of capacity, and its average weekly receipts were just under $1,400.[7] Had business continued at the pace established opening night, the weekly average would have been almost eight times as much. Clearly, the Camp Sherman theatre did not live up to its opening night promise of popularity and financial solvency.

Moreover, records of receipts and attendance for all the camps indicate that the Liberty Theatre at Camp Sherman enjoyed a degree of esteem and prosperity that was *above average*. The 42 army theatres offered space for over 26 million admissions between January 1918 and August 31, 1919.[8] Although 8.5 million admissions are recorded, this amounts to only one-third of the capacity of all the theatres. But popularity and debt-free operations are standards appropriate for a commercial theatre. Criteria for judging the success of the army theatres should include not only their purposes but also their adaptation to or resistance to the material conditions in which they operated. The durability of their legacy must also be considered.

* * *

Allen F. Davis' survey of the wartime achievements of a number of progressive reform movements concludes that the reformers scored their most impressive victory in the Army camps. There the CTCA applied social work techniques and programs and processes of the nascent recreation movement to the problem of entertaining soldiers and protecting them from the brutalizing effects of the traditional military experience.[9] Indeed,

Secretary of War Newton D. Baker came to believe that the CTCA, in providing places of amusement and recreation in the mobilization camps, had promoted a sense of community that would make returning soldiers better citizens. Speaking at the dedication of the Liberty Theatre at Camp Humphreys, Virginia, December 5, 1918, Baker suggested that the commission's programs, of which the theatres were the most visible manifestation, would elevate community life in America and infuse the nation with a "new sense of power of associated manhood." He also opined that these results might be some compensation for the terrible loss of life, labor and wealth caused by the war.[10] Raymond B. Fosdick, CTCA chairman, added that the theatre program was "an imaginative undertaking and one of the outstanding achievements of the Commission."[11]

Henry F. May has designated the period from 1912 to 1917 "the first years of our time."[12] From one perspective those years might be regarded as the time of the libertarian's nightmare. Progressives and those deeply influenced by progressive discourse advocated and achieved measures sharply increasing government intervention in business practices and in the economy. The Federal Reserve Act (1913) reformed the currency system and increased the government's power to regulate the economy. The Fed as it now familiarly known, became deeply involved in the nation's banking system, working to limit the threat of recurrent banking panics caused by overexpansion of credit, inadequate bank reserves, and inelastic currency. In 1913, the Sixteenth Amendment to the Constitution gave Congress the power to impose an income tax. A federal income tax quickly followed. In 1914 the Wilson administration helped create the Federal Trade Commission, empowered to enforce antitrust laws, prevent false and deceptive advertising, and investigate the workings of business to keep Congress advised of how well the antitrust laws were working. The Clayton Antitrust Act (1914) extended the government's regulation of big business, and the Keating-Owen Act restricted child labor, thereby limiting business and industry access to this cheap and malleable workforce.

The government that inserted itself into banking and business offices and into personal pocketbooks also created the Commission on Training Camp Activities. The CTCA interpolated itself deeply into the military culture with programs that have endured to this day. The CTCA's reform-minded bureaucrats also engaged in a struggle with the denizens of America's deeply fragmented and polarized theatre business. The resulting spectacle may be viewed as a comic drama in which the idealistic reformer, naïve but wrapped in red, white and blue, encounters the jaded entrepreneur, willing to respond patriotically but certain from experience what shape the response should take and reluctant to alter common production and distribution practices.

The good, clean fun provided in the Liberty Theatres was the result of the complicated, often strained, marriage of an avowedly lowbrow civilian entertainment business and a high-minded camp reform movement conceptualized by progressives in the administration of President Woodrow Wilson. The spectacle of CTCA managers steering the camp theatre program through the rocks and shoals of mobilization, complex daily operations, and swift demobilization illustrates what happens when idealistic agents of change clash with deeply recalcitrant exponents of the status quo. Unlike the revolutionary who pulverizes those who resist or respond with anything less than complete submission, the reform ideologue analyzes the situation, identifies the problems, proposes solutions to improve the situation (all done according to a vision), then begins a dialogue with defenders of the status quo. The dialogue is supposed to lead rational parties to discover and implement rational, consensual solutions. A common result of this process is that ideals are compromised or abandoned as the status quo envelopes and neutralizes them. Another outcome is a growing cynicism about reform. Philosopher Kenneth Burke has called this process "the bureaucratization of the imaginative" and an account of the Liberty Theatres illustrates it. Burke thought the bureaucratization of the imaginative was a basic process of history whereby agencies of utopian change become enmeshed in the very social texture they try to alter.[13]

As the Wilson administration's imaginative camp reforms came to full realization their new ideas of what the military training experience ought to be encountered older, established practices and attitudes. As the American entertainment establishment was asked to respond to the challenge of deploying their products in a new way to new audiences, the first response was enthusiastic but subsequent actions indicated resistance to change. Everywhere in the camp theatre project, the old became entangled with the new and differences and divergences cropped up. These encounters, sometimes acrimonious but often merely annoying, necessitated compromise, and that compromise often produced unintended by-products, the weight and force of which sometimes amplified the reform effort, but more commonly the old ways neutralized, distorted, or subverted the reforms.

In this respect, this book is guided in part by the observations of Robert Weibe, Warren Sussman and Michael McGeer about progressive reforms. Weibe's synthesis of the history of the "search for order" from 1877 to 1920 concluded that progressives developed an approach to reform but that they mistook the application of their bureaucratic methods for actual reform achievement. He claims that progressives might have been emotionally committed to reform objectives but their vision set those objectives at too great a distance from the status quo of the moment.[14] Sussman observes that America's social reformers could not sufficiently detach themselves from the world they sought to change, so they could not avoid being co-opted by that world.[15] Michael McGeer is still more emphatic in sustaining Weibe's thesis. A crusading middle class was driven by progressive ideals to promise utopian outcomes: the control of big business, the amelioration of poverty, and the purification of politics, but also the transformation of gender relations, the regeneration of the home, the disciplining of leisure and pleasure, and the segregation of genders, races and economic classes. McGeer argues that progressive reformers turned on popular culture because theatres, movies, dance halls, and ballparks promoted too much mingling. Recourse to these pastimes dislodged from the grip of the church and the home the shaping of personal identity. These venues were especially troubling because they offered women a new, freer identity and they exalted individualism and open sexuality.[16] Certainly, the CTCA set out to discipline the purveyors of amusement but at the same time they had to solicit the patriotic support of those they sought to drive toward a higher moral plane. The achievement of their dual goal was both impeded and abetted by structural changes occurring in the field of entertainment.

If the camp theatres were an element of military reform they were also a manifestation of a theatrical reformation that began about 1910. For the next two decades, until 1930, American entertainment passed through the first phase of a process through which it is still passing. The best way to comprehend the scope of the reformation of entertainment is to begin by looking briefly at what entertainment has become. Today, the mass-market products of the entertainment industry pouring out of Hollywood, Nashville, and New York, to name but three of the most fabled capitals of the new religion of entertainment and starworship, are designed and marketed for profit by corporations targeting very large market segments that are emotionally and economically malleable. Television and motion pictures, popular music, and trade publishing of popular books and mass-circulation magazines occupy positions in what French sociologist Pierre Bourdieu calls the "field of large-scale cultural production."[17] The field of cultural production is the site of an intricate system of relations among agents and agencies involved in the production, distribution, and reception of works that consist in part of symbolic goods. A Harry Potter novel and a James Bond movie are examples of symbolic goods produced and distributed in the field of large-scale cultural production. The Disney corporation's long-running Broadway hit, *The Lion King*, is an example of theatre for the large-scale market, whereas a critically celebrated *Killer Joe*, by Tracy Letts, winner of a Fringe First Award at the Edinburgh, Scotland, Fringe Festival, is an example of a work accruing capital other than economic. It was produced for an elite theatre audience in what Bourdieu has called the field of restricted production. *Killer Joe* has appealed to theatre connoisseurs and practitioners, acquired critical honors, and won for the author access to a worldwide collection of noncommercial theatres.

The American theatre of 1910 occupied a position in the field of large-scale cultural production similar to that now occupied by motion pictures, for instance: it was a business devoted to producing and distributing symbolic goods designed to give pleasure to a mass audience through its nationwide network of theatres featuring Broadway hits on tour. However, American theatre since 1910 has changed its position in the field of cultural production. Since then its commercial function has declined to a mere skeleton of what it once was, while theatre created by amateurs and professionals in organizations and venues supported mainly by unearned income has proliferated to become the theatre most Americans experience, if they experience theatre at all. Theatre has thus been repositioned from the field of large-scale production for the market to the field of restricted production for elite and specialized audiences.

By 1917 art and community theatres, early manifestations of restricted production, were beginning to emerge. These alternatives to commercial theatre included ethnic theatres catering to populations of Germans, Yiddish-speaking Russians, Italians, African Americans, Latin Americans, and Scandinavians. The era of World War I also witnessed the beginning of the study of drama and theatrical production in colleges and universities. Theatre as a laboratory for the teaching of dramatic art was another example of operations in the field of restricted production. Among these manifestations of restricted production one should also number the government's camp theatres. As will be seen, the camp theatres shared with community theatres and campus theatres a noncommercial, educational, and developmental mission. Interestingly, despite this avowed mission, mass-market products, notably live professional performances and motion pictures selected from among those readily available to civilian audiences, dominated the camp stages.

Observers of our modern theatrical scene can see that the direction of change in the mainstream has been away from "show business," in which theatrical products are marketed by profiteers, and toward the use of theatre as a recreational and educational instrument aimed at training and refining minds and hearts. Although for-profit commercial theatre is still alive, the theatre in 20th-century America has been undergoing a process of consecration. The once-pervasive view of theatre as a form of diversion has been challenged by a view of theatre as a means of enlightenment. The army theatres participated in this movement in its infancy.[18]

The camp theatres were also a manifestation of the progressive drive toward social purity. Nancy K. Bristow's recent study of the Commission on Training Camp Activities focuses on the commission's rhetoric of suppression and imposition. She writes that the CTCA was primarily devoted to the prevention of venereal disease, and "all of its programs—social hygiene, education, recreation, law enforcement, and prophylaxis—address this responsibility directly."[19] Certainly, the Military Draft Act made suppression of prostitution and control of the sale and use of alcohol in areas around the camps prominent CTCA objectives. However its founders believed that "young men spontaneously prefer to be decent," and that "wholesome recreation" was the key to transforming the camp milieu.[20] Accordingly, the suppression and control of vice became less important in reforming camp life than providing facilities and programs for the expression of "wholesome," creative, and positive motives.[21] The CTCA should be remembered at least as much for its theatres and libraries, its athletic leaders and facilities, its musical directors and songbooks as for its prophylaxis stations, its VD posters and films, its police efforts and its social work with women and girls in the cities near the camps.

The camp theatres of the Commission on Training Camp Activities exemplify a truly positive progressive reform, a social program dominated by a belief that camp conditions could be improved not only by the suppression of vice but also, and more significantly, by the addition of invigorating social and artistic activities as an alternative to vice. Moreover, it is clear from the published thoughts of Newton Baker that the commission's programs, as well as its support of the activities of private, faith-based organizations, such as the Young Men's Christian Association, were designed not only to alter military camp life but also to invigorate the whole of American society with a new sense of cohesiveness and solidarity. The camps were thus envisioned as model cities and the training experience of over 4 million Americans who passed through them was seen as a lesson in the rights and duties of citizenship. The Liberty Theatres were also a product of a public recreation movement coalescing in the years just before the European war enveloped the United States. Governments and volunteer societies such as the YMCA and the YWCA were beginning to try to exert social control in cities impacted by immigration by seizing control of leisure time and its activities. The movement drew energy from the adult education movement, from the efforts of cities to develop playgrounds, parks and green space, and from the founders of settlement houses.[22]

An identifiable "recreation movement" has since merged with other cultural movements promoting specific kinds of leisure pursuits. Recreation rhetoric has always stressed participation rather than spectatorship; mental, moral, and physical development rather than reckless hedonism or idle relaxation; and easily and cheaply accessible public parks and playing fields rather than commercial entertainment venues, such as sports arenas and stadiums, theatres, concert halls, and dance clubs. In this view the recreation movement was an early form of the anticorporate, antispectatorial, ecological and environmental green movements of today.[23] Recreational use of theatre has been long a part of soldier life, often in spite of prodigious barriers. The theatres in the training camps of World War I were conceived as an expression of the ideals of recreation leaders in the CTCA. Initially, the CTCA thought only of providing professional entertainment on stages in the camps, but a volunteer in the New York office of the CTCA, Kate Oglebay, persuaded the organization to develop a way to stimulate the production of soldier shows and to train a few soldiers to produce soldier shows when divisions were shipped to France. Oglebay's idea ultimately became the source of one of the CTCA's most enduring and pervasive legacies.

The tumults of the twentieth century have pervaded the lives of virtually every inhabitant of the planet: in the U.S. alone tens of millions of men and women have served in the military, navigating the potentially dangerous shallows between their independent moorings in civilian life and their place in the uniform convoys launched "to make the world safe for democracy." Most have been sustained in part at least by civilian organizations such as the Commission on Training Camp Activities or United Services Organizations (USO), established in 1941 and continuing to serve military personnel off base. The Special Services Branch, created in 1918, succeeded the CTCA, and today the U.S. Community and Family Support Center, headquarters for Morale, Welfare and Recreation, continues programs pioneered by the CTCA that have become a pervasive feature of today's army. The Liberty Theatres were a humanitarian, utopian enterprise that betokened remarkable changes in the political and social status of the U.S. armed forces. The Liberty Theatres and other projects of the CTCA stand at the head of a line of programs extending from 1917 to the present day, a line that includes cultural icons as widely known as the Bob Hope Christmas Show and the camp shows of World War II, the Korean War, the Vietnam War, and the recent conflicts in the Persian Gulf region. That heritage also includes social welfare programs for veterans now deeply imbedded in American life, such as the several editions of the G.I. Bill for providing postsecondary education for millions of veterans.

2

Old Soldiers

The diaries, letters, and recollections of the common soldier from the Revolution to this day testify to the deadly monotony of camp life. No matter how frantic or prolonged the combat, the soldier's hours between the battles and the years between the wars have been either tedious or empty. Fatigue duties—cooking, cleaning, building, repairing—and drill have seldom lightened the heavy hours. Isolation from friends and family, from civil companionship and the attention of women has been the cause of uncounted physical and spiritual casualties.

A list of the ways soldiers have responded to the drabness of camp life looks like a catalogue of humankind's pastimes. Some diversions have been beneficial, affording pleasures that sharpened the mind, refined the instincts, and cultivated the body. Others have won for the fighting man the off-duty reputation of drunkard, whoremaster, and gamester. These pursuits have too often led to mental and physical breakdown, disease, and crime. Moreover, not until recent times has military officialdom abandoned the policy of routine acceptance of the view of the common soldier as a brute and expressed an enlightened concern for that person's social and spiritual welfare.[1]

Members of the British army garrisoned in the American colonies before and during the Revolutionary War performed plays for amusement, charity, and profit. In 1753, in a move that might have been consciously contemptuous of local mores, British officers garrisoned in Albany, New York refitted a barn and presented George Farquhar's *The Beaux' Stratagem*. The play, one of the masterworks of the English Restoration, had been among those so vigorously and effectively attacked by Thomas Rhymer, Jeremy Collier, and others some 60 years earlier. It and others like it from the pens of George Etherege, William Wycherly, and William Congreve, had been all but expelled from the patent theatres of London. In Albany, *The Beaux' Stratagem* scandalized some who found it coarsely ribald and decadent. Later, a performance planned by the British garrison in Boston met with such strong resistance from locals that it was cancelled.

In the early years of the Revolution the British army controlled urban centers and made rather heavy use of the theatres located in them. The Continental Congress of October 1774 forbade all theatrical presentations in the colonies, condemning them as wasteful and dissolute. In spite of this edict and the harsh conditions of their encampments, Continental army troops presented plays. Col. William Bradford wrote to his sister that troops performed Joseph Addison's very proper heroic tragedy *Cato* at Valley Forge, Pennsylvania, on April 15, 1778. He noted that theatrical amusements would continue, and he named several plays from the standard British repertoire of the time. After the British evacuated Philadelphia, the occupying Continental troops gave performances in the Southwark Theatre in September and October 1778. In October 1778, the Continental Congress passed two more resolutions banning theatre, but officers and common soldiers continued to perform.[2]

The army that developed after the Revolutionary War was mainly a frontier constabulary, subject to austere funding that often failed to provide for pay, supplies, quarters, arms and munitions. In addition, the public feared a large standing army, and, in the words of one commentator, regarded those who served as "beasts and blockheads." Soldiers in the peacetime army spent most of their time building and maintaining frontier forts. They lived as did the civilian pioneers they policed, clearing land, building shelters and providing food and services for themselves, their comrades and their officers. Pay, food, and clothing came erratically. They farmed, hunted, and fished because they would have gone hungry otherwise. Hard labor, drill and garrison routine left soldiers little time for recreation or amusement.

Whiskey was part of a trooper's life. He received a daily ration and, often, an additional amount when on a work detail. Drunkenness was common. Traders offered more whiskey for sale when the soldiers were paid, and camp followers offered sexual gratification. Saloons and bordellos offered these services as the frontiers became more settled. Prostitution, drunkenness, and gambling were facts of the soldier way of life, tolerated by military authorities and accepted by the public as the usual pursuits of the men in blue.

Letters and diaries commonly note the monotony of garrison life filled with chores and punctuated by occasional training exercises. Where the terrain permitted, many pursued outdoor sports such as hunting and fishing. Checkers and card games were common barracks pastimes and soldiers organized occasional dancing parties. Any garrison included a few musicians, and an amateur actor was not uncommon. Music was an important part of soldiers' lives, and singing was popular, especially among soldiers from German ethnic backgrounds. Thespian societies flourished in garrisons throughout the 1830s, '40s, and '50s, but the existence of a theatre club does not necessarily mean that plays or skits were rehearsed and performed. At some posts soldiers converted unused spaces into theatres. No record indicating the nature or extent of theatrical activities before the Civil War has survived.

Soldiers had to have the initiative to seek opportunities for recreation, amusement, and expression. The only source for funding such efforts, outside the change in their own pockets, was the post fund, created mainly by payments from the post's sutler. Sutlers, who operated the post stores, paid for the privilege, giving the post fund from 10 cents to 15 cents per month for each officer and man in a garrison.

In the Civil War, Billy Yank and Johnny Reb were also eager sportsmen. Footracing, wrestling, and boxing built physiques and encouraged individual aggressiveness. Team sports such as football, cricket, lacrosse, and baseball ("bass ball" in the South) developed group spirit and filled otherwise dreary or dread-filled hours. Even juvenile pastimes such as marbles, hopscotch, and leapfrog were popular with men famished for diversion. Many leaders noted that unorganized playfulness could break out into aimless horseplay and violence, but few did anything about it. Homesickness, despondency, and mental fatigue were common, but officers gave little attention to nurturing the morale of their charges. Military commanders seemed to believe that the organization of group or individual sports was either beneath their concern or best left to the men themselves.

A like attitude prevailed toward other types of recreation. Reading was a common pastime in Union camps, and soldiers eagerly purchased newspapers, even though 10 cents per copy was often beyond their means. Cheap thrillers and dime novels flooded the camps, while civilian groups donated quality books and periodicals of value to units that maintained small libraries and reading rooms.

Music has always been a popular antidote to boredom. Johnny Reb seems to have been especially given to singing. Observers sketch the image of the warrior in gray singing quietly or boisterously to himself. John Howard Payne's "Home, Sweet Home" was reputedly most popular in both the North and in the South. Soldiers harmonized with informal groups or participated in a camp jubilee during which hundreds of soldiers would gather to sing. Several regiments had glee clubs, and bands were common, though seldom very accomplished. Minstrel bands made up of folk instruments and instruments improvised from camp utensils were often remarked upon.

Dramatic and theatrical offerings were popular in both the Northern and Southern camps. Variety shows included burlesques of many aspects of army life, as soldiers lampooned the compassion of surgeons, the honesty of quartermasters, the humanity and intelligence of officers, the palatability of food and the generosity of whiskey rations. Minstrel turns alternated with the trial scene from Shakespeare's *Merchant of Venice* or the first act of *Richard III*. The vast majority of the entertainers were amateurs—the soldiers themselves. Occasionally, though rarely, soldiers were entertained by traveling civilian performers. A young and promising Steele MacKaye, later an innovator in stage mechanics and a crusader for greater realism in acting, starred in soldier shows in the Baltimore area. James E. Murdoch, an eminent and versatile tragedian, abandoned his stage career for a time to entertain Union troops in camps and hospitals. The Lombard troupe entertained the Union forces at Vicksburg, and the Hutchinson family gave performances to troops in the East. But whether amateur or professional, the theatricals were officially regarded as superfluous, at best.

The camp life of Johnny Reb and Billy Yank was hard and the duty was dangerous, but the conscripted soldier or volunteer of the Civil War engaged a task with a seeming end and campaigned from a base of civilian and governmental support. The regular enlisted soldier of the following 40 years was not so blessed.

From the Civil War to the Spanish-American War, the U.S. Army policed the nation's western frontier and manned posts often built at great distances from any city. Poor mail service, crude quarters, nutritionally and aesthetically inadequate food, menial labor, and inadequate recreational services compounded isolation from home, parents, and friends. A typical squad room housing from 30 to 100 men was more like a dungeon than a home. Reading and writing were out of the question because of poor light from a handful of candles. Ventilation was poor and sanitary conditions were crude. Soldiers slept in pairs in rickety wooden bunks, piled two or three high. They used one blanket and one sack filled with straw or hay and an assortment of roaches and bugs. Apathy, fatigue, discontent, and demoralization prevailed in America's frontier garrisons.

The principal foods were beef, salt pork, bread, coffee, and beans, and there were no trained cooks to transform these staples into palatable meals. Quartermasters sold a portion of the soldier's rations and used the receipts to buy vegetables, condiments, and recreational equipment. Congress frequently threatened salary reductions and sometimes enacted them. One time Congress dismissed without making any appropriation for army pay. Foreign-born troopers recruited mainly from the crowded immigrant ghettos of the cities of the East made up 50 percent of the ranks of the army in the decade following the Civil War. This proportion declined to about 35 percent in the last two decades of the 19th century, but the dismissive or hostile attitude toward immigrants that has marred our nation's history meshed neatly with the view of the enlisted regular soldier as an outcast to deepen antimilitary antagonism. Civilians despised enlisted service, regarding soldiers as lawless wastrels or desperate dandies. A prejudice against army life was thought to be "wholesome — the aversion of every free man to become a machine."[3]

Gambling, drinking, and whoring continued to flourish, but, as before, there were other amusements — hunting, fishing, theatricals, dances, and holiday celebrations. Soldiers used military libraries and appreciated regimental bands. Baseball continued to be a popular game for soldiers in the period after the Civil War, and the excitement of sports — running, weight lifting, calisthenics — did much to break the monotony of garrison life. Soldier-run canteens and post exchanges, providing enlisted men a place to purchase necessities, eat, relax, read, bowl, or play billiards, replaced the sutler and the post trader.

Since the government did little to provide even the simplest athletic or game equipment, the men themselves generated most recreational activities to relieve camp conditions. They sang or played simple musical instruments; they read, when chaplains were successful in soliciting books, newspapers, and magazines from civilian sources. Athletics were popular, but inadequate equipment and space limited play. Amateur theatricals livened a few evenings during the winter months in spite of official indifference. But boredom and loneliness were perhaps more commonly relieved at the post trader's store, where rot-gut whiskey was readily available, and at "resorts" near the posts, where blowsy whores enticed, infected, and collected. Drunkenness and venereal disease were second only to desertion as the cause of inefficiency in the ranks.

Reform movements in the late 1870s and early 1880s brought some relief. Squad rooms were made more livable with the addition of oil lamps and single, steel-frame bunks. Steam laundries and sewage and bathing facilities were provided. Authorities officially sanctioned and promoted canteens, or social halls, offering the off-duty soldier a place for amusement and recreation. Quartermasters stocked post libraries and reading rooms; soldiers were given sports equipment and encouraged to participate in baseball, football, and lacrosse. The new emphasis on leisure was seen also in an increased number of minstrels and amateur theatrical events at some posts.

While these changes helped make garrison life more bearable, they were not revolutionary. Prostitutes still gathered in large numbers near major camps and drinking in the ranks was very heavy. In 1905 moralists and political commentators debated the advisability of selling beer and light wines in post canteens, and a *Nation* article noted the incidence of desertions, courts-martial and medical incapacitation for drunkenness and venereal disease and bemoaned the "low tone of the Army."[4]

Military life in 19th-century America, whether in periods of war or peace, was an enervating mixture of long days of tedious routine and brief hours of chaotic and dangerous exertion. To make matters worse, in peacetime the public disparaged enlisted service and regarded the army as a haven for society's dregs. Officials rarely paid any attention to the conditions of camp living. Officers and noncommissioned officers struggled to teach recruits the rudiments of tactics and weaponry. Once learned, however, these lessons were useless to bored, discontented, sick, or drunken soldiers. Something had to be done to offer the soldier constructive ways to use his leisure time.

The appearance of theatres and other recreational facilities in army training camps in 1917-1918 was, in a word, miraculous, given the nation's history of antimilitarism and indifference to the soldiers' welfare. Just as remarkably, two politicians noted for their distrust of the military, President Woodrow Wilson and Secretary of War Newton D. Baker provided the impetus to change a soldier's experience to make it more like the social and civic life he had presumably known as a civilian. Wilson and Baker vowed to themselves and to an antimilitary American public that they would keep alive the conscripted soldier's mind and spirit and heart through months of training and waiting for the battle despite isolation from sustaining civilian social forms. Moreover, they promised they would return the soldier to society bettered by his military experience rather than degraded.

Perhaps the most unexpected tool they used to achieve the ends they sought was theatre. Given patrician indifference to commercial theatre and the outright hostility toward theatre expressed in most progressive social reform movements, it is remarkable that theatre was included at all in the mixture of activities provided in the camps. But the astonishing fact is that building theatres in the training camps, sending commercial shows to them, and providing drama coaches to train soldiers how to produce their own shows was a key element of a campaign to assuage the nation's strong antimilitarism and to assure the citizenry that military service would not degrade soldiers but might lift them to a higher plane of social responsibility.

3

Camp Life Reforms in World War I

At the beginning of the European war in 1914, the image of the enlisted regular soldier was little changed from earlier times. He was better fed, better housed, and his social welfare was better attended, but he was still disparaged and discredited as immoral and violent. As the European strife continued and America was drawn nearer the maelstrom, military and political leaders viewed with dismay the conduct of the army's action against the Mexican rebel Francisco Villa. On March 9, 1916, Villa and a band of some 400 soldiers sacked the small town of Columbus, New Mexico. In the surprise early morning attack, the Mexicans killed and wounded citizens and soldiers stationed there, while suffering heavy casualties in the streets of the town and as they retreated down the road to the international border. Within a week Brig. Gen. John J. Pershing, commanding the garrison at El Paso, led 5,000 regulars into Mexico in pursuit of Villa. Tensions mounted between the two governments, and President Wilson mobilized 160,000 National Guardsmen from all over the U.S and stationed them in Texas, New Mexico and Arizona along the border with Mexico. The guardsmen patrolled the border and the regulars pursued Villa until February 1918, when the expedition was recalled to El Paso and the guard demobilized. The conflict involved only 11 skirmishes that left 15 American soldiers dead and 31 wounded. Many more casualties resulted from camp life conditions in the isolated posts along the Mexican border.[1]

Wilson had appointed Newton D. Baker as secretary of war in March 1916. Baker, a longtime friend of Wilson's from the days when they lived in the same boarding house near Johns Hopkins University in Baltimore, had established himself as an effective progressive reformer while mayor of

Cleveland, Ohio. Newspaper accounts of drunkenness and debauchery among the guardsmen encamped near San Antonio and along the border from Brownsville, Texas, to Douglas, Arizona, created a small crisis for the Wilson administration. They needed reliable information about the situation. Wilson suggested Baker send Raymond Fosdick to tour the camps, observe conditions and write a report.

Raymond Blaine Fosdick was a younger brother of Harry Emerson Fosdick, the noted preacher, professor of practical theology at Union Theological Seminary in New York, and, later, leader of a Modernist revolt against fundamentalism in the Baptist Church. Raymond was born of a family of few means in Buffalo, New York in 1883. He studied jurisprudence and constitutional government at Princeton University under Woodrow Wilson, and they remained lifelong friends. Following a master's degree at Princeton in 1906, Fosdick studied law at the New York School of Law, a course he completed in 1908, when he was admitted to the bar of the state of New York. While a law student, Fosdick lived at the Henry Street Settlement on the Lower East Side. There he taught history to settlement house clients and admired the urban reform principles and tactics of the settlement's founder, Lillian Wald. Wald started the Henry Street Settlement in 1894 as a visiting nurse service, but by the time Fosdick volunteered to teach there the settlement house included a savings bank and a library, and it offered vocational training for boys and girls and theatrical activities for adults.

Fosdick became assistant corporation counsel in the city government and later New York City's commissioner of accounts, a type of inspector general responsible for auditing the financial records of city offices. He served as counsel for a grand jury chaired by oil magnate John D. Rockefeller, Jr., investigating police corruption and prostitution in New York. Fosdick's service added Rockefeller to his circle of influential friends. In 1912, at Woodrow Wilson's request, Fosdick served as comptroller and auditor of the finance committee of the Democratic National Committee during Wilson's presidential race. Once Wilson was elected, Fosdick left politics to join the Bureau of Social Hygiene (BSH), newly established by his former associate, Rockefeller. For two years, Fosdick traveled through Europe studying how the police controlled prostitution, and in 1916 he published a book on the subject. He had also studied how American police responded to prostitution, but his war service delayed the publication of his book on this subject until 1920.

When Fosdick stepped off the train in San Antonio in July 1916, he carried the imprimatur of the president and his secretary of war. He was also an associate and personal friend of one of the wealthiest and most powerful men in America. And he was a seasoned investigator whose views were grounded in sweeping knowledge of his subject and in the idealism of a committed Progressive reformer.² Fosdick started his survey in San Antonio in late July 1916, and he traveled by rail and automobile to Brownsville and up the Rio Grande valley and along the international border in southern New Mexico and Arizona.

He found the conditions in San Antonio the worst. Regulars from Fort Sam Houston and guardsmen from Illinois and Wisconsin billeted at Camp Wilson crowded San Antonio's renowned red light district. Prostitutes solicited soldiers on the streets of San Antonio and on the country roads to and around Camp Wilson. Fosdick found the provost guard unable to exercise any control over the situation and the local police indifferent to it. The medical officer at Camp Wilson reported to Fosdick that his staff treated as many as 200 soldiers each day for symptoms of venereal disease.

Everywhere Fosdick traveled conditions were much the same: teeming sex ghettos, street prostitutes, disease, and drunkenness overseen by ineffectual or corrupt military and civilian police. Some commanders successfully restricted access to brothels and prohibited the sale and consumption of liquor; most either ignored the situation or abetted the panderers and purveyors by assigning military police patrols merely to keep order in the sex and saloon districts. The officers who ordered the patrols believed that troopers were restless animals who needed prostitutes and alcohol as antidotes to military discipline. For political reasons and because it hurt legitimate businesses, local civilian authorities uniformly opposed efforts to abolish or restrict saloons and brothels.

Fosdick suggested military police close the sex ghettos to any traffic by uniformed personnel. He recommended a strong anti-prostitution stance by the War Department to encourage local resistance, and he suggested Baker appoint a council of officers and physicians to formulate a unified and effective policy to be adopted by all division commanders.³ Later, Fosdick reported to the House Committee on Military Affairs that "the fellows went to the devil down there because there was absolutely nothing to do. The temperature was 100 or 120 sometimes, and there was no place where they could read and there was nothing for them to read.... There were no homes into which they could be received ... and out of sheer boredom they went to the only places where they were welcomed, ... the saloon and the house of prostitution."⁴ Fosdick's testimony emphasized recreational alternatives to vice, a priority he maintained when he was again called into national service in April 1917.

Fosdick discovered that military officialdom accepted bestial living conditions and behavior as a normal condition of warfare and service. He deplored this attitude as much as he despised the waste of humanity. He recommended radical changes in the soldier's life, and the reforms were launched less than one year later.⁵

Fosdick's ideas were realized so quickly because they were planted in the minds of men philosophically predisposed to change the army and powerful enough to effect widespread reforms. The administration of President Woodrow Wilson was apprehensive about the military, suspecting that militarism was essentially antipathetic to the institutions of a democracy.[6] Wilson had been reelected in 1916 after a campaign that stressed his success as a neutralist, and his appointment of Newton D. Baker as secretary of war further indicated his antimilitary bias. Baker made no secret of his strong prejudice against the army. He regarded war as an anachronism and professional soldiers as relics of a barbarous past. To Baker the West Point code of "Duty, Honor, Country" was a naive oversimplification and the soldier's commitments to brutal force an "over-extended adolescence."[7] Both Wilson and Baker looked upon the militarization of millions of young men as an evil whose effects should be minimized by all available means.

In a letter to President Wilson on the eve of America's entry into the European war, Baker suggested that the large army to be raised would encounter the same morale problems experienced on the Mexican border. He wrote that "homesickness, liquor, and cheap motion-picture shows seemed to be the greatest causes of military delinquency," and he proposed to do something to alleviate these ills. In early 1917, recalling Fosdick's report on conditions on the Mexican border, Baker sent Fosdick on a quick tour of Canadian training camps for more ideas about what might be done in the U.S. camps. Baker's supreme attempt to humanize military training was the creation of the Commission on Training Camp Activities, an entity initially suggested by Fosdick.[8]

Baker established the CTCA to deal with the political and social problems he and President Wilson believed to be associated with military mobilization. The nation was deeply divided over the wisdom of U.S. entry into the European war and over the necessity of conscription.[9] CTCA programs were in part an effort to make mobilization more palatable. Wilson and Baker acted to assuage concern that a generation of young men would be brutalized by military training and service, to say nothing of actual combat, in what was known to be one of the deadliest conflicts ever foisted on the people of the planet. More specifically, this Progressive administration was dedicated to reducing or eliminating the dangers of venereal disease and drunkenness, common elements of military camp life. Moral concerns apart, VD and alcohol abuses were known to be the leading causes of illness among soldiers and of failures of military preparedness, so the commission was assigned the difficult task of suppressing prostitution and the sale of alcohol in the civilian areas adjacent to the camps. Thus the CTCA was a political instrument shaped by antimilitaristic and moralistic energies. It was also an expression of a practical concern for the physical and spiritual welfare of men in training in the U.S. and in rest areas away from the front in Europe.

Baker's justification of the CTCA also revealed anxiety about other potentially corrosive effects of military training and service in a European war:

> These boys are going to France; they are going to face conditions that we do not like to talk about, that we do not like to think about.... I want them adequately armed and clothed by their government; but I want them to have an invisible armor to take with them. I want them to have an armor made up of social habits replacing those of their homes and communities, a set of social habits and a state of social mind born in the training camps, a new soldier state of mind, so that when they get overseas and are removed from the reach of our comforting, restraining, and helpful hand, they will have gotten such a set of habits as will constitute a moral and intellectual armor for their protection overseas.[10]

Baker's words reveal that the CTCA was born not only of a concern about the barbarous conditions of military camps and trepidation about the permissiveness and carnality of European culture, but of what the genteel, white, protestant, and male leadership regarded as the moral decay of the American cities hosting many of the camps.

Under Baker's reform leadership, the army's new training camps were conceived as model communities. They would be the entryway to a distinctly unconventional military experience. The new army would instill a new state of mind, different from the conventional military set of attitudes, different from the easy manner of the European, but also different from the relativistic, multi-ethnic, and secular ethos of urban America.

Nowhere did anxiety about the decay of cities become more evident than in the progressive era's response to prostitution. Mark Thomas Connolly has observed that in the first two decades of the 20th century "prostitution became a master symbol, a code word, for a wide range of anxieties engendered by the great social and cultural changes that give the progressive era its coherence as a distinct historical period."[11] Reform theory, especially as it applied to the campaign to purify the training camp environment, tended to reduce the problems of the camp environment to drunkenness and prostitution, and the reformers tended to see all sexual activity outside of marriage as some form of prostitution.[12] Antiprostitution and its bookend issue, temperance, were about sex and alcohol, surely, but they were also about much more. They were about the apparent undermining of the simple values of family, farm, and village, an ethos assuming cultural and ethnic homogeneity and thought to be an appropriate model for social development everywhere, including the congested, ethnically diverse and industrialized cities. Temperance and purity rhetoric and action grew out of the fear that the young of the nation, especially those of the "lower orders," meaning the urban immigrant underclass, were reeling out control in their pursuit of pleasure. Antiprostitution campaigns aimed to close red-light districts where teeming brothels huddled side by side with fetid, dank saloons dispensing beer laced with benzene to produce an epidemic of violent crime, venereal disease and alcoholism. But the campaigns also cast a disapproving eye on the proliferation of independent young working women in the cities, women who chose neither celibacy nor marriage. Antiprostitution rhetoric also drew on the alarmed belief that immoral (i.e., outside marriage) sexual activity was a plague and that sex was becoming depersonalized and despiritualized in direct violation of the ruling ideals of middle-class domesticity. Moreover, sex and alcohol ghettos violated the bourgeois presumption of cultural unity as much as did ethnic and class ghettos.

But antiprostitution and temperance movements also recognized the swelling volumes of economic, sociological and medical evidence of the rapid spread and horrible effect of venereal disease and the heavy social and economic cost of the abuse of alcohol.[13] The expenditure of public funds for camp theatres was part of ongoing "purity" campaigns aimed at containing sexual impulsiveness among the young by offering them "wholesome," "constructive" alternatives to the "cheap amusements" linked in the reformers' minds with vice. Progressive reformers in pursuit of social justice in the ghettos of America's cities viewed commercial recreation as a major contributor to social decline in the cities and the weakening of family bonds in tenement households. Settlement workers seemed to believe that an earlier generation of children had sought recreation out in nature: swimming, hunting, and fishing. Upon their return home fires lighted families taking meals together, praying together, singing and telling stories and developing connections that strengthened the children's moral fiber. Crowded tenement apartments and bustling city streets offered no space for such pursuits. The trouble began at the corner candy store where children ruined their bodies by filling up on sweets and learning to smoke, while they heard coarse talk and learned to gamble. The boys graduated to poolrooms and the girls to dance halls, then to saloons. Forms of street play and cheap theatre — vaudeville, melodrama, burlesque and nickelodeon movies — further stunted moral growth. Melodrama served up in "ten-twenty-thirty" (the scale of admissions) theatres offered sex and crime: visions of robberies and shoot-outs as well as sensually provocative love scenes. Cheap amusements substantiated an ethos very much at odds with the behavioral tenets of evangelical Protestantism, one of the ideologies underpinning progressivism.[14]

The connection between commercial amusements and moral torpor is evident in the observation of Richard Henry Edwards that commercial recreation degraded the young and joined with commercial vice "to form one great series of exploitations by which the vicious and criminal prey upon the innocent."[15] Edwards, a sociologist working for the Young Men's Christian Association at the University of Wisconsin, wrote a series of study guides, of which his *Popular Amusements* was one number, to be used by "community interest groups" discussing social problems and proposing solutions for them. Edwards was an exponent of the recreation movement, a political and social-action front dedicated to intervening in what they believed to be a positive way in the leisure choices of young Americans. Recreation reformers saw too many young men and women (they seemed especially concerned about young women) abandoning "civilized," Victorian morality to seek sexual adventures in dance halls, saloons, nickelodeons, and theatres, to name but a few of the venues the reformers proscribed. According to Jane Addams, co-founder of Hull House, Chicago, one of the first social settlements in the U. S., Americans had "turned over the provision for public recreation to the most evil-minded and the most unscrupulous members of the community."[16] Concerned that an emerging and uncontrollable mass culture had the potential to demoralize the youth of America, recreation reformers led a movement to organize programs to resist the new, hedonistic forms of popular play. Again, the words of Jane Addams, an eloquent and influential spokeswoman for the early recreation movement: "It is as if our cities had not yet developed a sense of responsibility to the life and the streets, and continually forget that recreation is stronger than vice and that recreation alone can stifle the lust for vice."[17]

Raymond Fosdick recruited leaders of the recreation movement when he assembled the Commission on Training Camp Activities, and they brought with them an antipathy for commercial amusements. Their attitude seriously complicated the process of mobilizing the commercial entertainment industry when the time came to build and supply camp theatres that would be an alternative to venues outside the camps.

4

The Purpose and Form of the Commission on Training Camp Activities

Localism and volunteerism were the cornerstones of Baker's political and social doctrine. He was generally opposed to the creation of new agencies that might place more power in federal hands, believing that the home front should be manned as far as possible by existing agencies.[1] Moreover, Baker also believed that social inducements were more effective than social restraints. He deemphasized law enforcement and suppression and accentuated the use of wholesome recreation to counterbalance the temptations of drink and sex.[2] Not surprisingly then he eagerly turned to established welfare and recreation organizations and somewhat reluctantly to the commercial entertainment establishment for the ideas, money, and manpower to provide a new kind of camp life for the men in training. The commission was intended to regulate and coordinate the activities of the independent welfare agencies and to stimulate volunteerism among other groups and individuals capable of providing vital camp services. The Army General Staff wanted to exclude civilian organizations from the camps, but Baker's policy prevailed.[3]

Fosdick asked Baker to appoint a single committee of about seven persons to advise him on training camp activities, and Fosdick offered 22 names of leaders in social welfare, recreation, and theatre who might serve on the board. Baker confirmed Fosdick's recommendations and made him chairman of the group.[4] The commissioners were to act as a "clearing house" for ideas about providing recreational and other facilities for men in training camps.[5] President Wilson took a personal interest in the work of the commission and regarded it in a similar light. Wilson claimed that the federal government promised the people that their men would be returned to them "with no scars except those won in honorable conflict," and he believed a democracy owed its defenders an environment within which bodies could be strengthened, minds enriched, and spirits enhanced.[6] The Commission on Training Camp Activities was the means whereby that debt could be paid.

Baker's selection of persons to serve on the commission further reveals his idea of the scope of its task, for he appointed members on the basis of past experience with the kinds of activities the commission was to supervise. Fosdick chaired the CTCA, and, because of his knowledge of police organization, he supervised the law enforcement functions of the commission.

Baker and Fosdick selected Lee Hanmer, director of the Recreation Department of the Russell Sage Foundation, to oversee the commission's recreation and entertainment programs. Hanmer was responsible for planning the camp theatre project and was its manager until February 1918. Hanmer was a spokesman for those in the recreation movement concerned with what they perceived to be the rapid growth of decadent forms of popular entertainment. His appointment to the commission reflected Secretary Baker's belief that degrading commercial amusements had undermined troop morale on the Mexican border in 1916. It also betokened the commission's antipathy toward the commercial theatre establishment to which it was soon to turn for shows for the camp theatres.

Hanmer's employer, the Russell Sage Foundation, was a national leader in the application of the methods of social science to the solution of the problems of cities caused by industrialization, urbanization, and immigration. Even before the formal declaration of war, officers of the Russell Sage Foundation met with Secretary of War Baker and others to offer the foundation's services in the coming conflict. Indeed the foundation's entire Division of Education and its Division of Statistics closed down in April 1917 and the staff of the Department of Recreation became the core of workers supporting the Commission on Training Camp Activities. The location of the headquarters of the CTCA in the New York offices of the Russell Sage Foundation underscores its alignment with the recreation movement.[7]

Hanmer joined the Russell Sage Foundation staff in 1907 as field secretary for the newly formed Playground Association of America, and he quickly gained a national reputation advising citizen groups across the U.S. about how to establish public playgrounds and parks. In 1911 he became a member of the General Committee of the National Board of Review of Motion Pictures, a body that attempted to censor films produced in the U.S. His office at the Russell Sage Foundation facilitated recreation surveys sharply critical of popular amusements, such as dance halls attached to saloons, motion picture arcades, and nickelodeons. He assisted and advised the author of a book called *The Exploitation of Pleasure* that sharply criticized the commercial entertainment industry of New York City.[8] Hanmer later became acting chairman of the CTCA when Fosdick made investigative and peacemaking trips to France.[9]

Malcolm L. McBride, president of a Cleveland, Ohio, mercantile firm, had been selected by Mayor Newton D. Baker to assist in drafting Cleveland's home rule charter. He also served on the Distribution Commission of the Cleveland Foundation, a trust fund devoted to the establishment and support of city parks and other recreational facilities. McBride was first charged with establishing general stores in the camps. Later, in February 1918, he focused his business management skill on the camp theatres, succeeding Lee Hanmer as the commission's entertainment manager.

Dr. John R. Mott, president of the Young Men's Christian Association, represented the YMCA and the YWCA on the commission. An aide, John S. Tichenor, actually directed the YMCA's huge camp welfare program and spoke for Mott. Joseph Lee coordinated recreational service in towns near the camps through the War Camp Community Services (WCCS), the wartime manifestation of the Playground and Recreation Association of America, of which Lee was president from 1910 to 1937. Lee was perhaps the most influential of the pioneers of public recreation. A proper Bostonian trained in the law, Lee acquired the reputation of a "muckraking radical" as he argued for the use of recreation not only to "Americanize" immigrants, but also to inculcate traditional small-town values in big city ghettos. He was a distinguished philanthropist and author of *Play in Education* (1915), a classical statement of the philosophy of the recreation movement.[10] His appointment to the commission was a strategic attempt to focus the energy of the recreation movement on marshaling the social and recreational resources of communities near the camps for support of the soldiers in training. Under Lee's leadership the WCCS helped communities arrange for housing camp civilian workers and visiting dependents of the soldiers, and to open swimming pools, barber shops, and eating establishments to soldiers on leave. WCCS also organized stage shows, dances, and movies for the men in training.[11]

Dr. Joseph E. Raycroft, professor of physical education at Princeton University and a leader in the movement for more intramural athletics on college campuses, administered the CTCA's athletic programs. His main task was to supplement calisthenics and close-order drill with competitive sports in a more comprehensive army physical fitness program. Raycroft assigned 44 athletic directors and 30 boxing instructors in various camps and had them build organizations in camp to get soldiers to play baseball, football, and soccer; to provide training in boxing and wrestling; and to involve soldiers in cross-country running. Raycroft oversaw the allocations of athletic equipment to the camps.[12] Each of these appointments emphasized Fosdick's and Baker's commitment to recreational, regenerative alternatives to police suppression as a means of improving the environment of the training camps.

In June 1917 Baker made more appointments that broadened the field of expertise on the commission. Gen. Palmer E. Pierce, Baker's personal aide, provided liaison between the commission and the War Department General Staff. Charles P. Neill, a noted labor authority and former United States commissioner of labor under presidents Roosevelt, Taft, and Wilson, supervised the construction of camp library buildings. Fosdick hired Jasper J. Mayer, a social welfare worker, as executive secretary and seated him on the commission. Mayer served until April 15, 1918, when W. Prentice Sanger replaced him.

Lee Hanmer at first worked with advocates and practitioners of amateur and noncommercial theatre, but they made little headway toward providing shows for the camp theatres. In August 1917 Fosdick added to the commission Marc Klaw of New York City, a partner in the theatrical booking agency of Klaw and Erlanger and president of the United Manager's Protective Association, an organization representing major New York theatre producers in their relations with organized labor. Fosdick later added two more members. Eliot Wadsworth, philanthropist and financier, represented the American Red Cross, and John G. Agar, noted for his ardent interest in municipal reform, spoke for the United War Work Campaign, fund-raiser for the civilian organizations serving the camps.

Baker's appointments precisely articulated his hopes for improving training camp life. A counterbalance to Baker's antimilitarism was his belief that military training, if properly conducted, could promote the realization of progressive social ideals and could sustain middle-class virtues of patriotism, respect for authority, energy and efficiency, reverence of women, chastity, temperance, and personal cleanliness.[13] Baker believed that the training camps should be more than mere replicas of the cities and towns from which the young men were to be drafted. They should provide the soldier many of the cultural and social advantages of civilian communities; moreover, they should be vast proving grounds for civic reforms only hesitantly and partially adopted in American cities.

The camps were to be what later generations of planners would call model cities. The military and the CTCA prohibited the sale of alcohol in or near the camps, thereby modeling prohibition as it would be prescribed in the Volstead Act in 1919. They also established tough, ground breaking measures to suppress vice and to prevent the spread of venereal disease. Finally, under the guidance of leaders of the fledgling public recreation movement the CTCA aimed to make the training camp experience a model of the planned use of leisure time.

The commission's members faced an enormous task and the pace of mobilization allowed them little time to accomplish it. Moreover every program they instituted from sex education to group singing was largely untested in application to so large and diverse a population scattered in 20,000- to 40,000-person segments around the country. Much had to be learned by trial and error, and there were many trials and many errors. The mobilization and training of the army was centered in 32 new camps, mostly in the Southeast, but also sprinkled throughout the Midwest and along the eastern and western seaboards. Conscripted soldiers were to be trained for service in 16 divisions, each composed of about 27,000 draftees. To accommodate mobilization of these divisions and the training of more thousands of replacements, the War Department built cantonments, each a hastily constructed city of about 1,500 unpainted, wood-frame buildings. They mobilized 16 divisions of the National Guard in tent camps located in the southern and southwestern states where the winters were warmer. The camps and cantonments were designed to accommodate 40,000 soldiers each so that levies of new draftees could be housed even as full divisions remained encamped. Construction of the camps began in June 1917, and by September draftees flowed into them, although they were not completed until November.[14] But these were not the only new camps called for in war plans. Huge debarkation camps were built at Tenafly, New Jersey; Mineola, New York; and Newport News, Virginia. Coast artillery replacements were training at Camp Eustis, Lee Hall, Virginia; field artillery at Camp Knox, West Point, Kentucky; engineer replacements at Camp Humphreys, Belvoir, Virginia; and army aviation pilots and crews were training at Kelly Field, San Antonio, Texas. All these eventually had CTCA programs, including Liberty Theatres.

The proliferation of new camps and the flood of trainees compounded the commission's problems, but so did the fact that the inductees differed in important respects from the citizen Baker and Fosdick had in mind when they conceived the work of the commission. Baker and Fosdick imagined that the "invisible armor" fitted to the needs and interests of the conscripted soldier would be like armor suited to the idealistic and well-educated volunteer already beginning to swell the army's ranks, especially in the Plattsburg camps. Named after a summer training camp established at Plattsburg, New York, in 1915 the Plattsburg-type camps offered basic military training to make better officers out of college students or business and professional men seeking or possessing commissions in their state militia. The Plattsburg campers were serious enough about their training to pay for it themselves, but the camps also offered cheerful camaraderie and healthy recreation for outdoorsmen. Additionally, the Plattsburg camps were designed to inculcate patriotic and nationalistic values in a select group of influential citizens with the hope that these citizens, whose love of country had been stimulated, would pass those values along to their civilian contacts.[15] Baker and Fosdick seemed to have believed that the training camps could do for the draftee what the Plattsburg camps had tried to do: provide lessons in citizenship and national unity, rudimentary military training, physical conditioning, and recreation in a wholesome, stimulating environment. Baker also likened the training camp to the college campus and the inductee to a college boy.[16]

The draftees entering the camps in the late summer of 1917 were much less educated and more ethnically diverse than anyone had anticipated. The typical soldier was young — just 22 years old — and unmarried. He came from the lowest economic levels and had little formal or technical education. Draft-age men with skill and education were often exempt and allowed to continue to work in war-related industries. One in five of the conscripts was foreign-born and spoke only street English at best. Three of 10 could not read at all or read too poorly to understand simple written instructions, so training, welfare, or recreation programs could not reasonably presume literate clients. Psychological tests given soldiers revealed little about native intelligence but a great deal about the low level of social sophistication of most draftees. The draftee was surprisingly naive about common pastimes of the middle class. Observers estimated that three-quarters of the men didn't understand the idea of play itself, so they had to be taught its value and the rules of organized games. The men enjoyed singing, but they knew few songs. Baseball and campfire crooning were unaccustomed modes of diversion. Urbanity, a presumed correlative of sophistication, was less evident among the draftees than had been anticipated. The typical soldier was either a farmer or had been raised on a farm. Moreover, soldiers from urban areas tended to be drafted into units and trained together so that urbanity might be very high in some camps and very low in others. The social and educational background of trainees posed a challenge to commission activities that depended upon the knowledge of middle-class mores and manners, literacy, urbanity and the homogeneity of camp populations.[17]

Baker was certainly aware that the scope of the commission's business precluded any easy success. He may have suspected that the real inductee would differ from his preconception, but he and his appointees were undaunted. The twofold task confronting them — to police the camps and to supply recreation programs— was vigorously assayed by volunteer organizations, termed the "seven sisters" by the men, and by special agencies created by the commission. The volunteer efforts were enormous.

On April 26, just one week after the commission was established, the Young Men's Christian Association offered to provide social welfare and recreational programs in the camps. Their campaign was extraordinary. The association built and staffed nine to 14 "huts" in each National Army cantonment and six tents in each National Guard camp. The YMCA located buildings so they could serve units of about 5,000 men. "Hut" suggests a small structure, but the YMCA buildings were equipped with a small auditorium, a stage, dressing rooms, classrooms, and social rooms, as well as with living quarters for the association secretary. The YMCA also built in each cantonment a large auditorium seating 2,800 and they fitted it to accommodate motion pictures, amateur dramatics, athletics, and games. By December 31, 1919, the YMCA claimed to have supplied, free of charge, over 240,000 entertainment programs of all types. Attendance, they claimed, was over 90 million. Nothing in their published histories suggests what they were counting as an entertainment program or what constituted an attendance or an admission. Local talent from nearby communities and from among the soldiers was the main YMCA attraction, though the YMCA hired and toured some professional talent. Motion pictures were popular as well. The YMCA extended its entertainment services to soldiers in Great Britain, France and in occupied Germany after the armistice through its Over There Theatre League and its Soldier Actor Division. The YMCA claims to have sent more than 1,000 civilian entertainers abroad. Association activities were supported by donations totaling $162 million, of which only a little over $129 million was expended.[18] All accounts indicate the YMCA was ubiquitously present both over here and over there.

The Playground and Recreation Association of America formed the War Camp Community Service (WCCS) in April 1917. Under the direction of Joseph Lee, the WCCS labored to create "a public spirit of hospitality and friendliness" in the 600 communities adjacent to the camps. The WCCS operated information bureaus, clubs and social centers; they guided soldiers to wholesome commercial amusements and to friendly clubs, churches, and fraternal orders; they also fought petty profiteering at the soldier's expense by forming Square Deal associations and Better Business bureaus. The WCCS also assisted organizations such as the YMCA in seeking local talent to entertain in the camps.[19]

Fosdick and Baker assumed the work of the YMCA would be nonsectarian. However, the War Work Council of the YMCA admitted no Catholics or Jews, a decision Fosdick could not get reversed. So, to avoid charges of sectarian bias and despite Army General Staff reluctance to multiply the organizations serving in the camps, the CTCA sanctioned the Knights of Columbus in May and admitted the Jewish Welfare Board in August. The Knights of Columbus also erected service buildings and tents (numbering almost 500) and paid over 1,100 male secretaries to staff them. The Knights, as did the YMCA, raised more money than they spent — total receipts to June 30, 1919, were about $31 million; they spent about $20 million on construction, salaries, recreation equipment, and entertainment for the soldiers. The Jewish Welfare Board (JWB) erected service buildings in only 16 camps, but they sent organizers to all camps. The YMCA, the Knights of Columbus, and the JWB were approved only after assuring the CTCA that recreational and educational services would be available to men of all faiths. Arrangements with these organizations made it difficult to deny access to other groups, and pressure built until January 1918, when the CTCA decided to allow any fraternal order to serve the camps as long as it held no secret meetings.[20]

As the mobilization gained momentum in the summer of 1917, so also did efforts to refine the camp environment. In the course of the war, the Young Women's Christian Association built almost 100 Hostess Houses. The sitting rooms, cafeterias, verandas, and nurseries of these big, brown bungalows teamed with men and women on visiting days. The American Library Association circulated almost 3 million books and maintained 24,500 periodical subscriptions in library buildings erected by the CTCA in 36 camps. Branch libraries located in service centers run by the YMCA, Knights of Columbus, and the Jewish Welfare Board made books and magazines easily available. The Salvation Army was allowed in 1918 to dispense in American camps the steaming coffee and fresh doughnuts that made it a favorite with British and American soldiers in France.

Social workers sponsored by faith groups inundated the camps. Professionals and volunteers working for the YMCA, the YWCA, the Jewish Welfare Board, the Knights of Columbus, and the Salvation Army formed a shadow army of the faithful, a sheltering ring of new camp followers. Their main purpose seems to have been to help the conscripted soldier maintain his religious identity, if he had one, and to moderate the depressing conditions of camp life with numberless opportunities for rest and relaxation, for spontaneous play and entertainment, for education and counseling. Despite the scope and intensity of their labors, Baker gave the CTCA the job of supplementing their efforts. He charged the commission with the task of supplying the "normalities" of life in the training camps and reestablishing "the old social ties" to which he assumed the young men had been accustomed. The commission was also to keep the camp neighborhoods "clean and wholesome" by suppressing licentious amusements, as well as drinking, prostitution, and gambling, three vices traditionally associated with military service.[21]

Fosdick and five assistants, called district directors, undertook the police tasks of the CTCA. The district directors investigated camp conditions and represented the commission to camp commanders. Ultimately, Fosdick formed a Law Enforcement Division of the CTCA consisting of 39 officers of the Army Sanitary Corps. These investigating officers gathered facts about the violation of laws regulating prostitution and the sale of alcohol in communities near the camps and presented these facts to responsible civic officials. CTCA investigators also coerced local authorities to do something about corrupt or lackadaisical police. They publicized violations in the civilian press, they threatened direct application of federal law by agents of the Department of Justice or by military police, and they closed uncooperative communities to soldiers on leave. By November 15, 1918, Fosdick could report that the commission had closed so many sex ghettos that the red-light district had practically ceased to be a feature of American city life. But, as sex ghettos were closed, prostitutes found other ways to solicit and service their clients. The CTCA then focused on the eradication of prostitution, a strategy that forced them to confront the difficult task of distinguishing between sexually active women and prostitutes. The Law Enforcement Division employed 141 social workers who were empowered to detain "delinquent" girls and prostitutes and to examine and treat those infected with venereal disease. The Fosdick commission urged the construction of detention houses where women so detained could be counseled, and it advocated the enlargement of programs to educate and reform offenders.[22]

Several CTCA divisions attacked the problem of keeping the soldier physically fit with more positive, constructive programs. The Social Hygiene Division, consisting mainly of Sanitary Corps personnel, used lectures, pamphlets, and motion pictures to instruct soldiers on the danger of venereal disease and the advisability of immediate treatment. The commission made a major commitment to programs designed to increase creative and healthful use of leisure time. Where the volunteer organizations stressed relaxation and spontaneous play, the CTCA tended to regiment recreation and leisure activities. The Athletic Division assigned athletic directors and boxing coaches who trained the soldiers to play football, baseball, and soccer, and they adapted children's games to camp conditions. The athletic programs, especially boxing, were expected to develop aggressiveness and improve discipline and physical conditioning. Most camp commanders allowed play breaks of 15 to 30 minutes during each morning and afternoon drill period. All camps set aside the time between the end of drill and the call to retreat (4:00 to 5:45 p.m.) for organized games and sports led by athletic directors. Commanders encouraged everyone to participate and the athletic games proved to be popular. Camps reported that the spectators and participants in athletic games equaled the camp population every 18 days on the average. The Department of Camp Music appointed 53 song leaders who organized competitive music activities. Finally, the Liberty Theatre Division built and maintained 42 theatres in the camps, equipped them with scenery and mechanical gear, and hired professional managers who planned motion picture programs and arranged regular performances by professional theatre companies.

The commission touted the theatres as "civic centers," hoping that nontheatrical use of the auditoriums by the military would more completely integrate them into the daily routine of the camps.[23] Camp commanders regularly used the theatres as classrooms.[24] Commission song leaders, bandmasters, athletic instructors, and dramatic directors used them for group singing, band concerts, and boxing matches, as well as plays and variety shows, often to raise money for other camp activities.

While the camp theatre functioned partly as a town hall, its main purpose was to provide an alternative to the "vulgar, licentious shows" in many new and some established venues in the towns near the camps.[25] The War Department seemed to have regarded only some commercial theatrical fare as too suggestive and coarse for exhibition in or near the camps, but experience, especially on the Mexican border, had taught that theatres near camps often provided only the most lurid burlesque and the cheapest vaudeville. Moreover, the CTCA specifically disavowed any intention to moralize from the stage. Instructions to those responsible for reviewing and selecting camp shows were quite explicit in this regard. Selections standards were to focus on the entertainment value of the shows invited to play in the camps.[26]

Though the policy was never stated, the theatres were meant to cater to the presumed tastes and pocketbooks of the men in the ranks. The private's income dictated that ticket prices be kept as low as possible and the private's supposed interests guided the selection of attractions. The CTCA consistently opposed the notion that the theatres were meant to serve officers to any significant exclusion of enlisted men and draftees by denying requests for officer's nights, box seats, or reserved sections for officers.[27]

The theatres were open seven nights a week for an admission well below the standard for commercial theatre. Military leaders favored free entertainment, but Congress appropriated no money for theatre operations, so an admission had to be charged. The commission tried to set ticket prices high enough to pay expenses but low enough to attract the private. Low-priced tickets necessitated sharp curtailment of expenses; this in turn called for a massive volunteer effort from military and civilian amateurs in and near the camps and from the professional theatre at large. The commission at first planned to use professional entertainment every night, but the theatres ultimately used professional performers only half the time, reserving the other half for local amateur shows and for motion pictures.

The commission grew steadily until March 1918, when it had a paid staff of 140, about half of whom were located in Washington. By November 1918 that figure had doubled and thousands of volunteers were contributing their services.[28]

Money to support the commission came from several sources. Private donors contributed almost $241,000 to the War Department Auxiliary Fund, most of it through the United War Work Campaign. Receipts from ticket sales and concessions at camp athletic events brought in $30,000 while the sale of books by the Camp Music Division yielded about $16,000. The commission received about $97,000 in other donations. Cash receipts of the Liberty Theatres amounted to about $1.8 million. The Smileage Fund, made up of cash accruing as civilians purchased coupons and sent them to the soldiers to be used to pay admissions to entertainment in and near the camps, took in about $1 million. Congress appropriated about $3.4 million for commission projects, mainly theatre construction and maintenance.[29] The total of this earned and unearned income, about $6.6 million, hardly compares with the $162 million available to the YMCA or the $31 million in the coffers of the Knights of Columbus. The "sisters" collected money well in excess of the $205 million reported by the secretary of war in 1919.[30] In all cases where figures are available, it is clear that spending by the volunteer social service agencies dwarfed government spending in the camps.

Frank Tannenbaum, an Austrian-born American and member of the radical Industrial Workers of the World (IWW), later a renowned history professor at Columbia University, condemned camp life for its tendency to destroy the most cherished ideals of civilian life: individuality and self-determination. Tannenbaum's experience in the camps led him to argue that camp welfare and recreational activities failed because they emphasized spectator events rather than programs to develop initiative and self-expression and because the programs reached but a small portion of the men in the camps.[31] He indicted the reformers with a lack of imagination and a helpless, antiquated attitude. Tannenbaum's charge that the camp programs failed to achieve their objectives is right but only as a matter of degree. He doesn't acknowledge that their very existence was revolutionary and his claim that the reformers lacked imagination is just wrong. They imagined grandly. That their attitudes were "antiquated" is also questionable. They were fighting a rearguard action against cultural changes that were to sweep over the country in the '20s and subsequently, but they were also daring and dauntless experimenters in social engineering of the kind that was to be the hallmark of the New Deal in the '30s. John Dickinson countered Tannenbaum's argument by observing that the welfare organizations were trying to ameliorate the very camp conditions Tannenbaum so appropriately condemned. Dickinson perhaps rightly noted that the camp recreation and welfare programs could not have hoped to reduce the "incidence of bestiality" below that in the civilian population as a whole. But Dickinson did underestimate the idealism of Baker and Fosdick when he maintained that the army did not aim to make each camp a democratic utopia.[32]

In kind and quantity the outpouring of energy, money, and material devoted to the improvement of the quality of camp life had no precedent. Wherever the new soldier turned in the new camp, he encountered evidence of the concern of his fellow citizens for his well-being. On a nearby corner stood a club building devoted exclusively to enhancing the quality of his leisure time. Built and operated by sectarian alliances, staffed by male volunteers who dispensed free stationery and religious counsel, the hut provided a clean, quiet place to rest, to talk with friends, to play a piano or listen to phonograph music, to think or write. Free newspapers, books, and magazines were readily available in libraries and reading rooms scattered throughout the camp. While the civilian volunteers showed motion pictures and organized talent shows, sing-a-longs, French classes, and athletic contests, they usually allowed the soldier to express his needs with minimal restraints and guidance. The new soldier also discovered a new official concern for his welfare. The government was literally reforming the city to which he retired on leave. Streetwalking companions and illegal liquor were available to anyone who looked long enough and paid the price, but many blatantly organized saloon and red-light districts were pressured out of business. Community workers labored to dispel the civilian's suspicion of uniformed men, and clubs, churches, and homes were opened. In camp, War Department employees offered health counseling, planned a wide variety of sporting activities, and scheduled and led group singing. Competent managers booked professional actors and actresses in the soldier's own Liberty Theatre, to which he could gain admission for one-fourth or one-half of the cost of a show in town. It's hard to imagine that any soldier found these amenities to be sufficient recompense for having been uprooted from his home and trained for deadly combat in a remote and seemingly endless war. Indeed, regimental histories seldom mention training camp recreational services, the usual exception being memories of the regimental band, of group singing, and of sports, especially boxing. Nevertheless, the new soldier could hardly have escaped the realization that the training camps were teeming with volunteers and dotted with buildings dedicated to wholesome recreation. He could believe President Wilson's assurance that "no army ever before assembled has had more conscientious and painstaking thought given to the protection and stimulation of their mental, moral and physical manhood."[33]

5

Commercial Theatres or Government Theatres?

Although the commissioners wanted to provide theatrical entertainment in the training camps, they did not immediately decide to build their own theatres. First they gathered facts about the cost of dramatic productions and the availability of volunteers. They also considered opening the camps to commercial concessions that would provide entertainment in privately owned buildings.

The Commission on Training Camp Activities held its first meeting on April 26, 1917, in an office at the Russell Sage Foundation in New York City. Lee Hanmer, coming from a background in public recreation, coordinated camp entertainment but focused initially on creating a music program. Hanmer later assumed more direct responsibility for the camp theatres, but at first he asked his assistant, Clarence A. Perry, associate director of the Recreation Department of the Russell Sage Foundation, to mobilize volunteers in the entertainment field. Perry's specialty at the Russell Sage Foundation was promoting the use of public schools as social centers and encouraging local school boards to cooperate with municipal authorities in arranging other uses of school buildings outside school hours. In private life he participated in amateur theatre in the New York City area, and, as a part of his foundation work, he had been organizing community playdays and pageants, especially those with patriotic and educational value, designed to take the place of dangerous fireworks displays on July 4.

Perry's initial efforts reflected his orientation toward noncommercial theatre or theatre for a restricted market. Perry first turned for help to the Drama League of New York of which he was a member. The Drama League of New York was an affiliate of the Drama League of America, an organization of devotees of amateur and noncommercial theatre that worked to improve the quality of both professional and amateur theatre in the United States. It was often critical of U.S. commercial theatre, finding much of it empty and tasteless. The Drama League established play-reading circles where members read and discussed the new English and European drama, looking to George Bernard Shaw and Henry Arthur Jones, for instance, as models of a more penetrating and substantial drama. They also published a quarterly journal espousing the cause of art and community theatre and providing some guidance to the groundbreaking plays of Shaw and the Scandinavians, Henrik Ibsen and August Strindberg. It also organized touring companies of professional performers bringing artistic but not commercially serviceable plays to Drama League centers all over the country. The Drama League persuaded performers to accept below-normal salaries so the shows would be affordable to all Drama League members.[1]

Initially, there seems to have been little or no interest on the part of the CTCA in sending professional touring shows to the camps. Perry fished in what was for him familiar waters, but how could he have supposed the catch would be big enough to serve the camp theatres? He had before him the YMCA model that called for a distinctly amateur focus. Entertainers in the YMCA auditoriums would be volunteers drawn from communities near the camps and some might be professionals, but none would be paid. The YMCA also instructed their secretaries in the camps to organize soldier shows made up of skits or demonstrations of individual talent. Finally, the YMCA auditoriums made an early commitment to heavy use of motion pictures.

The Drama League appeared to Perry to have access to volunteers whose services might reduce costs to the CTCA. The league's staff had some experience in organizing theatrical tours of organizations such as the Hull-House Players and the Irish Players and stars such as Minnie Maddern Fiske and George Arliss to locations remote from the nation's theatrical centers, to towns like Rockford, Illinois, and Des Moines, Iowa, near where camps would be built. Most importantly, the Drama League shared the anticommercial point of view so much a part of the vision of the CTCA. Perry asked the Drama League of New York to provide an estimate of the cost of sending entertainers to the camps and an assessment of volunteer potential in the theatre industry. This estimate has not survived, but it must have been no bar to the course chosen by the commission. Action on the matter of camp entertainment was deferred, not because it would be too expensive as at first conceived, but because the size of the camps had not yet been determined.[2] Perry and Hanmer continued to collect facts about the feasibility of camp theatres.

They also asked for help from the Stage Women's War Relief. These women of the theatre in New York devoted most of their volunteer efforts to producing benefit performances of Broadway hits and variety shows for the camps near New York and Washington, D.C. Playwright Rachel Crothers was a founder and national chairwoman of the organization. Crothers was a proponent of the "new woman," a woman liberated from obligatory domestication and free to openly express her political and social beliefs and her sexual preferences. Her plays were adroitly crafted and expressed a degree of social consciousness that made her stand out from her contemporaries. She promised Clarence Perry help in obtaining plays and actors at the lowest possible prices, basing her pledge on patriotic promises of generous support already given by theatrical managers.[3] However, Stage Women's War Relief was able to give only very limited support to the development of the Liberty Theatres partly because Crothers was overstating or overestimating the cooperative spirit of the theatre's business leaders. Her group was able to put together several fundraising performances by some of Broadway's biggest stars, but they were never able to offer the steady supply of entertainment the Liberty Theatres were to need.

The search continued for ways the mobilization camps could be provided with regular programs of professional entertainment. The commission considered granting concessions to private theatre owners who would build theatres in the camps at their own expense and run them for a large percentage of the profits. In effect this was an adaptation of the function of the sutler, a commercial businessman who ran a general store inside 19th-century army camps and shared his profits with camp officials, who in turn used the money (or so the plan went) to provide recreational facilities for the troopers. Malcolm L. McBride, commissioner in charge of the organization of Post Exchange stores in the camps, favored such a plan and he investigated the matter. The concession theatre idea was in line with Secretary Baker's general dictum that the CTCA coordinate the efforts of existing agencies rather than create new camp welfare organizations. Nevertheless, the potential for commercial profiteering troubled some commissioners.

On May 13, 1917, Lee Hanmer presented a proposal to provide vaudeville theatres in the camps from E.R. Seamens, representative of the Allardt Circuit, a chain of vaudeville theatres in the Midwest. Mr. Seamens touted his concession at Camp Hughes in Canada as a "highly satisfactory" commercial venture, providing him with a profit and camp authorities with a percentage of the receipts.[4] Seamens proposed that the Allardt Circuit build theatres in all the large training camps and, every other week, Allardt would provide vaudeville for 90 percent of the gross receipts.[5] Seamens would charge the soldiers 15 cents and 20 cents per admission for his vaudeville shows. He would also rent his theatre to producers of standard plays for 10 percent of the gross receipts. Seamens' proposition was tabled until repre-

5. Commercial Theatres or Government Theatres?   51

sentatives of the commission could examine the service he was providing at the Great Lakes Naval Training Camp, near Chicago, and see some shows in his regular circuit.[6] Before Seamens could sell his proposition, the CTCA abandoned the idea of privately owned theatres in the camps. The potential for profiteering by Seamens and other managers, coupled with the worries that these commercial managers would fill the camp stages with exactly the sort of cheap amusements Fosdick had witnessed on the Mexican border, made concession theatres seem too risky.

In mid–May 1917 Fosdick asked Senator Morris Sheppard of Texas, a member of the Senate Military Affairs Committee, to include money for recreation in the training camps in the Regular Army Act then under consideration. Fosdick suggested an initial appropriation of $500,000 for camp recreation under the item "Military Post Exchanges."[7] Sheppard promptly amended the bill, and the CTCA got its money. The commission decided to use the money, if appropriated, to construct its own multipurpose buildings, designed for athletics, physical training, and military instruction, as well as for motion pictures, vaudeville, and plays.[8] As plans developed, the commission abandoned the idea of designing the theatres for anything other than movies, vaudeville and plays. Their potential use as gymnasia was eliminated when the building's designer chose raked floors to improve sightlines and fixed seating to facilitate more efficient handling of audiences. The theatres could, however, be used for military instruction.

While waiting for passage of the Regular Army Act, the commission took steps to counter anticipated congressional and military objections to the construction of camp theatres by demonstrating the value of camp entertainment.[9] This they accomplished in part with a professional variety show at the officers training camp at Fort Myers, Virginia, on June 9, 1917. Rachel Crothers provided the financial backing and the Stage Women's War Relief secured the talent and supervised the production. George M. Cohan, Broadway's "Yankee Doodle Dandy," and the street's most popular performer and playwright, and Cohan's partner, Broadway producer Sam Harris, produced the show, in which Cohan introduced his new war song, "Over There." Vaudevillian Nora Bayes, then without a rival on the American stage in dramatizing and selling a song, belted out "Over There" at the Fort Myers show and went on to make it the most popular American song of the war period. Cohan also won a congressional medal for writing it. Another vaudevillian, the barrel-shaped princess of all working drudges, Marie Dressler, appeared in the Fort Myers show. Dressler continued contributing to the war effort through appearances in shows promoting the sale of Liberty bonds. Elsie Janis, one of the greatest stars of the vaudeville stage, also performed, the first of Janis's many appearances before the troops in the U.S. and in France, efforts that earned her the soubriquet, "Sweetheart of the

A.E.F." Crothers and the Stage Women's War Relief put together a powerful show using some of the most magnetic and dynamic talent then available to promote the cause of theatres and professional performers in the training camps. The CTCA announced the Fort Myers show as "the inauguration of a definite policy on the part of the War Department to provide theatrical entertainment of first class character for the officers and men of the Army." They added that carrying out this plan would be contingent on funding.[10] Days later, in thanking Crothers for her part in the Fort Myers experiment, Fosdick told her that officers in the War Department had reacted favorably to the idea of developing camp theatres.[11]

Congress passed the Regular Army Act on June 15, 1917, and it included $500,000 for theatre construction. The CTCA had its funding, but they had to get in line for scarce materials and manpower needed to build the theatres. Their position in that line was assigned by the omnipotent Council of National Defense, made up of six members of the president's cabinet and empowered to advise the president on industrial mobilization. Their Emergency Construction Committee coordinated camp construction. Ordinarily this project would have been the responsibility of the Quartermaster Corps, one of the permanent service bureaus of the War Department, but the quartermasters were overburdened with gathering war materiél and could not oversee camp construction. W.A. Starrett, a civil engineer, chaired the Emergency Construction Committee, which drew its members from the ranks of large contractors. Col. I.W. Littell's Cantonment Division of the Quartermaster Corps merely signed the construction contracts Starrett submitted to it. Starrett and Littell promised to help but said they could do nothing until the commission's architectural and management plans were more complete.[12]

6

Mobilizing the Commercial Theatre

Building the theatres was a daunting task, but in complexity it paled in comparison to the job of routing professionally produced plays and other entertainment through the camps. Before Lee Hanmer and his CTCA associates could build theatres and create an organization to manage them, they first had to win the patriotic support of theatre businessmen and managers, an establishment the commission had lately spurned for being too greedy. Further, the CTCA had to find enough money to pay the expenses, at least, of professional entertainers who might volunteer, since Congress had provided no money for the operation of the theatres. At each step the commission labored to overcome antagonism, ignorance, indifference, and misunderstanding in the military establishment, in Congress, and in the theatre industry, as well as in the ranks of the welfare organizations they coordinated. These human problems paired with material hindrances, such as those posed by the nation's distressed railway system and by harsh winter weather, threatened to sink the camp theatre project before it was fairly out of the harbor.

The commission expected to pay and pay handsomely for the cost of theatre construction. Contractors who were building the rest of the camp's structures built most of the government theatres. Builders operated under cost-plus contracts that essentially removed all incentives for suppressing costs. Laborers could thus be paid anything necessary to get the camps built quickly and contractors paid whatever was necessary in the heated market for building supplies. Labor and building supply costs skyrocketed. Concerns about profiteering were rampant but the urgency of the situation undercut them.

Ironically, the commission expected theatre professionals to cut rates or to volunteer services at no cost to provide the government theatres with inexpensive attractions. Again, commissioners had but to look, but not too closely, at the example of the YMCA for support of their position. By the time construction crews had cleared sites in preparation for building to start in June, the YMCA had readied construction plans. As military barracks and offices were going up, so were YMCA huts, so that construction workers could use them. As camp construction drew to an end in September 1917 and the first draftees were arriving, the YMCA huts were ready for service, providing free (albeit almost exclusively amateur) entertainment and free movies.

At no time did the commission calculate the economic value of the free or discounted services they expected from theatre professionals, nor were Hanmer and Perry quick to establish contact with leaders in the commercial theatre. The Drama League of New York, to which Clarence Perry had access, was critical and antagonistic toward the purveyors of pleasure, and the Stage Women's War Relief had only very limited moral authority in dealing with theatrical businessmen.

Kate Oglebay, a Drama League executive in New York City and an assistant to Clarence Perry, took the lead in this regard. Oglebay had trained as an actress in New York and had worked briefly on the Broadway stage. But her interests and talents led her to the Drama League. In 1916 she had chaired New York City's celebration of the Tercentennial of the death of William Shakespeare, acquiring in the process a fine reputation for raising funds and interest in community theatre.

Oglebay displayed her skill in first asking Otto Kahn for advice. Kahn was a New York financier whose association with the theatre scene included his being founder of the New Theatre (1909–1911), one of America's first attempts to establish a professional art theatre. He was also the chief benefactor of the New York's Metropolitan Opera Company and he was providing support for New York City art theatres such as the Washington Square Players and the Provincetown Players just getting established in 1917. In his time (he died in 1934) Kahn became the greatest individual patron of the arts the U.S. had yet known.[1] Kahn suggested to Oglebay that Baker or Fosdick should immediately appeal to Marc Klaw. Klaw was president of the United Managers' Protective Association (UMPA), an organization that functioned to "protect" producers and owners of theatrical real estate from the mounting pressure of organized theatrical labor. Apparently, Kahn thought the UMPA had the capacity to mobilize the commercial theatre establishment for the war effort.

A description of the sources and limits of Klaw's power in the theatre affords a measure of the enormity and complexity of the problem of providing professional entertainment in the camps. Marc Klaw was indeed a name to be conjured with in professional theatre circles. Following a legal education, he worked as a newspaper reporter in his hometown of Louisville, Kentucky. In 1881 he left Louisville for New York to become a tour manager then an advance agent for Charles Frohman, one of America's leading producers and purveyors of hit Broadway productions that were then replicated one or more times and sent on tours of theatres across the land. At the time, producers like Frohman supplied thousands of small-town theatres, referred to as "the road," with touring attractions mounted in the nation's theatre centers, the chief of which was New York City. Touring companies most often performed a single play for one to six nights in each theatre. Company managers and advance agents arranged to transport the company and its baggage from one theatre to another on the tour route. The advance agent arranged advertising for the show and lodging and local transportation for the company. The company manager kept watch to see that performances remained at an acceptable level. He collected the company's share from the theatres it visited, paid the performers' salaries and expenses, and he delivered the profits to Frohman. Experience working for Frohman led to Klaw's becoming an independent agent for touring theatrical companies.

In 1887, Klaw formed a partnership with Abraham Erlanger, another advance agent, and together they managed several successful theatrical tours of the South. In 1888, Erlanger conceived the idea of establishing a central booking agency in New York City to serve the theatres in the southern U.S., and Klaw assisted him in this venture.

Booking referred to the means whereby the local theatre manager was assured a flow of plays in his theatre and the theatrical company was assured a profitable route to road theatres. A booking agent was a broker or mediator, who, for a fee, usually 5 percent of the theatre's gross, contracted with a theatre owner to provide a regular schedule of productions. Booking agents also extracted fees from the productions they booked, and some agents charged a fee when they supplied the theatre owner with advertising materials. The booking agent then arranged the tours of theatrical companies so the theatre owners were supplied with attractions. Booking agents normally contracted with a group of theatres called a circuit, located along convenient lines of transportation in a limited geographic area.

Booking circuits of road theatres was lucrative for the knowledgeable and resourceful agent. Booking required a profound knowledge of the transportation services of a region or of the whole country, because the major booking problem was to create a tour without long and costly jumps from one performance venue to the next or periods of inactivity for the touring company. The ideal tour plan kept performers on stage every night of the week. Booking also required an immense amount of information about the activities of other touring companies, because a tour's profit could be cut if it were to follow a tour presenting the same kind of play. The booking agent had to know the staging facilities, the seating capacity, and admission prices of every house he served. He had to know about hotel accommodations in the road towns, and he was usually responsible for advertising, so he needed to know each road-town's printing and billing capacities and costs. The late 19th century saw the rise to fortune of several eminently successful booking agencies. One of the most successful of these was that of Klaw and Erlanger.

By 1896 Klaw and Erlanger had formed exclusive affiliations with over 200 theatres, mainly in the South. In the same year, they became key members of the Theatrical Syndicate or Theatrical Trust. The syndicate included as well Alfred Hayman, who leased the most important theatres in the West. Broadway star-maker and producer Charles Frohman was a vital member as were and Fred Nirdlinger-Nixon and Fred Zimmerman, who controlled key theatres in Philadelphia and the middle Atlantic region. The partners owned 16 first-class theatres and controlled the booking for 17 more in the principal cities of the U.S. These 33 theatres were the nucleus from which the Theatrical Syndicate extended its control over most of the major theatres and attractions in the U.S. By 1901 they had increased their holdings to approximately 65 first-class theatres. The syndicate branched into many other forms of control of the theatre industry, until they reached the ascendancy of their power between 1905 and 1910. Their control amounted to a virtual monopoly of the theatre industry during the first decade of the 20th century. Monopoly control meant that the fees charged to theatres and to productions mounted steadily as competition disappeared, to as much as 50 percent of the theatre's gross receipts and as much as 50 percent of the gross income of the touring attraction.[2]

Independent producers tried unsuccessfully to break the control of the syndicate in 1898 and in 1903-1904.[3] The syndicate was most effectively challenged by the growth of another organization somewhat like it. The Shubert brothers (Sam S., Lee, and J.J.) of Syracuse, New York, were inspired less by a desire to free the theatre industry from monopolistic control than by a desire to make money by exerting a new, different kind of monopolistic control. The Shuberts sought dominance through a corporation open to venture capital, while the syndicate held control through the cooperation of managing partners.[4] They began their theatre ownership in upstate New York, and by 1905 (the year of Sam S. Shubert's death in a train crash) they owned 15 theatres in the east and the Midwest. Since the syndicate controlled so many first-class theatres, the Shuberts challenged them as much by building new theatres as by leasing or buying older, less profitable ones. Up to about 1905, the Shuberts and the syndicate had more or less peaceful relations. Productions managed by the Shuberts played syndicate theatres, and the Shubert theatres booked through the Klaw and Erlanger Exchange. After 1905, with the death of Sam Shubert and the ascendancy of his brother Lee, they were rivals and competitors, and in the next 11 years they waged a series of economic battles from which the Shuberts emerged the victors and managers of a rapidly growing new "syndicate."[5] The twin titans battled on nearly equal grounds until 1909 when the Shuberts and their allied independent producers and theatre managers forced the syndicate to abandon its practice of demanding exclusive rights from both theatre managers and producers. Prior to this time the syndicate did business only with those theatre managers who would agree to accept only syndicate productions and with producers who agreed to place their shows exclusively in syndicate theatres. In 1913, during a deep slump in theatre business nationwide, the Shuberts negotiated an agreement with Klaw and Erlanger to limit their competition in several large cities, to close less profitable theatres and to pool and share the profits of those remaining in operation. The parties expanded the pooling agreement in 1915. The agreement binding the six syndicate partners expired in 1916, leaving the field to Klaw and Erlanger and to the Shuberts. The pooling agreement brought about a four-year period of relative peace based in part on a fragile balance of power and in part on economic necessity — both parties were faced with a complex phenomenon called "the decline of the road."

"Decline of the road" refers to a decline of the number of touring companies and a consequent decline in the number of road theatres presenting legitimate attractions. Broadway producer William Brady estimated in 1915 that 75 percent of the profits of a Broadway theatrical production came from its touring outside New York City. The decline of the road had disastrous effects on producers and on theatre managers throughout the country. And a prime cause of decline, Brady claimed, was the poor quality of the road show, which he said was too often a weak play or musical featuring performers from the lowest rungs of the profession performing in shabby costumes and before drab, worn scenery.[6]

In 1900, 339 legitimate theatrical companies toured the U.S. and Canada. In 1910, the figure dropped to 236, then in 1913, the first year of the Shubert-syndicate truce, it tapered to 178. The number of touring attractions continued to drop until there were but 77 shows on the road in 1917 and 41 in 1918. In the period 1910-1925, the number of road theatres declined as well, from over 1,500 to less than 700. Theatre owners clamored for attractions, and the resulting high prices for talent compelled many to convert their houses to cinema. Ultimately, even the largest central booking offices found it impossible to fill their own theatres because of the dearth of first-class attractions. By the war years of 1917-1918, the road had lost its status as the most financially lucrative sector of the theatre industry.[7]

The Theatrical Syndicate was almost universally excoriated and nowhere more consistently than on the editorial pages of one of the most influential theatre trade newspapers of the times, the *New York Dramatic Mirror*, owned and edited from 1880 to 1911 by Harrison Grey Fiske. Fiske was a dauntless opponent of the commercialism in the theatre, and he viewed the Theatrical Syndicate as an exponent of all that was destroying the artistic and socially aware theatre he loved. From the founding of the syndicate in 1896 Fiske editorialized against the cartel of managers who were choking the life out of the theatre in an effort to squeeze every last cent of profit from it. At their feet he laid the undermining of local autonomy in the selection of attractions, the sinking moral tone of the drama, and the destruction of the old stock company mode of management. Fiske was not alone in his view of the syndicate. Critic and proponent of modernism Sheldon Cheney likewise viewed the rapid commercialization of the theatre under syndicate rule as a movement toward a theatre of the "lowest common denominator," a theatre for which the people had lost all respect.[8] Arthur Hornblow, editor of the influential *Theatre Magazine* and formerly a correspondent for Fiske's *New York Dramatic Mirror* and for the *New York Herald* and the *New York Times*, echoed the idea that a perceived decline in the quality of the American theatre had been caused by its commercialization.[9] Hornblow and his fellow critic William Winter pined for the theatre of old and its repertoire of dramatic standards and classics, such as the plays of Shakespeare, and they argued that profit-motivated managers had displaced the more artistic-minded actor-manager of the late 19th century, epitomized by Augustin Daly. Fiske, Cheney, Hornblow, and Winter, all speaking from the perspective of the genteel tradition of white, college-educated managers of American media, articulated a deeply conservative nostalgia and anticommercialism that correlated neatly with the agrarian idealism and recreation orientation of the CTCA reformers.

Interestingly, CTCA chairman Fosdick had been helping set up an organization to help small noncommercial theatres get started and stay in business. The committee upon which he served included playwright Percy MacKaye, author of *The St. Louis Masque* (1914), a noncommercial event that was but one of dozens of community pageants (albeit one of the largest) produced in the U.S. between 1908 and 1920. MacKaye wrote and lectured widely on the value of the community pageant as a tool for stimulating a deeper understanding of democracy and for promoting community coherence. He had also written the Shakespearean pageant *Caliban of the Yellow Sands*, staged in 1916 in New York's Central Park as part of the city's commemoration of the 300th anniversary of the death of Shakespeare. MacKaye and Fosdick, among others on the committee, were trying to promote noncommercial theatre because they believed commercialization had stripped drama and theatre of its potential to promote social change. Powerful businessmen, such as Marc Klaw, had monopolized the American theatre and disenfranchised the public and independent theatre owners, stripping them of the power to choose what they wanted to show and see. According to sociologist John Collier, author of a series of influential articles in *The Survey*, the magazine of the Charity Organization of New York City, producers were imposing a destructive censorship of theatre and motion pictures, basing their choices not on a social or an aesthetic goal but upon what would attract the largest possible audience paying the most for tickets. Collier called his series of articles on theatre and motion pictures in society "The Lantern Bearers," thereby suggesting the priority of the social and spiritual functions of drama and theatre, functions that had been subverted in the transformation of theatre and motion pictures into entertainment and the marginalization of the public as consumers. The commercialization and professionalization of theatre had degraded the status of the amateur performer embedded in a community and participating in theatrical events celebrating the history and values of that community. Collier and other advocates of a "new theatre" found more life-altering power in amateur performances at European feast days and American civic pageants, in nonprofessional theatre such as was being produced by the Neue Freie Folksbühne (New Free Worker's Theatre) in Germany; by the Irish Players of Dublin; in Arnold G. Arvold's Little Country Theatre in Fargo, North Dakota; and in theatres like those at Hull House in Chicago and at the Henry Street Settlement in New York City.[10]

Fosdick, Hanmer and their colleagues on the commission were steeped in an ethic that stressed participation in performance events rather than consumption of entertainment. They were positioned within a socialist ideology that demonized the capitalist commercialization of entertainment. They were privy to the results of vice reports and recreation surveys of American cities being channeled through the offices of the Russell Sage Foundation, investigations that connected apparent social decay with commercial entertainment.[11] Moreover, recent experience on the Mexican border gave them good reason to be concerned about the potential for profiteering and about the quality of the professional attractions commercial managers might bring into the training camps. However, they seem to have had no recourse but to turn to Klaw or someone like him, given the speed at which mobilization was proceeding. The only sector of the theatre apparently capable of putting attractions in the dozens of new camp theatres was the commercial theatre establishment and its touring arm.

Marc Klaw's position as president of the United Managers' Protective Association gave him the superficial appearance of being the acknowledged leader of the theatre's most powerful group. The UMPA was organized on

May 31, 1914, with Marc Klaw as president and Lee Shubert as vice president. The members also elected a board of governors, with the Shuberts and the syndicate equally represented. The managers organized to protect their economic interests, and UMPA did present a united front to outsiders: actors seeking better working conditions, legislators trying to impose censorship and taxes, or rail companies threatening to raise rates. It was, however, totally ineffectual in mediating conflict among its members. For example, in August 1915, UMPA sponsored an agreement among the managers in New York City to eliminate the sale of cut-rate tickets. A majority signed the agreement, but it was in effect less than a month when Klaw and Erlanger cut ticket prices at two theatres. The UMPA Board of Governors rebuked them, but they insisted they had acted only after the Shuberts had broken the agreement. The managers finally decided to abrogate their agreement and conduct business as they pleased.[12]

Nothing in the records of the Commission on Training Camp Activities indicates anyone was aware of the fierce competition and business decline in the commercial theatre. Had they known of these disabling features, they would nevertheless have had no choice but to traffic with suppliers already in the market and to put the best face on the situation. The commissioners supposed that "minor" grievances could be set aside in a display of patriotism so that the managers of the theatre industry could cooperate to supply the entertainment needed in the camps. Under the circumstances, Klaw was probably the man to appeal to, but the circumstances in the theatre industry were such that even he could not be very helpful. Cooperation between the syndicate and the Shuberts, beyond that demanded by economic necessity, was next to impossible. Virtually every producer and theatre manager in the country was aligned with one or the other faction, so appeals for cooperation put every theatre worker in a position that might be seen as a betrayal of one or both of the kings of the industry. Moreover, years of rapacious booking and touring fees charged by the syndicate and exploitive relations between producers and theatre owners and the theatrical work force — writers, actors, stagehands — had created a hostile atmosphere in the theatre. Writing about conditions in the theatre industry as late as April 1918, Percy MacKaye claimed that the theatre was failing to adapt its structures and policies the better to discharge its wartime responsibilities. He condemned the theatre for civic apathy generated by decades of tawdriness, anarchy, greed, and speculation. MacKaye believed the theatre had the capacity to meet its obligations, but he charged that it was failing because business competition and personal enmity were making it impossible for the theatre establishment to unite and cooperate.[13] The theatre's fund of mutual appreciation and trust among segments of the industry required for the large-scale mobilization of volunteers had been drawn down to zero.

To further compound these problems there was the personality of Marc Klaw himself: vain and self-conscious of his power, sensitive of the smallest slight, volatile and vengeful when opposed. Otto Kahn warned the commission of Klaw's character and suggested that the CTCA's ambassador emphasize the privilege and honor accorded Klaw in the government's appeal. He thought Klaw would be flattered by the request, but only if the theatrical potentate were assured that no "lesser people have been fooling with the proposition." Kahn suggested that whoever visited Klaw should carefully deprecate the efforts of the Stage Women's War Relief as "a little experiment that touches only the officers' camps," and assure Klaw that the CTCA needed his help in the large conscription camps. The messenger should also point out that the request for aid came from the secretary of war and was directed to the managers as the only source of the type of excellent entertainment needed in the camps.[14] Assuredly, the United Managers controlled the theatre business of the country. They owned or controlled a large share of existing theatrical real estate; they possessed the capital necessary to acquire the rights to produce new dramas, to hire actors and technicians, to buy scenery and costumes, and to pay the rising costs of producing and touring a play. In a real sense, the Shuberts and Klaw and Erlanger owned the commercial theatre industry. They dictated the terms under which the rank and file theatre laborer could work and their choices as to what to produce determined what audiences could see. Kahn correctly argued that the commission could develop no camp entertainment program without their assistance. Clarence Perry suggested to Raymond Fosdick that "it is important we make them feel that we know they're 'it' as soon as possible."[15]

Hanmer and Fosdick approved Otto Kahn's suggestion, and Fosdick himself immediately wrote to Klaw, explaining briefly the work of the commission and asking him whether he would be willing, as president of the UMPA, to use his influence with the managers to make theatrical entertainment available in the camps.[16] Klaw's response has been lost, but it must have been favorable, because Perry reported at the next meeting of the CTCA on May 26, 1917, that plans were being made to secure the active assistance of leading theatrical managers in securing shows for the conscription camps.[17]

Rachel Crothers became responsible for liaison between Klaw and the commission. She reported to Fosdick that Klaw would meet with Daniel Frohman, Sam Harris and a few other leading managers to discuss how to supply shows to the camps and that Klaw could plan larger meetings with theatre managers and with motion picture executives.[18] A few days later these conferences had taken place. Her report suggested a breakthrough and a movement toward theatrical unification in the war effort, but no specific plans were being made.¹⁹ She also reported that Klaw had received assurances of cooperation from several New York managers, especially B.F. Keith, head of the most powerful vaudeville booking agency, the United Booking Office. The United Booking Office, under the management of Keith and E.F. Albee, was to the vaudeville stage what the syndicate and the Shuberts were to the legitimate stage.²⁰ Actually, Klaw conferred almost exclusively with managers aligned with the Klaw and Erlanger Exchange and included the Shuberts and their associates only superficially.

Klaw made little immediate progress toward providing entertainment for the training camps. On June 21, he told Fosdick he was forming some concrete ideas about the camp theatres. He added that the theatrical people with whom he conferred seemed perfectly willing to cooperate but he warned that they didn't grasp the scope of the problem of putting shows on the camp theatre stages.²¹ In Hanmer's view, the industry was fragmented into one group of managers and another looser grouping of performers and other functionaries, a kind of labor-management split, and Hanmer feared these factions might not be able to unite in the patriotic cause.²² In any case, the commissioners were learning that the professional theatre was so splintered into contentious factions that the mobilization of volunteers was going to be slow and tedious and might be impossible.

When Klaw finally outlined a plan, he rightly rejected the idea that volunteer performers could supply the entertainment needs of the government, and he argued that someone would have to pay for professional talent if the camps wanted a large number of good productions. Klaw thought the War Department should supply initial operating funds for the theatres, and he believed the soldiers would have to pay an admission to defray the expenses, although the commissioners had hoped the shows would be free. The commission also wanted the theatre industry to supply dramatic entertainment each and every night, but Klaw advocated a scheme in which the presentation of legitimate drama was only a part of the theatre program.²³ His plan, presented to the commission on June 28, called for a large "amusement hall" (theatre) in each of the 16 National Army cantonments, the program of each to vary from week to week. Professional companies would perform the first and third weeks of each month; managers would make arrangements locally for entertainment the second and fourth weeks. Klaw expected a charge of 20 to 35 cents per admission to cover expenses. Klaw's scheme seemed workable and affordable to all concerned, so the commission accepted it.²⁴ It was vitally important to at last have an idea, an outline of a plan because camp construction had already started in most locations.

Meantime, Lee Hanmer asked Klaw for help reviewing plans and cost estimates submitted by architects, scenic artists, stage equipment suppli-

6. Mobilizing the Commercial Theatre 63

Liberty Theatre, Camp Devens, Ayer, Massachusetts. The "THEATRE" sign is enhanced with light bulbs. Billboards announce coming attractions, the major form of advertising (courtesy National Archives, 92-Construction Division Completion Reports, Box 70, Photo #22).

ers, and chair seating contractors. Klaw assigned an architect and theatrical designer from his staff, F. Richard Anderson, to work with Hanmer. In mid–July, the commission asked its architect, Edward Lippincott Tilton, already designing library buildings for the camps, to design the government theatres. Tilton was highly regarded. With his first partner, William A. Boring, he won a government competition to design the Ellis Island Immigration Station in 1891. Boring retired in 1916 to become the dean of the School of Architecture of Columbia University, and Tilton continued in practice with Alfred Githens, specializing in libraries and museums, for which he won several medals for design. At his death in 1933, Tilton was one of the foremost library architects in the country.[25] He presented his theatre plans to Lee Hanmer in early August and Hanmer and Anderson, Klaw's man, quickly approved them.

Tilton's building seated 2,400 on the main floor and about 600 in the balcony, and it cost only $28,000. Hanmer and Tilton estimated $4,500 would purchase and install lighting, scenery, stage fittings, and miscellaneous equipment in each theatre. The total cost of each was thus $32,500.[26] Fosdick took the plans to the Emergency Construction Committee of the Council of National Defense, and they promised to select sites for the auditoriums, make the necessary contracts, and supervise the builders.[27] However, they needed specifications and blueprints from Tilton to determine independently whether the 16 buildings could be built and equipped for $500,000. Fosdick instructed Hanmer to press Tilton for the completion of the plans.[28]

Hanmer approved the idea of letting the Emergency Construction Committee supervise construction, but he believed someone on the commission should keep a close watch on the project. He suggested the name of Charles P. Neill, a noted labor authority. Neill, a recent addition to the commission, had supervised the construction of library buildings in the camps, and he knew both Tilton and Maj. W.A. Starrett, chairman of the Emergency Construction Committee. Although Neill said he would accept the additional assignment, Fosdick ultimately assigned the task to his personal secretary, Jasper Mayer, who had been observing the process of theatre planning and construction and reporting to Fosdick. The theatres were being built with appropriated funds, the largest body of such funding the commission would receive, and Fosdick wanted his own man close to the project.

As Tilton finished plans for the building, Klaw completed the details of his scheme to provide shows and submitted it to the commission on July 19. For three weeks he waited for a reply. His patience frayed, Klaw wrote a grumbling letter to Fosdick. He petulantly suggested that the idea of camp entertainment must have been dropped since he had heard nothing. He went on that his plan was neither an argument that camp shows should be provided nor the only way it could be done — it was merely an illustration of one way to organize the camp theatres. He then huffily informed Fosdick that he would not come to Washington as an advocate for his scheme, but he would allow the commission to use his ideas as they pleased.[29] Klaw also asked about completion dates for the theatre buildings, for without this information, he argued, he could not begin booking talent. The request yielded no information on when the theatres would be ready, but the complaints prompted Fosdick to assure Klaw of the government's sincerity by offering him a seat on the commission. Klaw was appeased by the honor and accepted the offer on August 23.[30]

Conditions at the beginning of the camp theatre venture promised no quick and easy successes. The commission had money to build theatres but no money to operate them. The planning of the buildings was largely in inexperienced hands. F. Richard Anderson was experienced in designing and developing theatrical real estate and Edward Tilton was a more than competent architect, but Mayer was a social worker with no knowledge of building and equipping theatres. The commission's public recreation-oriented philosophy indisposed them in their dealings with the theatre businessmen, and the CTCA tried at first to organize entertainment without professional assistance. When at last they appealed to the theatre industry they unwittingly cast their lot with an individual, Marc Klaw, so embattled as to be only marginally capable of mobilizing the commercial theatre establishment and the motion picture business. Moreover, the theatre business was torn by competitive strife and struggling to counter the effects of rising costs, declining productivity and decreasing demand for its products. That the venture ever got beyond these planning stages testifies to the strength of the convictions of Raymond Fosdick, Lee Hanmer, Jasper Mayer, and Marc Klaw, if not to their efficiency and managerial acumen.

7

Tents, Theatres and More Theatres

By September 1, 1918, the National Army cantonments were nearly built and the first levy of draftees was arriving. The commission efficiently developed law enforcement and recreation programs, and the volunteer organizations, such as the YMCA, built huts and auditoriums and created large and diverse welfare and entertainment programs, but the government's camp theatre project stalled. The building program faltered in the planning stages as Lee Hanmer conferred with commission architect Edward Tilton over the design of the camp auditorium. The CTCA was six weeks away from being able to begin construction of the camp theatres.

Moreover, camp commanders were not fully aware of the existence and function of the CTCA. In June 1917, Secretary Baker informed commanders of departments, the geographical divisions into which the War Department divided the country for the army's administrative purposes, of the work of the CTCA and its sanction in law, but, later, the adjutant general had to reconfirm the CTCA's existence and purpose.

When it became apparent that commission theatres would not be ready for the earliest draftees, the CTCA reversed its earlier rule forbidding concession theatres in the camps. At the same time Secretary Baker warned camp commanders that the CTCA would have to approve concession theatre contracts and that the commission's local representative would supervise commercial entertainment on or adjacent to camp property.[1] Commercial managers built four concession theatres as a result of this measure.

As a further stopgap, the commission arranged with the Redpath Lyceum Bureau of Chicago, Illinois, a circuit chautauqua booking agency managed by Harry P. Harrison, to supply entertainment in tents Harrison would transport to many camps. Furthermore, the chautauqua booking offices had the tents and the talent to meet the CTCA's immediate needs. The chautauqua agents knew the transportation facilities in the areas where the camps were being built, so tent theatres seemed a good temporary remedy. Lee Hanmer arranged with Harrison for Redpath to provide tents to several National Army cantonments and especially to the National Guard camps in the South, where the commission had made no provision for entertainment.

September 8, one week after the close of the regular chautauqua season, Harrison had entertainers and tents bound for the army camps with the largest populations. Redpath managers represented the commission in the camps at no profit to the Redpath Bureau. Harrison calculated that admission charges of 10 cents and 25 cents, according to the character and expense of the entertainment, would cover Redpath's expenses. Any surplus was to be given to the Post Exchange or used as the camp commander desired.

Almost without exception, camp commanders welcomed the tents, but several had reservations about charging the soldiers, so Hanmer had to delay the shipment of tents until the camp commanders consented to the collection of admissions.[2] The tent theatre plan encountered further unspecified delays, for by the end of September, tents were up and operating in only three camps; however, by the end of October tent theatres operated in 17 camps.[3] The CTCA sent the tents to the National Guard camps in the warmer southern and southwestern regions of the U.S., although tents did operate at Camp Grant, near Rockford, Illinois; at Camp Sherman, near Chillicothe, Ohio; at Camp Devens, near Ayer, Massachusetts; and at Camp Custer, Battle Creek, Michigan. Cold weather forced the discontinuance of tent operations at the northern cantonments in late November.

Despite an apparent need for camp shows, tent chautauqua was a strategic and financial failure. Soldiers did not attend the shows and the cost of managers, performers, tent rental, and transportation far exceeded gate receipts. Many tents closed after only a few weeks' operation, but a few continued for several months and often up to the opening of a Liberty Theatre in the camp.

Several factors contributed to the failure of the chautauqua tents, not the least of which was the competition from other forms of entertainment. The presence of the chautauqua tents in some of the camps caused some friction with the YMCA, which had engaged Paul Pierson of the Pennsylvania Chautauqua Circuit to organize similar entertainment in their auditoriums. Neither the YMCA nor the Redpath programs were attracting soldier interest, but Harold Braddock, director of the commission's field activities, felt sure that the dearth of entertainment in the cities adjacent to these southern camps assured the success of the camp enterprises.[4] However, it was soon apparent that the tents could not compete successfully with the auditoriums, huts, Knights of Columbus halls, and concession theatres. Neither the YMCA nor the Redpath operations met expenses. However, the YMCA could better afford to shoulder the expense than could the CTCA, which had no reserve to cover deficits.

At the commission's weekly meeting of November 21, Lee Hanmer asked Harrison and Pierson to cooperate.[5] The YMCA removed its tents in the southern National Guard camps and agreed to use the Redpath tents three days a week, while granting the CTCA and Redpath the use of the YMCA auditoriums in the National Army cantonments in the North for three days a week.[6] The Redpath activities and the YMCA Triangle Entertainments were consolidated under commission auspices and known thereafter as the Liberty Entertainments.[7] Harrison agreed to provide attractions for the joint program from his offices in Chicago. Aside from the competition, the tent business suffered in unseasonably cold fall and winter weather across the nation. In mid-January, Harrison reported to Fosdick that snow and cold had ruined business.

The number of tents used and their distribution is uncertain, as is the fare that played in them. More certainly, however, the commission spent over $114,000 more than it received from tent theatre business. To keep the tents open Harrison borrowed $20,000. By mid-February 1918, Harrison reported a total loss on Redpath tents of $102,000, one-fifth of which the CTCA owed Harrison's own Redpath Bureau for tent rental.[8] Fosdick initially disavowed responsibility for these losses but the CTCA eventually repaid Harrison.[9]

* * *

Chautauqua tents and concession theatres offered no workable solution to the problem of providing government-sponsored professional entertainment in the camps. The huts and auditoriums of the YMCA, the Jewish Welfare Board, and the Knights of Columbus presented amateur entertainers, a few volunteering professionals, and soldier shows while the government theatres being built to offer professional entertainment at least half the time were held up.

Hanmer, Mayer, and Tilton struggled to start theatre construction. By August 31, Tilton had provided the Emergency Construction Committee the necessary blueprints and specifications, and Hanmer estimated that the theatres could be operating by the first of October.[10] Things seemed to be proceeding smoothly, when the Quartermaster General's Cantonment Division informed Mayer that Tilton's theatres would cost significantly more than had been appropriated to build them.[11] Tilton had to redesign the auditorium to eliminate the balcony and to reduce the construction cost by about 20 percent. Tilton finished the new plans on September 18, and on the 25th Baker approved them and allotted the commission $432,000 to launch the project.[12] Another three weeks passed as the Quartermaster General prepared duplicate plans, instructions, and authorizations for Camp Constructing Quartermasters.[13]

Delays in preparing suitable plans postponed the beginning of construction until early October 1917 when camp construction was almost complete. The theatre plans arrived just as the civilian contractors were leaving, and many seem to have regarded the job as an anticlimax. More delays resulted from construction errors and confusion as contractors interpreted plans for a type of building with which they had little experience. In the northern United States one of the worst winters in decades made construction, especially excavation, nearly impossible. Cold weather often isolated the camps from the nearby towns where construction workers lived. When the workers could get to the camps, the cold slowed their labor. The weather also slowed or halted the delivery of construction materials, as railroads, already hard-pressed to move men from the camps and strategic goods from markets and factories to the East Coast debarkation ports, were tied up in blizzard-bound Midwestern rail yards. When the trains were running material and equipment was often misrouted or damaged during shipment. Occasionally, steel for theatrical rigging and copper for electrical equipment was not available. Finally, outbreaks of sickness in the training camps forced camp quarantines that halted the movement of construction workers to their jobs.

In early October, the CTCA began construction of 16 theatres. By late October, camp construction crews had started only four theatres.[14] Colonel Littell, Cantonment Construction Division commander, assured the CTCA that many of the theatres would be completed by mid–November.[15] However, by the end of the first week of November construction had not yet begun at three of the 16 camps.

In an effort to reduce the cost of construction and of rigging equipment, Tilton had designed the theatre to function without a gridiron, a reinforced gridwork ceiling high over the stage to which scene-shifting equipment and lighting instruments could be attached. In eliminating the gridiron, Tilton followed well-established theatre construction practice. Furthermore his design was more efficient since it reduced the weight to be borne by the loft above the stage, thereby reducing the amount of reinforcement the loft required.[16]

Apparently CTCA construction coordinator Jasper J. Mayer did not understand Tilton's plans. Mayer heard from a consultant in Portland, Oregon, that the theatres would need a gridiron from which to hoist and operate scenery and he believed him.[17] A ludicrous spectacle of bureaucratic bungling followed. Mayer reacted without checking with his architect. He asked the Cantonment Construction Division for more money for each theatre to cover the expense of adding the gridiron but he failed to discuss this change with Tilton. Fosdick instructed Constructing Quartermasters to leave scaffolding around the stage loft until revised plans could be prepared.[18] When word of the change reached Tilton, he objected, but Mayer ignored him and listened instead to H. Robert Law, whose firm was building stock scenery for some of the camp theatres. Law insisted that a theatre could be equipped less expensively if it had a gridiron. However, Law's cost estimate was lower because he proposed providing less rigging equipment.[19]

The government saved no money on the change, but H. Robert Law made a great deal, since his company won the contract for rigging a number of the camp stages. The addition of the gridiron caused further construction delays because plans had to be redrawn and specifications rewritten. The theatres ultimately cost no more with the gridiron than without, but they were less completely equipped and adding the gridiron unnecessarily delayed completion. Mayer's management of theatre construction was uninformed and ineffective at best, but, with the episode of the added gridiron, it reached its nadir.

Camp Taylor, Kentucky, and Camp Sherman, Ohio, were the first to open their theatres on December 3. Both used locally arranged entertainment. On December 6 the theatres at Camp Devens, Massachusetts, and Camp Custer, Michigan, were opened, likewise using local talent. On December 13 the theatre at Camp Pike, Arkansas, was ready. The first official opening was at Camp Sherman on January 10; others followed quickly until 11 were operating on February 20, 1918, when plans were announced for the construction of several new camp theatres of a new type.

The delay occasioned by the gridiron misunderstanding was but an episode in a story full of mistakes and bad luck. The construction of the theatres was poorly managed from the beginning. Crucial decisions about the camp auditoriums were dictated by naive preconceptions about the camp populations and about the ease with which shows and entertainers would be sent to the camps. Moreover, economic necessity meshed with these presumptions to lead the CTCA to build at least 20 quite dysfunctional buildings. When the commission decided at its first meeting to provide professional touring attractions, the size and equipment of the stage area was set. It would have dressing rooms, electrical fittings, scenery, and scene-shifting apparatus, including a loft, to provide minimal accommodation for legitimate attractions such as musical comedy. The theatres had to pay their own way on admissions. The military expressed disappointment that camp shows would not be free, so the commission had to keep

7. Tents, Theatres and More Theatres 71

Interior, Liberty Theatre, Camp Grant, Illinois. View from near the back of the auditorium to the stage suggests that seeing and hearing stage action could be impaired by distance to the stage and the size of the stage opening. An olio curtain shows a fashionable country setting and one can see advertising panels on the sides and across the bottom of the curtain (courtesy National Archives, photo no. 165-ww-565b-27).

prices well below the scale of commercial theatres. To pay expenses while charging low admission prices, they needed a large auditorium. The twin necessities of a stage equipped to handle large touring attractions and an auditorium large enough to enable low admissions to pay expenses thrust a stern economic demand upon the CTCA. Theatres meeting these requirements had to be built and equipped from an appropriation of a half million dollars and no more seemed available. That there were to be 16 theatres, one in each National Army cantonment, was unquestioned, so the cost per structure was determined.

The Class A theatres were structurally all alike, although the wood frame buildings varied slightly from camp to camp depending on the geographic features of the site and on the whim of the builder. The wood frame building rested on concrete piers. The stage house floor was a commodious 76 feet wide but only 26 feet deep. The fly tower or stage loft, where the troublesome gridiron was located, was 60 feet high, an adequate height for scenery to be lifted off the stage floor and hidden from audience view. The proscenium arch (the frame through which the audience viewed the action) was 35 feet wide and 25 feet high. An orchestra pit 52 feet wide occupied 13 feet of the auditorium floor and afforded exits to the stage and to a cellar beneath the stage, where the hot water heating plant was located. Six small dressing rooms, sized eight feet by four feet, lined one side of the backstage area; four sized six feet by eight feet lined the other. The dressing rooms were unheated and had no water supply, but thoughtful managers added these conveniences in most of the theatres. A small lobby, flanked by a ticket booth and office, four living rooms, a bath and men's and women's cloakrooms, fronted the auditorium. No vestibule was planned but most managers added large folding doors to partition the lobby area from the auditorium. Builders sealed the walls to the roof trusses with beaverboard, a cheap paper-composite material, but they left the rafters exposed. Nine stoves in the auditorium and two on the stage just behind the proscenium wall heated the building. Most were also equipped with exhaust fans and 12 large ceiling fans to improve ventilation. Local managers spent money from admissions to furnish the theatres, and the CTCA supplied a set of stock scenery, rigging apparatus for shifting it, lighting instruments, and an asbestos motion picture booth, a projector, and a screen.[20]

The auditorium was oversized according to the standards of its day. It was 120 feet wide and 131 feet deep and it could seat up to 3,000 on plank seats with plank backs. Eleven new theatres built in the Times Square theatre district of New York City in 1917-1918 seated from 800 to 1,200, the most common size of theatres built at that time for legitimate attractions. An auditorium seating 1,200 to 1,800 was considered large.[21]

The Class A theatres were also unsafe. Tilton had designed the auditorium floor to bear 70 pounds per square foot, but this was well below the standard for buildings of this type.[22] When the builder of the theatre at Camp Meade, Maryland, complained that the theatre would be unsafe with such a weak floor, the Construction Division ordered the modification all theatre floors to withstand loads of at least 100 pounds per square foot.[23]

The wood frame structures were fire hazards. They were equipped with 13 exits, each with panic bolts, but any other fire safety equipment was added piecemeal. For instance, the Constructing Quartermaster at Camp Merritt, New Jersey, informed the commanding general that the theatre was poorly designed and inadequately equipped for fire safety. Although it was fitted with some fire protection equipment there were no fire-fighting water lines in the building. The proscenium opening had no asbestos curtain, a standard fire safety feature in place to delay the spread of a fire onstage to the auditorium. Moreover, the wood frame and paperboard partition between the stage and the auditorium was no deterrent to the spread of a fire. Finally, neither the gallery nor the dressing rooms had exterior exits. Camp Merritt's quartermaster recommended that the theatre remain closed until the faults were corrected. E.L. Tilton acknowledged that the frame building was not in compliance with any municipal fire code but he argued that the size and placement of the lobby spaces, exits, and staircases had been based on the New York code.[24] The commission's supervisor of maintenance and construction, Allen C. Minnix, supported Tilton, suggesting that no further precautions needed to be taken, and he noted that "the fire equipment will take care of any fire that could be taken care of." He concluded that a "fire that cannot be handled by the present equipment, could not be handled in time to save a building of the type of structure that the Liberty Theatre is."[25] Minnix was probably right about the speed with which a fire would consume the wood and paper structure, but his comment seems to express callous disregard for the lives of people who should happen to be in the building when a fire broke out. Nevertheless, the quartermaster's request was denied and the Camp Merritt theatre opened on schedule.

The Class A theatres seem also to have been structurally unsound, especially in the stage house frame. The proscenium arch was weak and could buckle out toward the auditorium.[26] Other design features made the stage loft, a tower above the stage floor, weak and subject to buckling and twisting under wind stresses.[27] Constructing quartermasters in two camps complained that roof trusses over the auditorium were weak, and the theatre manager at Camp Meade had to strengthen the trusses in the stage loft to better sustain the weight of the gridiron, rigging, and scenery.[28]

In almost every case, the Class A theatres cost more than the planners had estimated.[29] Civilian contractors working under cost-plus contracts built all the Class A theatres except those at Camp Upton, New York, and Camp Lee, Virginia. The contractors purchased the materials, conveyed them to the site, hired the laborers and supervised the construction according to plans drawn by the Construction Division. The contracts provided for a maximum profit of 10 percent sliding to 6 percent of the cost of the work as the total cost increased. The cost-plus contracts were widely criticized because they afforded no effective cost controls, in part because contractors could be vertically integrated through separate ownership of building supplies, labor pools, and trucking firms. They could then purchase or lease goods and services from themselves at exorbitant prices, thereby staying within the cost limit of 10 percent but actually realizing a much larger profit because they also owned the sources of material and labor supply. After the war, then Gen. Isaac Littell of the Construction Division defended the cost-plus contracting before a congressional hearing into War Department expenditures. He claimed that actual profits were about 2 or 3 percent.[30] Cost overruns on the theatre contracts may have resulted as much from CTCA mismanagement and from inflation as from profiteering by the contractors because all three factors were at play in the situation.

Although the commission proposed a multipurpose building, useful both as a civic center and an entertainment center, Tilton's theatres could accommodate little other than large audiences viewing theatrical productions. Fixed bench seating and a raked floor rendered them unsuitable for athletics and physical training. They were also too large to be usable as classrooms or social halls; a plan to use curtains to partition areas of the auditorium was rejected because it was impractical and expensive.

Moreover, the size of the auditorium limited its usefulness as a theatre, for its acoustics and sightlines were poor. Theatre architect A.S. Meloy recommended that the auditorium depth should not exceed 75 feet if the human voice were to be heard without strain. Class A auditoriums were 131 feet deep. Managers complained that speaking voices could not be heard at the back of the auditorium, and the authors of the official report of the work of the Liberty Theatre Division admitted that the buildings were acoustically inadequate for any except the loudest musicals.[31] The auditorium was much too wide, so sight lines to the stage from the sections to the far right and far left were poor. About 16 percent of the seats in side sections were useless because pillars obstructed the view of the stage. Another 16 percent offered an unobstructed but poor view because they were so far from the center of the auditorium. Because of the positioning of pillars, the narrowness of the proscenium opening and the excessive width and depth of the auditorium only about 45 percent of the seats offered an unobstructed view of the stage in a seat from which one could hear actors speaking.[32]

The theatres were rickety fire hazards and far too large for the uses to which they were actually put. However, the largest Liberty Theatres were imposing structures, always among the largest buildings in camp and therefore the most visible manifestation of the work of the CTCA. By December 31, 1918, the War Department had built 19 such structures at the following locations:

> Camp Custer, Battle Creek, Michigan
> Camp Devens, Ayer, Massachusetts, north of Boston
> Camp Dix, Wrightstown, New Jersey
> Camp Dodge, Des Moines, Iowa
> Camp Funston, Fort Riley, Kansas, near Junction City
> Camp Gordon, Atlanta, Georgia
> Camp Grant, Rockford, Illinois
> Camp Humphreys, Belvoir, Virginia
> Camp Jackson, Columbia, South Carolina
> Camp Kearney, San Diego, California
> Camp Lee, Petersburg, Virginia

Liberty Theatre, Camp Cody, Deming, New Mexico. An example of the smallest camp theatre, designated Class B, seating 1,050 but with a fenced yard where soldiers could stand to look at a stage show or movie through upward opening doors in the sidewalls of the theatre (courtesy National Archives, 92-Construction Division Completion Reports, Box 56).

>
> Camp Lewis, Tacoma, Washington
> Camp Meade, Baltimore, Maryland
> Camp Merritt, Tenafly, New Jersey
> Camp Pike, Little Rock, Arkansas
> Camp Sherman, Chillicothe, Ohio
> Camp Stuart, Newport News, Virginia
> Camp Taylor, Louisville, Kentucky
> Camp Upton, Yaphank, Long Island, New York[33]

• • •

Even as the first theatres opened in late January and early February, the CTCA felt pressure to build more theatres. Commanders of the large debarkation camps near Hoboken, New Jersey, and Newport News, Virginia, and of the aviation camps near San Antonio, Texas, demanded recreation and entertainment facilities. And the public complained that large numbers of troops in camps without Liberty Theatres were unable to redeem Smileage coupons, admissions prepaid with the money raised in fund drives all over the country.[34] The commission decided in early February 1918 to build several "more or less temporary" theatres in National Guard and embarkation camps.

Economic considerations, in addition to public pressure and complaints from camp commanders, figured significantly in the commission's decision. At the time the commissioners decided to build more theatres, the camp theatres were turning a weekly profit of approximately $200 while operating at about half capacity. (See Appendix B, Liberty Theatre Expenses, and Appendix C, Gross Receipts and Estimates of Attendance.) It looked like a smaller theatre in the National Guard camps could pay its own way, for experience showed they didn't have to accommodate capacity crowds to pay expenses. In addition, the Military Entertainment Committee of the CTCA decided to book the small theatres with variety acts and motion pictures rather than legitimate plays and musicals, so the new theatres could be smaller and built without the space and machinery for shifting the sets used by touring plays and musicals. Vaudeville acts and movies cost less so the small houses could meet expenses even with very low-priced tickets. There was some logic in building very different theatres in the most of the National Guard camps.

E.L. Tilton designed a small theatre, designated Class B, to seat 1,050. The War Department authorized 19.[35] Seven were cancelled because concession theatres in and near the camps were supplying the entertainment needs of the soldiers. Camp commanders cancelled two more because they wanted larger theatres. Ten were finally built at the following locations and seven of these were later remodeled to provide a larger auditorium and a fly loft over an enlarged stage:

> Camp Beauregard, Alexandria, Louisiana
> Camp Bowie, Fort Worth, Texas
> Camp Cody, Deming, New Mexico
> Camp Doniphan, Fort Sill, Oklahoma, near Lawton, Oklahoma
> Camp Fremont, Palo Alto, California
> Camp Hancock, Augusta, Georgia
> Camp Logan, Houston, Texas
> Camp MacArthur, Waco, Texas
> Camp Wadsworth, Spartanburg, South Carolina
> Camp Wheeler, Macon, Georgia[36]

The Class B theatres, like the larger Class A buildings, were little more than rude frame shelters over an auditorium filled with rough benches. Initially the small theatres had only a packed earth floor, but wood floors were added later, and they had no loft over the stage area. Large windows with upward swinging doors permitted soldiers standing in the enclosed yard around the theatre to see the stage. The buildings were about 113 feet long and 60 feet wide. The theatre had a wide but slender and shallow orchestra pit. The proscenium opening was 30 feet wide and 16 feet high and the playing area behind it was roughly 36 feet wide and 25 feet deep, which provided plenty of space for the vaudeville shows and motion pictures to be presented in them. There were small dressing rooms and toilets right and left backstage.³⁷ The Class B theatres were much less expensively equipped than the Class A theatres, although they were given a supply of stock scenery. Preliminary estimates indicated the theatres could be built for $4,000 each, but they actually cost more, averaging about $6,000 each. The buildings were small and simple, so the construction problems encountered earlier never developed. Seven Class B theatres were operating seven weeks after they were authorized.

The commission acquired a small theatre at Camp McClellan, Anniston, Alabama, where soldiers had converted a canteen to a motion picture and vaudeville house. The commission assumed management of the theatre in April 1918 after the War Department purchased the building from the men of the 112th Field Artillery for $2000.³⁸

In a similar move, but at the direction of the adjutant general of the army, the commission assumed the operation of the Buffalo Auditorium, a 2,500-seat theatre built at Camp Upton, Yaphank, New York, by the Welfare League of the 367th Infantry, a Negro battalion recruited in the New York City area. The theatre opened in early February 1918, and the commission took it over on May 21. Net profits from the operation of the theatre were forwarded to the commanding general of Camp Upton for transmittal to the treasurer of the 367th Infantry Welfare League, who was responsible for the redemption of the bonds floated to finance the construction of the building. The commanding general of Camp Upton, using camp funds, purchased the Buffalo Auditorium from the Welfare League of the 367th Infantry in April 1919.³⁹

During the spring and summer of 1918, the commission acquired three theatres operated inside camps by commercial amusement companies. The commission had allowed camp commanders to engage private amusement companies to provide entertainment in the camp or on its perimeter. Concessionaires built four private theatres; complaints about three of them caused the CTCA to take over their operation and buy the buildings.

An entrepreneur at Camp Sevier, Greenville, South Carolina, offered burlesque shows in a tent theatre during the autumn of 1917, then continued the same fare in the Hippodrome, a 2,500-seat theatre he built inside the camp. The commission's chautauqua tent competed with the Hippodrome, but failed to attract the soldiers. In January 1918, the camp's YMCA secretary protested to his national organization that the camp's chief of staff had been burlesqued in a show at the Hippodrome. Camp authorities also reported that civilian watchdogs complained of suggestive and objectionable dances in the theatre and of sexual relations and marriages between the soldiers and girls of the burlesque company. Finally, camp welfare workers asked the camp commander to revoke the concession contract and assume direct control of the Hippodrome. The CTCA considered purchasing the Hippodrome, but took no immediate action, although the theatre seems to have been its concession nightmare come true.[40]

D.B. Traxler, the Hippodrome's owner, made some efforts to censor his shows, but the complaints continued, finally reaching the ears of Samuel J. Nicholls, representative to Congress from South Carolina and member of the House Committee on Military Affairs, before which R.B. Fosdick appeared on March 14, 1918, to request money for the CTCA. Nicholls interrupted Fosdick's testimony about the operation of the Liberty Theatres with a question about what he was doing about "improper shows at the camps." Fosdick replied that only a few private concession theatres had been troublesome, one of which was the Hippodrome at Camp Sevier. Nicholls remarked that he too had received numerous complaints, and he believed that "it would be foolish to try to upbuild the morale of the troops on the one hand while permitting institutions like this to tear it down on the other." Fosdick agreed, but noted that the complaints were very recent and that the management had reformed its shows. Fosdick added, however, that he was not "convinced of the permanency of the reform."[41]

Their funding threatened, the CTCA took over the Hippodrome and renamed it the Liberty Theatre No. 1. The commission also seized the Gayety, another Traxler theatre devoted to motion pictures and vaudeville, and renamed it Liberty Theatre No. 2. The CTCA paid Traxler $16,500 for his two buildings, giving him a generous price considering that the new, smaller theatres were costing about $6,000 each. Ultimately the former Hippodrome was razed, while the Gayety was rebuilt to become the camp's only theatre.[42]

The commission also purchased the Majestic Theatre, built by the Interstate Amusement Company of Chicago in Camp Travis, San Antonio, Texas. Karl Hoblitzelle's Interstate Amusement Company pledged 10 percent of the gross receipts of the Majestic to the commanding general for use in the camp as their part of the concession agreement. The theatre, seating 1,942, opened in January 1918 with Interstate's best vaudeville. The venture was at first unprofitable, but about March 1 Interstate engaged a musical comedy stock company and soon started making money.

At the time the government claimed the Traxler theatres in South Carolina, commission representatives inquired about purchasing the Majestic. The theatre was making money, but Interstate claimed it wasn't making enough. Furthermore, Interstate specialized in vaudeville, so they felt they were not comfortable managing the musical stock companies that provided the kind of entertainment that attracted soldiers to the Majestic. Hoblitzelle offered the Majestic to the government for about $47,000, but the CTCA rejected the price as too high. Negotiations stalled until mid-May when the

Liberty Theatre, Camp Bowie, Fort Worth, Texas, one of the smallest theatres, was enlarged to include a new stage, stage house, and lobby. It was designated "Class C (Reconstructed)." The men are not identified. The billboard announces the mind reader Mercedes and his vaudeville troupe (courtesy National Archives, 92-Construction Division Completion Reports, Box 36).

commission received a report from the Ministerial Union of San Antonio, Texas. It claimed that visitors to the camp theatre had discovered performers of "apparently dissolute character" telling low, coarse jokes and scantily clad actresses leaving the stage to sit on the soldiers' laps and kiss them.[43] After weeks of negotiations filled with charges of immorality, Hoblitzelle sold the Majestic to the CTCA for $32,000.[44] McBride pressured Interstate into selling at the commission's price, but by the time it was sold the theatre wasn't turning a profit, so Hoblitzelle was out of a shaky, troublesome investment with a tidy bundle of cash.

By June 30, 1918, the CTCA was operating 31 theatres in camps across the nation. Virtually all the new, small theatres profited from the first week of operation, primarily because of their low cost of operation. When the Class B theatres were all completed and operating, they raised the total monthly capacity of all Liberty Theatres to 1,550,000. The theatres continued to be marginally profitable through June 1918, even though estimated attendance was only 39 percent of capacity. Thirty-one theatres were grossing only a little over $1,000 per week on the average, but they were paying only about $800 per week for talent and other expenses.

In August and September 1918, the commission enlarged the theatre program by approving the construction of 13 Class C theatres costing about $25,000 each.⁴⁵ They built only one, at Camp Franklin (part of Camp Meade) near Baltimore, Maryland. The Class C theatre seated 1,300 and had a fly loft above the stage floor for lifting and lowering scenery. It cost about $26,000.⁴⁶ The CTCA also allocated $45,000 to enlarge Class B theatres at camps Beauregard, Bowie, Cody, Hancock, Logan, MacArthur, and McClellan. The reconstructed Class B theatres with a fly loft, larger stage, and larger auditorium were designated Class C (Reconstructed). Their wood-floored auditoria seated 1,300; enlarged lobby spaces were also floored over. These reconstructions cost about $15,000 each, about three times the preliminary estimate. The scenic equipment in the Class C theatres was standardized, as had been that in the Class A and B theatres.⁴⁷

From mid-August through late October 1918, the CTCA authorized 10 new Class D theatres seating about 1,600 each. Construction on eight of them was suspended just after the armistice. Three were completed. The one at Camp Mills, Mineola, New York, opened January 2, 1919, and the one at Camp Eustis, near Lee Hall, Virginia, opened February 22, 1919. The CTCA provided the plans and $28,000 for materials and soldiers built their Victory Theatre at Camp Lee, Petersburg, Virginia. It opened January 13, 1919. The Class D theatre, designed by R.C. Chapin, was quite different from the other Liberty Theatres. Instead of being a rectilinear frame building, the Class D theatre was shaped like the longitudinal half of a cylinder resting on its flat side. The resulting arched roof required no internal pillars, so sight lines were better. It had more backstage floor space, hence more off-stage storage area than in the Class A theatre. The proscenium opening was smaller than in the Class A theatre and the auditorium was just three-fifths the width of the Class A auditorium. The new theatre's stage house was also more substantially wind-braced than the old. The CTCA provided standard scenery that cost about twice as much as that put in the Class A theatres.⁴⁸ Class D theatres were projected to cost about $43,000, but the actual cost of each, except that at Camp Lee, exceeded $61,000.⁴⁹ Appendix A lists known opening and closing dates of all the army's Liberty Theatres.

Large Liberty Tents, seating 1,600, were used at Camp Greene, Charlotte, North Carolina; at Kelly Field, San Antonio, Texas, where two were open in June 1918 and one was open in July and August 1918; and at the Field Artillery Training Center at Camp Knox, West Point, Kentucky. The CTCA also operated an amphitheater at Las Casas, Puerto Rico. This, the only Liberty Theatre outside the continental limits of the United States, seated about 3,000 before a stage 72 feet wide and about 30 feet deep. It cost the commission a little less than $5,000.

7. Tents, Theatres and More Theatres 81

Liberty Theatre, Camp Eustis, Lee Hall, Virginia, was a D class theatre. Patrons entered up a ramp to the rear of the auditorium and the auditorium floor inclined toward the stage. Note the size of the building relative to surrounding structures, mostly barracks (courtesy National Archives, 92-Construction Division Completion Reports, Box 93).

After the CTCA was demobilized August 31, 1919, the army built three theatres the same size as the Class D theatres, but they were more permanent structures, finished with carpets in the lobby, runners in the aisles, and opera chairs instead of bench seats. Builders equipped them with an asbestos curtain and a firewall between the stage house and the auditorium, assets not enjoyed by audiences in the earlier, less permanent Liberty Theatres. Although the army completed them, the CTCA had allotted $175,000 for their construction.[50]

The Morale Division of the War Department General Staff later built several Class G theatres at posts along the Mexican border. They were the same architectural form as the Class D theatres, but smaller, seating about 1,200 on one floor, with exterior decorations in Spanish mission style.[51] By February 1920, the Morale Division had 23 theatres planned or in operation.[52]

The Commission on Training Camp Activities spent a total of $1.5 million for theatre construction and approximately $150,000 for theatre equipment.[53] Throughout 1918 the CTCA became more efficient in planning, building and equipping new theatres, but it continued to experience enormous cost overruns. The first 11 Class A theatres overran their original allotments by 33 percent. They could not escape the effects of the soaring cost of construction during the war years. Later construction projects were even more troublesome in this respect.[54] Costs exceeded initial allotments by 50 percent in the case of Class B construction and by 100 percent in all other projects. The record indicates no reasonable explanation for the cost overruns, although a combination of profiteering, inflation, and mismanagement is the likely suspect. Moreover, one fails to see the logic of spending money to enlarge buildings already too large for the demands placed on them, as was done with the theatre reconstructions in the National Guard camps. Finally, the need for theatres as large as those in Class D, seating 1,600, was not born out in attendance numbers. See Appendix C, Gross Receipts and Estimates of Attendance.

At the time the commission decided to reconstruct the small theatres and build more and larger ones, barely one-third of the available capacity of the camp theatres was being used. On the other hand, the theatres were profitable. See Appendix B, Liberty Theatre Expenses, and Appendix C, Gross Receipts and Estimates of Attendance. In August 1918 theatre operations turned a total profit of $67,000. In September profits remained high at about $40,000. The major cause for this was that the commission paid the least ever for talent, only $550 per week in August, and just $620 per week in September. The impending end of the war slowed the flow of troops leaving the camps for France. Resultant high camp populations hiked attendance to 52 percent of capacity, equaling the best months in early 1918. November 1918 was thus the best month ever at the gate, with the theatres grossing over $240,000, or about $1,750 per week per theatre.

Why did the commission continue to seek and spend money for construction and enlargement of camp theatres when those already in service were so poorly utilized and when the affiliated civilian organizations, such as the YMCA and the Knights of Columbus, were opening recreational buildings? Profit is a recurrent theme in the commission's external correspondence and internal memoranda. A survey of profit and loss figures indicates that the theatre venture was profitable despite low attendance, a feat the commission accomplished by cutting the cost of talent as attendance went down. It is truly ironic that a commission so suspicious of commercial entertainment and wary of the potential for profiteering could have become so clearly driven by the motive it feared in others. It is an irony that those once so skittish about "cheap amusements" would have resorted to stringent cost-cutting measures in order to maintain profitability.

When the final flurry of construction was completed with the opening of the theatre at Camp Eustis, Virginia, on February 22, 1919, Liberty Theatres were operating in 35 camps and had a total monthly capacity of almost 2.2 million. However, attendance was steadily dropping as the American Expeditionary Force demobilized and divisions in training were released from duty. During the period between January 26 and March 1, 1919, attendance at Liberty Theatres was only about 500,000, or 23 percent of the total capacity for the period. In March and April it was up slightly to 26 percent, but it dropped steadily thereafter.

Despite the lack of attendance, the camp theatres returned a steady profit until late April 1919.[55] As demobilization emptied the ranks of the military, the theatres remaining open experienced steady operating losses from April through August 1919. Ultimately, however, the commission realized a profit on all theatre operations from September 1917 to September 1919 of about $270,000.[56]

8

Money Matters

The CTCA had money to build the theatres but none to pay for talent to entertain the troops. In the summer of 1917, theatre producer Marc Klaw gave the CTCA personal advice, made tentative arrangements with other theatre producers, and volunteered the services of his office staff, but he continued to complain that Hanmer and Mayer would not answer his questions about how the theatres were going to operate.

In early September, Klaw appointed a committee of prominent theatrical producers and artists to assist in mobilizing the theatre industry. Lee Shubert consented to serve, as did producer and lyricist Arthur Hammerstein, composer Irving Berlin, and producer and director Arthur Hopkins, all aligned with the Shubert interests. E.F. Albee, head of the United Booking Office, a powerful vaudeville agency, and Guilio Gatti-Cazazza, producing manager of New York's Metropolitan Opera Company, joined Klaw's committee. So did Sam Scribner, president of the Columbia Amusement Company, which at the time exercised a virtual monopoly in the production and exhibition of "high-class" burlesque, shows Scribner touted as suitable for family entertainment. But Klaw packed the committee with his friends and associates. He enlisted his partner Abraham Erlanger, his son Joseph (an accountant and apprentice producer at the Klaw and Erlanger Exchange), and two Klaw employees, W.L. Lillard and F. Richard Anderson. He also appointed several producers who used Klaw and Erlanger theatres exclusively: David Belasco, Henry W. Savage, Sam H. Harris, George M. Cohan, John Golden (who contributed money and time to the Stage Relief Fund and the Stage Door Canteen during World War II), Al Woods, and Winchell Smith. Then, to legitimize the camp theatre venture and increase its social credibility, Klaw appointed another advisory committee made up of 21 distinguished financiers, educators, and philanthropists. It included Otto Kahn, whom Klaw asked to be chairman; August Belmont, Jr., president of the Interborough Rapid Transit Company, New York City's first subway line; world-famous graphic artist Charles Dana Gibson; mining industrialist Daniel Guggenheim; and wealthy New York cotton merchant August D. Juilliard.[1] Klaw asked Otto Kahn to head the committee that Klaw regarded as "a good balance wheel for a theatrical committee." He also advised Kahn that the committee might not be called upon.[2] Indeed, it was called upon, but not for advice. Even as their names were being announced, Fosdick was asking them for money.

In late September, Klaw began to agitate for money to secure the contracts of performers to play the camps. He feared the theatres would be finished before he could arrange attractions to fill them if he could not immediately start writing contracts. He also argued that performers wanted partial payment in advance and assurances they would be fully and promptly paid at each engagement. His demands simply reiterated common themes in the business of theatre, but suspicion and disappointment abounded on all sides. The commissioners thought the monetary concerns of theatre managers meant they were either greedy or indifferent to the needs of the men in the camps. Klaw doubted the government really wanted professional entertainers in the camps, since they seemed unwilling to pay anything to get them; and producers of tours doubted they could economically route shows to many of the training camps in remote locations. The commission's only response to Klaw was the approval of his suggestion that the camp auditoriums be called Liberty Theatres. They also let him order the Smileage tickets that would be sold in advance of the theatre openings.[3]

Klaw directed his complaints at profound difficulties in the organization of the CTCA and in the laws by which it was empowered to spend public money. The CTCA struggled with the problem of paying for all kinds of personal services. Congress earmarked the appropriation of $500,000 for theatre construction and stipulated that none of it could be spent for personal services. The commission itself had no appropriation for personnel. Until October 16, 1917, its employees, mainly drafted from the Education Department of the Russell Sage Foundation, were paid from private contributions to an Auxiliary Fund. The CTCA made no allocation from this fund to operate a booking office or to pay theatrical performers.[4] As the deadlock persisted, Marc Klaw renewed his promise to book attractions for the camp theatres, but he vowed he would not solicit funds for them.

Hanmer prepared a letter for Fosdick to send to dozens of prominent individuals requesting loans to finance the Liberty Theatre operation, but Fosdick sent it only to those who happened to ask how they might be able to help with the commission's activities. Hanmer repeatedly asked Fosdick if he had located money for organizing the camp entertainment service, but

Fosdick had none. Fosdick made a brief appeal, at Klaw's suggestion, to H.S. Braucher of the American Playground and Recreation Association, whose organization had some donated funds to be used for camp welfare projects, but he got no money. Finally, on October 25 Klaw threatened to quit. He complained to Hanmer that he could get nothing done, and he worried that the theatres would be finished and there would be no shows booked for them. He needed the authority to issue contracts and the money to back his offers to performers and directors.[5]

Hanmer immediately sent Klaw's letter to Fosdick promising Fosdick he would try to keep Klaw engaged, but Hanmer was far from conciliatory: "If he declines to play the game, we can probably hire a good man to manage the bookings. Mr. Harrison could do it. We can make motion picture houses of the theatres if we have to. This is surely *war*."[6] Fosdick was not so willing to dump Klaw. Hanmer asked Klaw to wait for a few more days, and Fosdick wrote him a strongly apologetic letter, promising to renew his efforts to get money for the theatres.

At the same time, Klaw named the members of his two committees in an article in the *New York Times Magazine*, November 4, 1917, under the headlines "Real Theatres in Every National Army Camp" and "Soldiers in the Cantonments Will See Best Plays and Leading American Actors Each Week — Highest Ticket Price Twenty-five Cents." Klaw's picture of high-profile and solvent camp theatres was a fantasy, but the exaggerations seem to have been floating on Klaw's high hopes for his scheme to sell advance admissions to the general public, theatre passes called Smileage that citizens could give to soldiers, and on Raymond Fosdick's attempt to raise seed money from wealthy Americans. Klaw's threat to quit had worked to move Fosdick to action. On November 2, he began his promised campaign with a letter to over 30 prominent American philanthropists, including those on Klaw's blue-ribbon advisory committee. Fosdick wrote that the CTCA needed $50,000 to pay the preliminary expenses of booking shows for the camp theatre, and he promised the commission would repay everyone out of the receipts from the theatres. Fosdick also pointed out that the theatrical booking firm of Klaw and Erlanger had already contributed $20,000. Fosdick probably exaggerated the support of Klaw and Erlanger to sweeten the loan appeal. However, Klaw and his staff had been consulted about theatre construction and were working to identify performers and productions that might be routed to the camps, a not insignificant contribution. On November 15, Klaw began charging the CTCA $250 per week for office space and clerical help in his New York headquarters. At this rate, Klaw's contribution prior to November 15 could have been valued at about $4,000.[7]

The loan drive succeeded. By November 17, benefactors had pledged $67,000. Horace de Lisser, founder and chairman of the board of the Ajax

Rubber Company, offered $5,000, as did James Couzens, a founder and long-time general manager of the Ford Motor Company, in 1917 serving as police commissioner of Detroit, Michigan. Fosdick quickly redeemed $50,000 of these pledges, but Klaw saw none of it. The day the drive ended, Fosdick promised Harry P. Harrison $15,000 to cover some of Harrison's losses on the operation of chautauqua tents in the camps.[8] By February 16, Fosdick had paid Harrison $72,000, including all the money solicited for Klaw's booking operation.

Needless to say, Klaw was piqued by Fosdick's action, which he believed to be a misuse of the theatre guarantee fund. But Fosdick really had no alternative. Failure to pay Harrison's debts would only further damage the commission's reputation with lenders and supporters. He could not use government funds to cover Harrison's losses, and the Auxiliary Fund, his only remaining source, was not large enough to support such an expense as the tents had incurred.[9] The only money available was in the theatre guarantee fund. To make matters worse between Klaw and the commission, Fosdick had to further impose on Klaw's generosity, for the CTCA was unable to pay Klaw the $1,000 per month he needed to cover the cost of rent and wages in the New York booking office. In early December, even as the first theatres neared completion, Klaw was still waiting for the money needed to confirm engagements for the camp theatres, and Fosdick was still trying to find it.

Delays in launching the program for the Liberty Theatres adversely affected all the commission's efforts. An inspection tour in November 1917 revealed that the commission's programs and purposes were little understood or appreciated. The situation could hardly have been otherwise, given that what the CTCA proposed for the camps was a radical departure from common military practice based on well-established traditions. Commissioner Malcolm McBride was especially concerned about the inspection report and wrote to Fosdick and Hanmer to ask them to visit the camps personally and offer commanders assurance of the earnestness of the commission's efforts to provide recreational facilities. McBride feared the total failure of the recreation program of the commission, upon which most of their appropriation was being spent.[10]

Neither Fosdick nor Hanmer made the tour McBride suggested. Instead, Jasper J. Mayer, the commission executive secretary and Fosdick's man in charge of theatre construction, toured the construction sites in early December. His report substantiated McBride's fears and once more alerted commission executives to the danger of further temporizing over the theatres. However, Mayer laid at least part of the blame for delays at Klaw's feet. Mayer confirmed that the theatre was the most conspicuous building in the camp. Indeed, the theatre was the only part of the commission's direct effort that was materially visible. Mayer reported being received cordially, but he also found officials doubtful that the theatre would ever be functional. He expressed resentment that Klaw could not or would not begin booking attractions without a financial reserve, and he recommended that Harry P. Harrison book Redpath Lyceum programs into the camps where that was feasible; otherwise local managers could book whatever was available to them locally. He was adamant that shows appear on the Liberty Theatre stages at once, because delays were undermining the credibility of the commission.[11] But Mayer's efforts to heap blame for the crisis on Klaw can be seen only as the craven act of a man whose failures in administering theatre construction were manifestly the root cause of the delays damaging the CTCA's reputation.

Klaw had not demanded a "large financial reserve," as Mayer had charged. He needed concrete information about material conditions in the theatres and their environs. He was doing no less than any booking agent would do in trying to guarantee his clients they would not lose money when they toured the camps. By the 10th of December, Klaw was at his wit's end. He had equipped a Liberty Theatre booking office and he was paying three salaries to keep it open. He had solicited commitments from directors and other artists needed to assemble shows for the camps, but he couldn't get the specific, reliable information about the camps and about transportation and baggage hauling so vital to a smoothly working tour. Newspapers were also pressuring him for information and he had nothing definite to give them. He was embarrassed and angry and he threatened to abandon the project at the end of December if something weren't done.[12]

Klaw's threats to quit and to expose to the press the shambles of the commission's Liberty Theatre program must have perturbed Fosdick, for his response to Klaw's understandably immoderate and threatening letter illustrates the degree to which Fosdick and the CTCA at large disdained Klaw and his business and its practices. Klaw had repeatedly said he would book attractions for the Liberty Theatres, but he would not solicit funds for them.[13] Nevertheless, Fosdick secured a letter from Secretary of War Baker to give to Klaw to use as collateral to borrow $50,000 to finance the first production of shows for the Liberty Theatres, with repayment guaranteed from box office receipts.[14] But Klaw needed specific, accurate and timely information about the camp theatres—how to get to them from nearby railheads and what tour managers might expect by way of accommodations near and at the theatres—as much as he needed money to guarantee artists' contracts. Klaw made no use of the letter from Baker. The fact that he did not resign immediately and as publicly and noisily as possible is a monument to his forbearance.

In early December 1917 the Liberty Theatre project seemed doomed to failure. The CTCA was building theatres, but the government had no money to staff them or supply them with talent. The commission seriously considered discontinuing the project and assigning the auditoriums to local camp authorities or turning them over to private businessmen. Ironically, they had a solution in hand that they were not using; Klaw had invented it, but Harry P. Harrison had to devise a way to apply it to the problem.

Since mid–September 1917, Klaw had been trying to organize an advance sale of Liberty Theatre admissions. He wanted to sell special coupons to private citizens who could then give them to friends and relatives in camp. He followed the example of America's railway companies, which sold discounted mileage coupons to passengers who could later redeem them for rail fare at the advertised rates. Since the theatre tickets were to be used to brighten the lives of soldiers, Klaw called them Smileage coupons. Klaw's ticket plan also necessitated a name common to all the camp theatres to simplify the printing of the coupons and to protect the venture against the misrepresentations of commercial theatres, so all camp auditoriums or tents were called Liberty Theatres.[15]

Klaw had coupons printed with the total face value of $400,000, but, true to his promise, he made no special effort to sell them and would have abandoned the idea had not others stepped up to market the coupons.[16] Beginning November 24, the Stage Women's War Relief sold Smileage at a patriotic exposition called Heroland at the Grand Central Palace, an exhibition hall near New York City's Grand Central Station. The "bazaar" drew 12,000 visitors daily and took in nearly $600,000 in support of the war effort, including some undisclosed amount for Smileage.[17] However, Harry P. Harrison was convinced that Smileage was workable if the commission organized volunteers to market the coupons. Harrison believed that civilian subscriptions could maintain the whole chain of camp theatres. Advance ticket sales would provide the money Klaw needed to make his booking office fully functional, and the tickets would release the soldiers from having to buy admissions out of their very shallow pockets. He explained the idea to Fosdick and in mid–November Fosdick gained Secretary Baker's approval to go ahead with the plan.[18]

But the CTCA had no money to begin a sales campaign until about December 1, when Harrison negotiated a loan of $50,000 from the Central Trust Company of Chicago, Illinois. Central Trust at first insisted it be repaid from Smileage sales before receipts were used for anything else. Harrison balked at this, knowing such a repayment plan would further impede the flow of cash needed immediately to book talent for the camp stages. The bankers retreated to a demand that the War Department guarantee repayment in the event the Smileage drive failed entirely. Fosdick could make no such promise, so Harrison secured the bank loan personally.

On December 12, Harrison met in Washington with leaders of the International Association of Rotary Clubs and the managers of the chautauqua-lyceum bureaus to plan the nationwide Smileage campaign. They decided the sale should begin January 1, 1918, and they appointed Harold Braddock, formerly supervisor of CTCA field activities, as its director. Braddock brought valuable experience to his new post. He had been associate director of the first Red Cross War Fund drive in the summer of 1917, and he had helped the American Library Association solicit money to buy books for camp libraries. Secretary Baker suggested Fosdick appoint a committee to assist Braddock, particularly with the initial distribution of the Smileage books. Baker then named the people he wanted to serve on the Military Entertainment Council. James Couzens, a contributor to the theatre guarantee fund, was named chairman. Council members included Asa G. Candler, founder and chairman of the board of the Coca-Cola Bottling Company; F.W. Woolworth, variety store magnate; and Otto H. Kahn.[19]

By mid-January, Braddock had contacted campaign managers in several states.[20] He distributed the stock of coupons Klaw had printed, and, since the campaign goal was $1 million, Braddock ordered more coupons with a face value of $3.4 million. Globe Ticket Company of Philadelphia delivered the coupons on January 19, and Braddock sent them to the campaign chairmen in the states in time for an intensive sales campaign the week of January 28.

The Smileage campaign in the state of Iowa was typical, and it illustrates the means by which the coupons were distributed to civilian purchasers. Braddock appointed a state director, Clifford DePuy of Des Moines, publisher of *The Northwestern Banker*. DePuy appointed a chairman for each of the 11 districts into which the State Banker's Association divided the state. The district chairmen appointed chairmen for each of the counties included in their district. The Smileage organization varied throughout the state, being organized locally to suit local conditions. Linn County, seated at Cedar Rapids, for instance, had chairmen for each township. County and township chairmen asked committees from high schools, women's clubs, civic organizations, and chambers of commerce to canvass their areas. Businesses and manufacturers bought Smileage for their employees in the service. Not all localities were canvassed — in some areas banks, newspaper offices, and stores offered the coupons for sale. The volunteer sales agents collected cash for coupons and returned it via channels to Washington, where commission accountants credited the Smileage Fund. The campaign was hindered at first by a shortage of books, but Iowa was finally able to contribute nearly $36,000 by the end of 1918.[21]

The sales campaign was hastily but well organized, but Braddock devised no effective system for getting the coupons from the civilian pur-

8. Money Matters   91

Lobby and box office, Liberty Theatre, Camp Grant, Illinois, with a sign promoting the use of Smileage coupons, another warning away civilians not the guests of soldiers, and a third reminding patrons to telephone for reserved seats. The bill posted on the theatre entry door, left, announces Mercedes, a mind reader, headlining a vaudeville troupe that visited camps in June and July of 1918 and again from December 1918 through late February 1919 (courtesy National Archives, photo no. 165-ww-565b-26).

chaser to the soldiers. In some cases, individuals purchased coupons and sent them to friends or relatives in camps. In other cases, a community-wide appeal for contributions netted money used to purchase Smileage in the name of the community. The community then sent the coupons to the commanding officer of the camp where the community's National Guard or National Army contingent was training. Camp officials then distributed the coupons.

The books of Smileage coupons were worth $1 and $5. The soldier attending the Liberty Theatre presented his 5-cent or 25-cent coupons at the box office where they were accepted as cash. Here began the time-consuming bureaucratic redemption process. Periodically, the theatre sent the coupons to an office in Chicago, where they were recounted then sent to Washington. There the Smileage Fund was charged for the face value of the coupons, less 10 percent set aside to pay expenses such as printing and postage. From Washington the cash made its way back to Chicago and thence to the theatres where the coupons had been collected. Theatre managers could then write checks to pay for talent and other operating expenses.

The Smileage sales campaign was much more successful than the planners had hoped. By February 15, the commission had repaid the loan of $50,000 to Central Trust Company, and by mid-March over $200,000 had flowed into the Washington office.[22] Distributing, selling and redeeming Smileage was cumbersome, but the coupons got the Liberty Theatre program going and kept it solvent. The *Report of the Military Entertainment Committee* indicates that Smileage accounted for 60 percent of the receipts of the Liberty Theatres in 1918, (p. 60) but this is an exaggeration. Theatre receipts up to December 28, 1918, were approximately $1.5 million. Smileage redemption as of the same date was only $630,000, or approximately 40 percent of the receipts.[23] Smileage sales stopped a week after the armistice, although camp theatre box offices accepted the coupons until September 30, 1919. As of that date, Smileage sales were $1.038 million; redemptions totaled $635,000.[24] While 10 percent of Smileage receipts were set aside to pay the cost of the sales campaign, it cost over $150,000, or about 15 percent of receipts.[25] Ultimately, Smileage paid for 2.3 million of the estimated 8.5 million admissions to Liberty Theatres, or 27 percent.[26]

While Smileage sales provided a capital reserve in Washington, local managers paid the immediate, day-to-day operating expenses of the theatres from cash received at the box office from the first day of operation to the last. They deposited cash, after talent expenses were paid, in a local bank and they sent a check to Washington each week for one-half the bank balance. The remainder in the local account formed a small cash reserve with which the managers paid local operating expenses. Beginning in September 1918, managers began accepting canteen checks, a form of script issued by camp canteens to soldiers who mortgaged their future pay. Liberty Theatres accepted canteen checks as cash and then redeemed them at the canteen for 90 percent of their face value.

Klaw based his initial plans for Liberty Theatre operations on estimates that the expenses of the venture could be met by a general admission of 15 cents with a few choice seats at 25 cents.[27] Klaw observed that a civilian theatre paying salaries for a full staff could not operate so cheaply, but military theatre expenses could be minimized if only a manager were paid and other staff were detailed from the camp.[28] It soon became apparent that the theatres could not be self-supporting on admission rates of 15 cents and 25 cents. New plans called for higher prices of 50 cents for the best seats and 25 cents for all the rest. Movie tickets cost 10 cents.[29] The local manager determined admissions to local entertainment. CTCA policy dictated no reserved seats in any theatre.

In total, the camp theatres were self-supporting, taking in more in cash, canteen checks, and Smileage than they paid out for talent and miscellaneous operating expenses. From January 10, 1918, through August 30, 1919, attendance was good enough that receipts of over $2.4 million exceeded total expenses (not including the cost of constructing and equipping the theatres) of a little over $2.1 million. Major expenses were $1.6 million for talent, $400,000 for miscellaneous operating expenses, and the $114,000 lost on the chautauqua tents and programs in 1917.[30] This netted the CTCA a profit on Liberty Theatre operations of just over $270,000, for a profit ratio of 11 percent.[31] The War Department spent Liberty Theatre profits on theatre operations after the CTCA was demobilized. Money left in the Smileage fund because coupons were not redeemed was used for recreational facilities at Walter Reed Army Hospital, Washington, D.C.[32]

Liberty Theatre managers spent an average of $245 for operating expenses each week. These costs included $18 per week to supplement the manager's CTCA salary of $1,800 per year and about $25 per night for small salaries paid to soldiers assisting the manager. In addition, the CTCA levied a booking charge of 5 percent against the weekly receipts of each theatre (they averaged receipts of $1,055 per week) and used the money, about $50 collected from each theatre each week, to pay the expenses of the commission's New York booking office. The CTCA also charged each theatre $25 per week to finance theatre management operations in Washington including salaries paid to executives and their staff.[33]

The greatest single expense of the Liberty Theatre venture, aside from the cost of construction, was the expense of talent, including motion picture rental. For the most part, local managers paid talent in cash after each performance. In the early months of operation the local manager paid film rental fees, but the New York booking office paid them in the last year of operation.

Out of gross receipts of $2.4 million, the booking office and the local managers paid slightly over $1.6 million for talent. The War Department paid approximately the same amount from appropriated funds for theatre construction and theatre rigging and equipment. The average weekly talent expense was almost $18,000 for all theatres, or approximately $830 at each theatre. The large theatres booked more expensive talent and paid somewhat more, on the average; the smaller theatres, using vaudeville and motion pictures, somewhat less.

During the first 17 weeks of operation, January 10, 1918, to April 26, 1918, before the smaller theatres in the National Guard camps were fully operational, managers paid about $1,600 each week for talent at each theatre. This outlay proved to be unsustainable in the long run and was cut back to maintain solvency and profitability. From April 27, 1918, to August 30, 1918, when many theatres used volunteer vaudeville acts and motion pictures, the weekly average for talent dropped sharply to $600. In the next 12 weeks, August 31, 1918, to December 27, 1918, before the smaller theatres were reconstructed to enable them to host bigger, more expensive touring companies, the average rose to $730 each week. From December 28, 1918, to May 31, 1919, millions of soldiers returned from France and filled the camps as they waited to be discharged. In this period of higher-than-normal theatre attendance, the CTCA paid an average of $930 each week for talent in each theatre. During the final three months of Liberty Theatre operation under the Commission on Training Camp Activities, June 1, 1919, to August 30, 1919, a period during which attendance dropped rapidly, the CTCA paid $600 each week for talent.[34]

The Theatre Fund was heavily burdened from the start, but the camp programs attracted enough soldiers with cash or coupons to meet and exceed most expectations. Klaw never received the money he needed to secure performers in advance of the Liberty Theatre openings. He managed, however, to locate touring companies in the region where a camp theatre was opening and he persuaded them to pledge a booking without an advance or a guarantee. Marc Klaw's work with the CTCA was both a poignant example of Percy MacKaye's charge that the theatre would not be able to pull together in wartime and, at the same time, a remarkable exception to MacKaye's claim that theatre businessmen were wartime slackers.[35] Klaw was perhaps too well-known in the theatre business to bring its disparate and combative parts together; he was too much a part of the culture of competition and connivance that dominated entertainment businesses. Moreover the support he needed from CTCA officials came too late and was too little. Yet he persevered long after a less-tenacious person would have abandoned the camp theatre project, and he managed to induce enough cooperation to get the theatres staffed with competent managers and their stages filled from among the few touring shows that were available. Harry P. Harrison's willingness to guarantee a bank loan of $50,000 to launch the Smileage sales campaign is also noteworthy. Moreover, the camp theatres were untried markets in new territories, so tour managers assumed considerable risk in accepting such a contract. Those managers must also be accorded a measure of recognition for their willingness to operate at risk.

Jasper Mayer's discovery that camp commanders regarded the Liberty Theatres as the "flagship" program of the CTCA may have come as a shock to the commissioners, given the persistent difficulties encountered in getting them built and filled with attractions. But Fosdick and his colleagues might have been gratified by the news as well, for those outsized and rough buildings were tokens of their commitment to positive recreational programs providing soldiers in training with a constructive alternative to saloons, prostitutes, and "cheap amusements." However, except for the appropriation to support theatre construction, decision after decision of the War Department and the CTCA expressed either indifference, ignorance, or contempt for theatre business practices and the managers and artists who would have to be mobilized to deliver the good, clean fun. The CTCA both coveted and spurned entertainment and entertainers, viewing theatre as simultaneously important and trivial, desirable and repugnant. The Smileage campaign solved the CTCA's money problems, but it was really only an ingenious exploitation of patriotic fervor in imposing what was essentially a tax surcharge on the families and communities from which soldiers were drawn so that the government theatre program could pay its talent expenses.

9

Discord

The relationship between Marc Klaw, the theatre mogul, and Jasper J. Mayer, the social worker from Goodland, Kansas, was uneasy from the start. Klaw believed that he needed more power and a wider scope of responsibility, and he resisted being Jasper Mayer's subordinate. Hanmer and Fosdick uniquely empowered Mayer and he served as a buffer between the manager of commercial entertainment and the recreation-oriented CTCA. This use of Mayer articulated the anticommercial ideology of the recreation movement, but it constituted an abuse of Marc Klaw, a potentially valuable volunteer, and a dysfunctional distancing of the business of entertainment from the Liberty Theatre program.

Fosdick asked Mayer to coordinate construction when Lee Hanmer shifted his attention from the theatre program to recruiting song leaders for the camps. Knowing Mayer had no experience in theatre or in construction contracting, Fosdick must have wanted his close assistant to be his eyes and ears in this phase of the commission's business. Unfortunately, Mayer became Fosdick's mouth as well, but without the guidance of the chairman's wide knowledge and immense tact.

Klaw specifically disclaimed any personal interest in the details of construction, but he had assigned architect and costume designer F. Richard Anderson of his office to advise Tilton, Fosdick, Hanmer, and Mayer on technical matters.[1] Nevertheless, as theatre construction got underway, Klaw worried that the buildings were being thrown up without the oversight of someone with theatre construction experience, and he warned Hanmer that the commission needed people in the camps to supervise construction and coordinate the purchase and installation of theatre equipment. A month later, Klaw offered to send Anderson to the camps to supervise construction and to see that equipment was installed correctly. This seemed a good idea since the theatre managers to be assigned could not be expected to be competent to oversee construction details. He also wanted the CTCA to send an agent to the camps to gather the information about how baggage could be hauled to and from the camps and how performers could be boarded and transported.[2]

Mayer apparently heard Klaw's warning, but he declined Klaw's offer to send Anderson to the camps. Instead, he busily planned his own inspection tour. When Klaw asked Mayer for approximate dates that theatres might be completed, Mayer at first ignored him, then he explained that he had asked an aide to send progress reports, but the aide just never mailed them. Finally, he suggested that he would advise Klaw of the progress of construction only if Klaw came to Washington to get the information.[3] Mayer was scornful of Klaw's temperament and his status in the entertainment industry and his attitude allowed him to make choices that undermined Klaw's efforts to enlist talented performers to go to the camps.

And Klaw could expect no help from Lee Hanmer, who remained adamant in his suspicious view of Klaw and in his estimate of Klaw's marginal value to the commission. In a personal letter to Raymond Fosdick on December 21, he reconfirmed his understanding of the status quo in Liberty Theatre management: Jasper Mayer was general manager of all the Liberty Theatres and in charge of their construction and outfitting. Furthermore, Mayer should appoint the managers of the theatres, and the managers should be directly responsible to Mayer. In Hanmer's view, the scope of Mayer's involvement was large and complex; that of Marc Klaw simple and sharply proscribed. Klaw was to furnish talent for every second week, and there his job ended. In Hanmer's view the local managers arranged programs on alternate weeks and organized other uses of the buildings, as local conditions demanded, without clearance from Klaw. But Hanmer failed to realize that such neat compartmentalization of the theatre schedule hampered Klaw's efforts to book scarce touring companies. Such companies as might be available could appear in the camps only when their scheduled tours of civilian theatres permitted. Klaw needed unrestricted access to the camp theatre stages, and he needed the full cooperation of camp theatre managers if touring attractions were to efficiently dovetail with local attractions. It's hard to believe Hanmer didn't know what Klaw needed; rather, it seems likely that he interpreted Klaw's demands as a nefarious effort to seize power so that big profits could be wrung out of the camp theatres. Hanmer finally suggested that Fosdick appoint a supervisory committee to coordinate the commission's growing and now ungainly theatre program.[4]

On December 28, Klaw again threatened to resign. This time he cited Mayer's ignorance and recalcitrance and his own reluctance to suffer further discourtesies from Hanmer and Mayer.[5] Klaw's threats prompted Raymond Fosdick to intervene, but Fosdick's remedies did little to promote better relations between the CTCA and the commercial theatre. Following Hanmer's suggestion, Fosdick organized the Military Entertainment Committee (MEC) to coordinate and supervise all entertainment programs in the camps. At its head he placed Lee Hanmer, whom he gave rather broad powers, but he directed Hanmer to involve the chairman of the CTCA in matters of policy and in accounting for the expenditure of public funds.[6] He appointed Marc Klaw, Harry P. Harrison, John J. Eagan, and Jasper Mayer as members. Harrison remained in charge of the chautauqua tents and programs, while Eagan supervised the entertainment programs for naval training stations and the ships of the fleet. Fosdick ordered Mayer to supervise theatre construction and Klaw to book professional talent for the camps. Fosdick's committee simply calcified relationships among those dealing with theatres and entertainment, although it placed Hanmer in clear control of the volatile situation. Klaw immediately expressed concern that Harrison might assign chautauqua shows to theatres Klaw had already booked, so he asked the MEC to centralize camp booking by asking Harrison to advise Klaw of all his contacts with professional talent. The committee quickly granted this supervisory power.[7]

But on the critical question of the relative status of Mayer and Klaw and their authority over the local managers, Fosdick's directive simply reaffirmed the status quo as it had emerged since he had assigned Mayer to watch over construction. Mayer was to supervise theatre construction and the local theatre managers. Mayer would be directly responsible to Klaw in dealing with theatrical talent, but in all other cases, Mayer was to report to Hanmer.[8] Klaw's influence in vital relations with local theatre managers was sharply curtailed. Astonishingly, Fosdick's intervention momentarily appeased Klaw. Perhaps Klaw believed he could do his job in spite of the restrictions Fosdick placed on him.

The relationship between Mayer and Klaw was most strained over the appointment and supervision of Liberty Theatre managers. In January and February 1918, the CTCA opened 11 Liberty Theatres. Klaw and Mayer interviewed and hired the managers in November and December, Klaw contacting some of the managers and Mayer employing others. Sometimes Mayer and Klaw conferred before offering an applicant a job and sometimes they did not.[9] Klaw balked at being granted partial control of the local managers, warning Fosdick that "there must be one final authority and these managers should understand that I am in control." Klaw believed he could not make the theatres financially self-sufficient unless he could run them with a tight rein. He needed not just information about receipts and attendance but also more subjective opinions about the entertainment value of every touring show appearing in every theatre. Klaw wanted to know if the soldiers liked the show and the prices, and he wanted the manager to estimate the potential popularity of the attraction at subsequent stops on the army circuit.[10] Mayer's orders to the managers mentioned only Klaw's need for information about receipts and expenditures, leaving out any call for information about the quality of the shows and the nature of audience reactions.[11] Mayer and Klaw needed to define lines of authority and establish efficient business procedures; they succeeded only in befuddling the men they placed in the camps.

Klaw's demands disturbed the other members of the MEC. Fosdick and Hanmer insisted that Mayer should supervise all uses of the theatre except for the displays of professional talent.[12] Klaw objected to the division of power, but his alternately blunt then obtuse manner served only to lead the other commissioners to suspect the meanest motives. Ultimately, Fosdick withdrew from the dispute with a note to Klaw expressing the hope that he and Hanmer could settle their problems with Mayer.[13]

To make matters worse, Klaw did little to assure the local managers of the integrity of their bosses. He instructed them not to advertise Liberty Theatre attractions in local commercial newspapers, lest it appear the camp theatre wished to compete with the town theatres.[14] Conversely, Mayer and Hanmer had instructed managers to try to win the soldiers away from commercial shows in town, because the recreation-oriented executives believed those shows were likely to be unwholesome. However, Klaw was booking attractions for the camps from the same pool being drawn upon by commercial managers in the cities near the camps. There is no indication in commission records that Klaw applied any special selection standards. He simply looked for shows with available time touring cities in the vicinity of the camps. Furthermore, while Klaw asked managers to report the quality of the attractions he booked, he reprimanded a manager for submitting a bluntly negative criticism.[15] Klaw's practices demonstrated that he did not share other commissioners' concerns about town attractions. And his sensitivity about negative criticism of shows he had booked had the potential to further confound and demoralize the local managers.

Despite efforts by Fosdick and Hanmer to clarify the division of duties, Klaw and Mayer continued to clash over who should manage the camp theatres. Klaw chafed at the idea that Mayer should have broader authority than he, and insisted he should have the authority to hire and fire managers at will, though Fosdick had specifically assigned this task to Mayer.[16] On February 2, 1918, the New York *Herald* ran an article on the delayed opening of the Liberty Theatre at Camp Dix, New Jersey, in which the reporter referred to Mayer as "general manager" of the camp theatres. Klaw immediately complained to Fosdick. Mayer's announcements were uninformed and confusing and Klaw insisted again that Mayer could not be an effective general manager of the theatres and that "Washington," i.e. Fosdick, should correct his delusion.[17]

These conflicts and misunderstandings suggest the scope of managerial disorganization in the early months of the Liberty Theatre venture, and they also illustrate the insidious suspicions of managers in social welfare and recreation toward their commercial theatre agent, Marc Klaw. Mayer ignored or misunderstood Klaw's legitimate requests for information and offers of help. Klaw refused to accept Mayer's leadership in the wholly appropriate belief that Mayer was an inept and inexperienced manager of theatrical affairs. Nevertheless, Hanmer and Fosdick continued to support Mayer with efforts to minimize Klaw's influence over the local managers. These incidents suggest that Mayer, Hanmer, and Fosdick feared or disliked Klaw's commercialism, so they discounted Klaw's skill and knowledge. Similarly, events suggest that Klaw never understood the philosophical and practical differences between the commercial theatre he knew and the recreational theatre the CTCA was trying to establish in the camps. Thus, discord grew out of divergent views of the basic function of the camp theatres. Profit, which in Klaw's view flowed upward only in tightly managed theatres and touring companies, was central to Klaw's philosophy and that motive informed all he did. The government men said they wanted a theatre that might reform and enlighten the audience, but they acted like they simply wanted to insulate the theatres from commercialism, and, ultimately, they acted like they too were driven by a profit motive. They faced a complex problem of finding and distributing shows to the camps, one that demanded the best, better than the best, the commercial theatre establishment could provide, but their prudential negativism and their own professional parochialism kept the camp theatre project teetering on the rim of failure.

10

The Iron Hand

Duplication of authority and blurring of lines of responsibility on the Military Entertainment Committee continued until February 21, 1918, when Malcolm McBride, a commission member from Cleveland, Ohio, interceded to take charge of the CTCA entertainment program. The ineptitude and inefficiency that had plagued the Liberty Theatre project of the CTCA was typical of many of the War Department's mobilization efforts. Transportation and military procurement were disorganized, bound and gagged by the red tape generated by proliferating civilian committees assigned to carry on tasks beyond the ability of the traditional bureaus of the War Department. In mid–December 1917 Congress launched an investigation of the War Department and was soon demanding that Newton D. Baker resign. Congressional pressure stimulated profound changes throughout the War Department.[1] In this environment the Commission on Training Camp Activities tightened its organization to increase efficiency, and McBride reformed the Liberty Theatre venture to remedy many of the faults troubling it since its inception.

McBride believed his job was to stabilize and unify a fragmented organization unclear about its purposes and uncertain of the means to attain them. His approach to solving the problems facing the camp theatres was a mixture of rigid centralization and decreased reliance upon the theatre business establishment of New York City. He quietly removed Mayer as general manager of Liberty Theatres and began looking for a more theatrically experienced aide, one who would be knowledgeable about theatre and comfortable as a bureaucrat. Believing that Klaw had assumed responsibilities and executive powers more properly residing in Washington, McBride's communications to him made clear that all decisions about policy and procedure in the entertainment ventures of the commission would be McBride's to make. He wanted authority centralized in his Washington office and he wanted a booking office that simply collected lists of available plays and dates when they would be on tour near the camps. From these lists McBride or an assistant would pick the plays and engagement dates for each camp. The New York booking office would then negotiate the proper contracts. The procedure McBride envisioned turned out to be impractical and unworkable. More immediately however, these procedures made Marc Klaw a mere functionary, a role his temperament hardly suited him to play.

The effronteries Klaw had experienced before McBride took over continued in the new regime. Upon arriving in Washington, McBride promptly asked Klaw for a complete and up-to-date statement of expenditures with all vouchers as well as a detailed salary list for the company of *Here Comes the Bride*, a Klaw and Erlanger production scheduled for an exclusive tour of the Liberty Theatres. McBride also requested information about the percentages paid all companies playing the Liberty Theatres, and he suggested that the Klaw's booking office adopt a more "honest" policy of offering the same percentage to all companies.[2] Standardizing contracts in this way was contrary to established commercial practice and certainly not more "honest," but the use of the word made evident that Hanmer's skepticism would be carried on in McBride's relations with Klaw.

Klaw's reply was cordial, but Klaw did not give McBride the information he wanted. McBride again asked Klaw for a detailed report of his camp theatre bookings. This time he wanted a list of all plays booked for the camps, with the name of the manager and the names of each cast member of each one of the companies. He wanted to know how much scenery they were carrying and he wanted to know what percentage of receipts had been negotiated for each company. He wanted the names of all plays contemplated for camp booking, and he especially wanted an estimate of all the projected expenses of each of the three companies the commission's New York office was assembling for exclusive camp tours. He wanted an account of every detail of all the expenses of getting up these shows and touring them.[3] McBride made these demands of a man who at one time was among six agents who controlled the first-class commercial theatre in America and who was still one of the most powerful people in the business! Klaw answered, again with noteworthy restraint, that McBride was asking him to submit to a centralization scheme that would make Klaw's plans "impracticable."[4]

A third time McBride asked Klaw for details of his booking operations. This time McBride confronted Klaw over an issue that was personal as well as professional when he suggested that Klaw's son, Joseph, should not be paid for his work in handling the camp theatre accounts in the New York office. Klaw had just cleared this arrangement for his son with Hanmer and other commission members about three weeks earlier, but McBride's insistence that all the road company finances be handled in Washington essentially nullified the arrangement.⁵ McBride also suggested cutting the overhead expenses of the New York booking office by renting less space and paying for less service from Klaw's staff. Finally, he demanded that the commission establish a fixed percentage for the company share in all Liberty Theatre bookings.⁶

The following morning, March 5, Klaw angrily resigned from the Military Entertainment Committee. His annoyance with McBride was so intense that he submitted his resignation to Hanmer, the past chairman with whom he had maintained somewhat more cordial relations. He rightly complained to Fosdick that McBride's final request for information "reeks with suspicion or ignorance."⁷ Klaw was especially angered about McBride's objection to Joseph Klaw's salary, which, Klaw maintained, barely paid his son's expenses of staying in town a number of nights each week. Whatever Klaw's reasons for resigning might have been this time, Fosdick immediately wired an acceptance. He added that he hoped Klaw would continue to advise and assist with the entertainment program in the camps. ⁸

McBride offered a polite expression of regret, then explained in tones of thundering condescension that he was merely acting as any "business man" would under the circumstances.⁹ He hoped that the New York office would continue under Hollis Cooley, the aide Klaw had assigned to book shows in the camp theatres, but he complained that Cooley had changed bookings from time to time without informing the Washington office, so McBride asked Klaw for a complete, revised schedule of shows booked in each theatre. He also asked that Cooley be instructed to provide Washington with a list of possible plays and dates for McBride to approve.¹⁰ McBride badgered Klaw to emphatically assert his dominance in booking operations and he must have known that his demands for detailed reporting would drive Klaw away from the CTCA. McBride's actions suggested even more emphatically than his arrogant tone the contempt and mistrust that sullied relations between the camp reform bureaucrats and the agents of the commercial theatre.

Fosdick wrote to Klaw of the commission's debt for his work in launching the theatre program in the camps. He also promised to ask the secretary of war to write an official expression of gratitude, and he tried to minimize the appearance of malignancy in McBride's communications ¹¹ Raymond Fosdick seems to have exercised the charm of Svengali over Marc Klaw, who was partially mollified by Fosdick's explanation. He consented to advise McBride until he was no longer needed.¹²

Fosdick had reasons other than growing tension between Klaw and McBride to so readily accept Klaw's resignation. Pressures exerted upon Marc Klaw had made it increasingly difficult for him to provide effective liaison between the theatre and the War Department. Just as the camp theatres were nearing completion in December 1917, the Klaw and Erlanger Exchange became involved in a theatrical booking war with the Shubert Theatrical Corporation.

In 1913, the Shuberts and the Klaw and Erlanger Exchange had agreed to eliminate costly competition in the largest cities of the U.S. in a deal brokered by George B. Cox. Cox, the former Republican boss of Cincinnati, Ohio, and a major stockholder in the Shubert Theatrical Corporation since 1905 had mediated several conflicts between the Shuberts and the syndicate. Cox died in July 1916, leaving a fortune including several theatres to his widow. She continued to support the Shuberts with a large loan, but she exercised none of her husband's peacekeeping authority. In December 1917, the Shuberts sued Klaw and Erlanger and Klaw and Erlanger countersued. The suits ended the 1913 accord, and brashly publicized Shubert attacks signaled to theatre businessmen everywhere that the Klaw and Erlanger Exchange had been neutralized as a major force in the American theatre. J.J. Shubert told a reporter for the *New York Sun*, "Klaw and Erlanger are only booking agents and have few clients, while we own and control our own theatres. As far as we are concerned, we consider Klaw and Erlanger two old and antiquated men, whom the procession has passed. They represent such a small portion of the theatrical business that they can no longer be taken seriously."[13] The fracas spelled the end of any hope that Klaw could compel the cooperation of the theatre industry in providing professional touring attractions for the camps.

The effect of the hostilities reverberated throughout the Liberty Theatre venture. In the first place, a civil action against the Shuberts demanded a good deal of Marc Klaw's time. Other visible signs of the booking war came in a story printed in the *New York Review* stating that the Liberty Theatre venture was entirely Klaw's enterprise, booking only Klaw and Erlanger productions. The newspaper story further suggested that the general outlook for the government theatres was poor. Hanmer saw the story and complained to Klaw about it, noting incidentally that it was inaccurate to suggest that Klaw was entirely responsible for the government theatre project.[14] Klaw replied that the *New York Review* could never be expected to treat him or the government theatre project fairly, because it was "a weekly circular of Shubert attractions, published *by* the Shuberts *of* the Shuberts and *for* the Shuberts."[15] He was exactly right in his claim, and he might have added, although he did not, that the Shuberts had founded the *New York Review* in part to counter anti–Shubert rhetoric in the syndicate's newspaper, the *New York Morning Telegraph*.

Klaw told Hanmer the Shuberts lied in claiming only Klaw and Erlanger productions were being booked into the camps. He explained that he had sent Cooley to the Shuberts to see what they had available for the camp theatres precisely to illustrate that Klaw was fair and inclusive. According to Klaw, the Shuberts refused to see Cooley and refused to cooperate in providing attractions.[16] On the contrary, however, Cooley told Jasper Mayer that he had seen Lee Shubert on January 2, 1918, and Shubert had suggested five productions available upon the end of Broadway runs.[17] Klaw made no booking agreement with the Shuberts, so it seems clear that hostility between Klaw and the Shuberts damaged the government venture, denying attractions to the camp theatres when there were already too few available.

As Klaw became more deeply embroiled in responding to the collapse of the 1913 agreement, he became less able to provide adequate bookings for the growing chain of Liberty Theatres. In an effort to forestall criticism of the government theatre venture, Klaw quit booking the productions of managers privately affiliated with Klaw and Erlanger management.[18] This move further limited his access to the resources of the American theatre, for he was left with only the productions of the independent managers. However, independent managers could reasonably fear that any sign of cooperation with Klaw might be taken as faithlessness by the Shubert interests whose star was in ascendancy. A manager with a patriotic motive of providing entertainment for the troops in the camps could be denied access to Shubert theatres. Conversely, those who did not cooperate could find themselves frozen out of Klaw and Erlanger theatres.

Klaw's resignation did not go unnoticed by the Shuberts. The *New York Review* of March 9 printed an article asserting that Fosdick forced Klaw to resign when William A. Brady, a manager aligned with the Shuberts, "demonstrated that leading legitimate and motion picture producers would not cooperate as long as Klaw was in authority." According to the *Review*, Klaw had rented offices for the commission in his own New York Theatre building and had "placed a number of antique, behind-the-time Klaw and Erlanger road managers and others of his adherents in charge of amusement activities in the various camps."[19] Klaw was understandably alarmed by this story and quickly wired Fosdick to ask him to issue a disclaimer. Fosdick responded immediately that the article was "absolutely false," and he wired the *New York Review* requesting a correction or a retraction.[20] Klaw threatened a libel action, but he did not sue. In this he made a wise choice, for the substance of the *Review* article was true, although the tone was harsh. Conflict with the Shuberts had resulted in Klaw's being unable to enlist the full cooperation of the professional theatre.

The claim that Klaw had been unable to mobilize the motion picture industry to provide films for the Liberty Theatres was also true in large part. In June 1917, William A. Brady, president of the National Association of the Motion Picture Industry, had appointed the War Camp Motion Picture Committee, a subcommittee of the War Cooperation Committee of the Motion Picture Industry, to cooperate with the commission, but as late as the middle of August, Klaw had not yet seen their representative. It should be noted, however, that Brady had long been closely aligned with the Shuberts, who owned half the stock in William A. Brady, Limited, of New Jersey, a company established in 1910 to produce plays and acquire theatres in partnership with the Shuberts, as well as a controlling share of the World Film Corporation, of which Brady was president.[21] Brady's man in charge of the War Camp Motion Picture Committee insisted he be allowed to bypass Klaw to work with Raymond Fosdick, then he informed Fosdick that Klaw was "of the legitimate theatre" and not connected with the motion picture industry, so film producers simply would not submit to his leadership.[22]

Fosdick made no effort to placate Brady. He consented to back whatever method Klaw could devise for providing motion pictures for the camp theatres, even if it meant ignoring or opposing Brady's organization as Klaw had earlier suggested.[23] In November Brady capitulated by appointing a new group, the Producers and Distributors War Camp Motion Pictures Committee, under the chairmanship of Mr. P. A. Powers, treasurer of the Universal Film Manufacturing Company of New York, with whom Fosdick and Klaw were able to establish more cordial relations. Powers acknowledged that the motion picture industry was not providing films for the camp theatres, but he explained rather lamely that their reluctance was "due to the many interests desirous of showing activity in this direction."[24] Fosdick himself had very little confidence in the medium, believing along with Secretary Baker that cheap motion pictures had contributed to the moral desolation of the Mexican border camps in 1916. Klaw's position as well as Fosdick's belief account in part for the fact that it was mid-December 1917 before Fosdick directed Lee Hanmer to coordinate the work of renting films for presentation in the camps.[25] The *Review*'s claim that Klaw was unable to work efficiently with the motion picture industry was true, although their conclusion that Fosdick forced Klaw to resign was not true. The prickliness of Klaw's relations with the motion picture industry and with the Shuberts may account for a measure of Fosdick's ready acceptance of Klaw's resignation, but Klaw tendered it of his own volition.

Furthermore, Klaw did not act as if he believed Fosdick — or McBride — had forced him out of office. If he did, he responded with uncharacteristic good humor at having been rejected, for he pointedly assured McBride of his continued support. He also expressed his admiration for Fosdick and Hanmer, with whom he claimed somewhat ingenuously that he had always had good relations. In the week following Klaw's resignation, McBride asked him to continue on the Military Entertainment Committee, but Klaw refused in terms that clearly indicated no ill feeling for McBride, Hanmer, or Fosdick. He did, however, leave a final warning about working with Lee Shubert, who could not be trusted, Klaw believed, to honor any agreement or contract. He also said that members of his personal staff were severing their connections with the commission.[26]

Klaw believed he had suffered a moral defeat, not at the hands of colleagues on the commission, but at the hands of his competitors in the theatre profession. Some commissioners may have misunderstood his motives and techniques, but his business associates had defied his authority and frustrated his efforts to provide entertainment for the camps. He seemed not to have recognized the potential loss of professional status brought about by his experience with the commission. If he did, he swallowed the affront and continued advising commission agents in the New York booking office for at least another month.[27]

11

The Tightened Rein

Malcolm McBride ran the Military Entertainment Committee as if it were a failing organization without aim, order, or discipline. To establish control of the Liberty Theatres he centralized all administration in Washington. He also made appointments and established procedures that tended to insulate the government theatres from the influence of commercial entertainment interests in New York. Fosdick backed him wholeheartedly by forming a Liberty Theatre Division, the creation of which was part of a commissionwide effort to give various activities formal administrative status, and he made McBride head of the division. Measures taken in the spring and summer of 1918 so reformed the government theatre program that it became necessary to appoint a new Military Entertainment Committee. McBride had replaced Lee Hanmer, Klaw had resigned, Harry P. Harrison had become involved in the Smileage campaign, Jasper J. Mayer had left the commission, and John J. Eagan, responsible for entertainment activities on Navy ships and shore stations, had never associated with the old committee, although he had had some success in his assigned duties. McBride's new committee included Daniel Frohman, a Broadway manager aligned with the Klaw and Erlanger interests; Kate Oglebay; his personal assistant, J. Howard Reber, former president of the Drama League of America; Franklin Haven Sargent, a noted acting teacher and founder of the American Academy of Dramatic Art in New York City; and Augustus Thomas, a playwright and staunch Wilson supporter. Frohman had for some time been an unofficial adviser to Reber, who had taken Marc Klaw's position as head of the CTCA's theatrical booking office in New York. Oglebay, like Reber a Drama League of America officer, was a volunteer assistant to McBride. She headed the League's Entertainment Committee, a group soliciting volunteers to direct amateurs in plays to be presented in the camps, collecting vaudeville sketches suitable for camp presentation, promoting soldier shows (entertainments by and for soldiers), helping YMCA secretaries produce shows in their huts and auditoriums, and organizing recreational activities in towns near the camps. Her presence on the Military Entertainment Committee signaled a sharp turn away from the use of professional touring shows.¹

Since Mayer's departure, McBride had been looking for an assistant with a background in theatre management but with no obligation to the commercial theatre establishment in New York. Harry P. Harrison recommended Richard R. Smith, of Lincoln, Nebraska. Smith had managed chautauqua companies for the Redpath Bureau, a booking office in Lincoln, and, most recently, the San Carlos Grand Opera Company, a touring organization. Harrison then persuaded Smith, in Washington working for the War Camp Community Service, to contact McBride.² On March 1, 1918, McBride made Smith the business manager of all the Liberty Theatres except those in New Mexico, California, and Washington. Smith also took over Smileage sales from Harry P. Harrison.

Smith announced in *Variety*, a leading entertainment industry newspaper, that he was looking for an assistant with no "conflicting interests" in the theatre profession.³ He hired Dehull N. Travis of Detroit, Michigan, an acquaintance of James Couzens, who had made a large donation to support the Liberty Theatres. Travis had some experience with professional theatre as a leading man in stock and with road companies, but he had given up the theatre to study law. Upon being admitted to the Michigan bar, he became an aide to the governor of Michigan, then chairman of the Michigan State Board of Pardons. He continued making public appearances, however, as a lecturer on the New Penology for the Redpath Lyceum Circuit. Travis continued as assistant director until July 15, when he was made director of the newly formed Publicity Department of the Liberty Theatre Division. Howard O. Pierce, who continued to serve until April 1919, took his place in July 1918. Pierce had managed the Liberty Theatre at Camp Taylor, Kentucky, before coming to Washington.

Smith exercised telling influence in the Liberty Theatre venture through his appointment of managers. A comparison of the theatre managers Smith selected with those appointed by Klaw and Mayer further illustrates McBride's efforts to move the camp theatres out of the legitimate theatre's sphere of influence. Fifteen Klaw and Mayer appointees for whom biographical information is available had wide experience managing legitimate theatres and commercial touring attractions. R.R. Smith's appointees had somewhat different backgrounds. Biographical sketches of 25 of his over 60 appointees indicate that seven had significant recent experience as chautauqua managers; 11 had managed vaudeville and motion picture houses; six had managed legitimate theatres or legitimate theatrical touring companies; and only one had no practical theatre management experience.[4] Smith's shift away from appointing managers connected to the Broadway legitimate stage is pronounced.

McBride's tendency to appoint men from outside the legitimate theatre establishment is seen once again in his appointment of a new head of the New York booking office. The day of Klaw's resignation, McBride asked J. Howard Reber, of Philadelphia, to become the CTCA's booking agent in New York. Reber assumed the position in March. Reber and McBride agreed that Hollis Cooley from the Klaw and Erlanger Exchange would continue to solicit applications from theatrical tour producers for time in the camps, then submit possible bookings to Reber, who would select the shows the CTCA would book. McBride thus granted Reber an authority he hadn't given Marc Klaw.[5]

McBride chose Reber for two reasons: Reber was not affiliated with either of the leading factions in professional theatre and he was sympathetic with the aims and purposes of the commission's theatre program. Indeed, Reber had no prior experience with professional theatre. He had been a founder and president of a Philadelphia community theatre, Plays and Players, and he was active in the national community theatre movement through the Drama League of America. His position in the Drama League suggested his affiliation with reform forces in the American theatre. The league, founded in 1909, viewed the commercial theatre as a corrosive social force and they set out to reform it from the grass roots. They did so by promoting the "best" European and British drama for production in amateur theatres. The league also tried to improve audience tastes through drama study groups, the members of which might be able to pressure the commercial theatre to produce more intellectually compelling plays. Reber presided over the league at a time when it included about 20,000 members in a 100 centers through the country.[6]

Reber came to the commission as a volunteer, receiving $1 a year for his services. As head of the New York booking office under McBride, he picked attractions for the Liberty Theatres from a list of possible bookings submitted to him by Hollis Cooley and he provided liaison between the professional theatre establishment and the government. Reber's appointment was shrewd in that it lifted the commission's booking office above the intramural quarreling in the theatre industry without utterly abandoning the commercial theatre; it insulated the commission from the taint of commercialism that always spoiled their relations with Marc Klaw; and it further centralized McBride's authority.

McBride took steps to strengthen the commission's bargaining position along the Rialto by announcing a stringent show previewing process.

Reber's appointment gave the commission a responsible reviewer of the kind and quality of entertainment booked for the camps, so McBride announced that an attraction would be booked for camp time only after the commission had determined its entertainment value.[7] According to McBride's plan, Reber, one of his assistants, or a member of the Play Review Committee should review the script of a proposed production and preview the production itself at least once at a performance outside the camps. The reviewers were then to report their conclusions, with recommendations for cutting or revision, to the booking office.[8] The reviewer was supposed to assess the quality of the acting, the scenery, and the costumes, and to judge whether the play or musical suited the tastes of the men in the camps. Reber's only instruction to his reviewers was to avoid melodrama, except when it was of exceptional quality. "Sensational" melodrama had an even lower reputation among social reformers than sex farces. Melodramas typically shown in the cheapest legitimate theatres were thought to treat too lightly violent crimes and its perpetrators and to revel in rather than to scorn the awful fate that befell victims of "white slavery," the code word for prostitution, and the users of drugs and alcohol. He also urged reviewers to avoid all plays that might have a "depressing effect" upon a soldier audience. Reviewers were to screen the scripts and performances for indecencies, which were not defined, and they were to look for language offensive to any religious faith, race, or nationality. They were asked if the acting was good, the scenery and costumes new, and the girls pretty. The play review report form was a jumbled collection of questions that would have been very difficult to fill out and interpret had it been used very seriously. Finally, each Liberty Theatre manager was instructed to report to New York on each attraction appearing in his theatre to see that the show maintained its original standard, because proscribed language and behavior could and did slip into shows as ad lib additions.[9]

Reber reminded reviewers that entertainment value alone was the basis for selection. Reber's standard of selection seems anomalous when it is considered in light of the broadly educational mission of the camp theatres as an alternative to the "cheap amusements" the CTCA assumed to be the standard fare in commercial theatres catering to soldiers near the camps. Why wasn't the play selection committee advised to apply the standard of "patriotic fervor" or "moral uplift?" Such standards might have aligned the play selection process with the broad justifications for the CTCA announced at its inception by Secretary of War Baker and by Raymond B. Fosdick. Here again one observes the discontinuity between broad founding ideals and the conventional practices through which camp life reforms were actually realized. Although the camp theatre venture was born of repugnance for commercial theatre, commission executives quickly found that the legitimate theatre establishment was the only entity capable of delivering entertainment that the soldiers in training would actually use. Tent chautauqua had the reputation for delivering morally uplifting performances, but tent chautauqua failed to attract a soldier audience. More conventional theatrical fare had to be used if the camp theatres were to succeed. His background in the anticommercial Drama League of America to the contrary, Reber recognized that soldiers seemed to want entertainment — girls, jokes, and music — not demonstrations of the triumph of good over evil. Indeed, Reber told the Drama League of New York meeting in New York City in December 1918 that his experience booking shows for the camps had persuaded him that the Drama League was too highbrow in its communications with its members.[10] Kate Oglebay, the only woman (and an actress) on McBride's committee, seconded Reber's choice, but she recalled years later having to fight her "highbrow friends" who wanted "the boys entertained by the Isadora Duncan Dancers" (as, in fact, they were!).[11]

The review process was long on procedure and short on substance. Announcements of the process implied that reviewers would apply some standards, but those standards were never articulated. Indeed, the review process seems to have been publicly announced to impress the casual observer but to in no way regulate the flow of shows into the camps. Not surprisingly, it was ineffective because it failed to account for important elements of theatrical production and distribution. In the first place, scripts were not as easily available as a theatre outsider might have supposed. Actors learned lines from sides, booklets recording one character's lines and the cues for speech. Musical scores existed in manuscript, if they existed at all, and singers and dancers learned melodies, lyrics and movements in rehearsal. Scripts were costly to produce, and many productions were mounted from typescripts that were often radically altered in the production process and never printed or produced in multiple copies so that readers could have access to them. Reber's reviewers rarely read such scripts as existed before rehearsals began. Script review was a time-consuming process and a dubiously effective form of control over the entertainment quality of the production that resulted from the theatrical realization of the script.

Just a month after Reber became booking agent, McBride cautioned him that he was not using the Play Review Committee as originally planned. McBride believed they should report on every play suggested for camp booking regardless of its critical acclaim. Reber had found it impractical to review every production before it arrived at its first camp engagement, and he found that some managers would withdraw an offer to play the camps if the commission insisted on a preview performance.[12] Some productions were previewed before they went into the camps but many were booked without a preview. Nevertheless, the Military Entertainment Committee cautioned the theatre profession that they reviewed every play they booked, and that alone may have had the effect of making the camp shows seem to be censored and sanitized, but they were not.[13]

Camp theatre managers were also inconsistent about submitting reports on attractions. Reber emphatically reminded them to report after the first night of each show to assure the booking office that the company was still playing the same show the Play Review Committee had passed. Reber cautioned them that "weekly reports of attractions are absolutely essential," and he reminded them that they should not hesitate to use their authority to eliminate "suggestive or indecent lines" that might slip in after the company had been on the road for some weeks.[14] Script reviewing and production previewing and reporting offered a semblance of control but little more.

To maneuver the commission into a stronger bargaining position with theatrical managers, in July 1918 McBride established a Publicity Department in the Theatre Division. Dehull N. Travis was its director, and his main purpose was to stimulate the cooperation of the theatre profession by publicizing the efforts of those participating in the government's theatre program. Those failing to cooperate would thus be made more conspicuous as well. Shortly after the Publicity Department was established, special columns devoted to news of the Liberty Theatres began appearing in the *New York Dramatic Mirror* and in *Variety*, the most widely read theatrical trade papers of the day. Travis later edited a weekly publication called "Liberty Theatre News" that circulated through commercial theatre offices in New York City.

McBride's tight rein extended to the camp theatre managers. From December 1917 to about May 1, 1918, the local manager exercised some discretion as to what was presented in his theatre. That freedom was sharply curtailed during McBride's regime. In this regard McBride's drive to establish in Washington a central, regulating authority for the camp theatres had the effect of limiting the effectiveness of those theatres.

The camp theatre manager had wide-ranging responsibilities that required his familiarity with the camp and its environs. He supervised soldiers employed at the theatre and he scheduled all uses of the theatre and all maintenance and repair. He advertised Liberty Theatre attractions in camp newspapers (he was not allowed to advertise in civilian newspapers), in his own printed theatre program, and, where allowed, on bills and signboards at the theatre and throughout the camp. The manager met each traveling company and helped them arrange transportation and baggage hauling as well as board and room in town. He also supervised the performers while they were in camp. All members of the company were subject to military regulations while in camp, and the military could punish them for any misbehavior. Smoking anywhere in the theatre was prohibited. The manager had to see that performers neither carried liquor into the camp nor allowed any officer or private in a dressing room at any time and that no female member of the company was "entertained" in the camp.[15]

Managers were most successful when they maintained cordial relations with the camp's military staff and when they widely advertised the theatre's bill of fare. Managers depended on the goodwill of company commanders to assign soldiers to operate the theatre. The camp quartermaster and the camp utilities officer helped the manager maintain and repair his building and transport touring companies. The camp theatre manager had to be sensitive to military protocol and capable of adjusting to a military society in which he was an outsider. The best managers had theatrical experience and business acumen and they were also tactful and winning.[16]

In addition to his function as chaperone and housekeeper, the local theatre manager selected the motion picture program in his theatre from lists of films approved by the booking office in New York City. Under McBride, this was the single respect in which the manager chose the fare offered in his theatre. Agents in New York and Washington booked the legitimate and variety program, the most popular and expensive. New York and Washington solicited the manager's complaints or comments on the appeal and quality of the touring shows but seldom gave them any credence. The centralized organization of the Liberty Theatre venture stripped the person most likely to understand the desires and reactions of the camp audience, the local theatre manager, of the responsibility of adapting the program of his theatre to the tastes of the men in the camp.

The *Report of the Military Entertainment Committee,* written under McBride's direction, cites "centralized control of the business management and in the selection of entertainment" as the key to the "success" of the Liberty Theatres. Their evidence of success is that the theatres paid all expenses, including the operating expenses of the New York and Washington offices. Agents in New York and Washington estimated the future needs of the camp theatres on the basis of information contained in daily box office reports and weekly reports of attendance and receipts. It is hard to believe that such statistical and schematic information could properly inform a booking agent, neither one like J. Howard Reber, who had no commercial booking experience, nor especially one like Malcolm McBride, who had no theatre management experience of any kind. Reber maintained that the variety of tastes within each camp and camp-to-camp variation made adapting fare to the tastes of the men a "virtually an impossibility." He thought the CTCA had no reliable indicators of the sophistication, urbanity, or literacy of men in the army.[17] But, in the whole theatre operation, those with the greatest professional experience and competence were ostensibly the individual managers of the various camp theatres. Unfortunately their professional skills were almost entirely ignored. Amateurs, bureaucrats too far up in the hierarchy to maintain meaningful contact with the camp audiences, ran the operation from the top down, while the professionals were largely reduced to the status of custodians and receptionists. The results might have been better had the objective of centralized booking authority been abandoned and the local managers been allowed to form functional regional circuits and to cooperate with commercial theatres in their region.

The marginalization of the theatre managers further typifies relations between the utopian idealists who conceived the camp theatre program and the commercial theatre functionaries who possessed the means to realize the ideal. Reform rhetoric demonized commercial theatre, but the reformers had no choice but to deploy commercial producers, performers, and managers competent in the very practices they so deeply distrusted. McBride's harsh insistence upon centralizing authority assured that the theatre program operated blindly and insensitively.

12

Camp Shows

Tent Chautauqua

In the fall of 1917, before more permanent theatres could be built in the camps, the CTCA contracted with the Harry P. Harrison's Redpath Lyceum of Chicago to provide entertainment in tents in several training camps. Chautauqua circuits of the type Harrison managed developed in the United States in the first decade of the 20th century. Circuit chautauqua provided educational and morally edifying lectures, musical concerts and stage entertainment in tents in small towns in rural areas. Harrison's was one of several booking agencies that hired speakers, musicians, song leaders, and actors, organized these performers as a "course," a term more acceptable than "show," and routed it through the small towns in the circuit. A typical chautauqua program involved the use of seven tents in each of seven small towns in rather close proximity to one another. Acts circulated around this small wheel so that a patron could see a different show every afternoon and evening all week long. A typical program included about five acts. Circuit chautauqua tents were about 90 feet wide and 130 long and would seat 1,000 people on folding wooden benches. They were lighted with naptha lamps hung from the tent's support poles.[1] Of the several booking offices in the United States, the most prominent was Harrison's Redpath Lyceum Bureau of Chicago.[2]

Chautauqua programming proceeded from the assumption that the audience for chautauqua was homogenous within a geographic region, unconflicted, and stable. Chautauqua booking companies, like Harrison's, tended to serve a single geographic area. Harrison's Redpath Bureau covered states east of the Mississippi to Ohio and south to the Gulf of Mexico. Keith Vawter, also based in Chicago, focused on states in the upper Midwest west of the Mississippi. Paul Pierson's organization served the state of Pennsylvania, and other agents booked circuits in New England and in the mid–Atlantic coastal region.[3] Accordingly Harrison's talent agents booked acts they thought, or knew from experience, would please rural and small-town, white, Protestant audiences in the upper Midwest and in the Southeast.

The fact that the American public and the young men in the camps drawn from its ranks were ethnically and culturally heterogeneous and divided along economic, racial, and ethnic lines was not lost on CTCA reformers. However, they seem to have believed that the events and ideas on the stage or on the screen could function as a beacon or a lamp lighting the way for the audience to move toward cultural unification. CTCA leadership elected to offer not diverse entertainments to a diverse audience but rather homogenous entertainment reflecting the values and interests of the hegemonic class so that the objective of the camp theatre program might be realized.

The camp shows were to be gently, benevolently coercive, and with this general aim in mind, circuit chautauqua seemed an ideal expedient. Chautauqua shows were proper, decorous, restrained, and reasonable and therefore ideal for the camp theatres, given the position of these theatres in a plan to provide an alternative to the debasing and demoralizing spectacle offered in conventional houses of commercial amusement.[4]

Before the U.S. declared war on the Central Powers, circuit chautauqua avoided references to war and preparedness to avoid offending the Midwestern rural audiences that firmly supported Wilson's policy of neutrality in word and in deed. Moreover, in the years before the U.S. entered the European war, circuit chautauqua steered a course away from controversial social and political causes and toward light humor and entertainment. However, when the U.S. entered the war, chautauqua executives like Harrison urged their managers toward greater displays of patriotism and support of Wilson's proposition that the nation's involvement in the war was a step toward ending the war.

Managers booked lectures delivered by soldiers, mostly Canadian and British, using motion pictures and slides to inform the public about what this war was like in presentations that sometimes undercut conventional ideas of the glory associated with combat. Red Cross nurses who had worked in Europe spoke about the treatment of injured soldiers. Some perennially popular orators such as Russell Conwell, famous for his "Acres of Diamonds" speech about the treasures one finds in one's own back yard, and William Jennings Bryan, whose popular "Prince of Peace" oration touted creationism and spread doubt about scientific explanations of the origin of life, adapted their presentations to emphasize faith in God as vital equipment for winning a war and how democracy should stand firm against German imperialism.[5]

The CTCA's Lee Hanmer and Harrison planned to deploy all 106 tents used on the Redpath circuit. They also planned to select from among the 106 Redpath programs offered in those tents enough theatrical and concert performers and inspirational orators to make up 32 programs for the 16 National Guard camps and the 16 National Army camps.[6] No record of what Henry P. Harrison's Redpath Lyceum presented in the tents in the training camps has survived, but there are ample records of what Harrison and other agents were booking in the summer of 1917, so the best guess as to what acts played the camps is to judiciously project the summer offerings onto the fall and winter program for the camps. It is likely that the availability of performers was critical for program selection. The Hanmer-Harrison plan for 106 tents would require that dozens, if not hundreds, of entertainers be retained, and the best place to begin looking would be among those already under contract. Certainly, not all the best chautauqua performers could preempt commitments to be a part of the initiative in the camps. Nevertheless, acts appearing in Harrison's tents in the summer of 1917 were probably most evident among the shows sent to the tents set up in the training camps.

The camp offerings most likely included the patriotic lectures, supported by motion pictures and slides, given by Canadian and British soldiers who had seen action in Europe. Red Cross nurses speaking about the medical treatment available to wounded soldiers would have been a likely choice. The remainder of the chautauqua offerings of the summer of 1917 was not so clearly adapted to the likely interests of the soldiers in the camps. Chautauqua programming typically stressed the discussion of strategies for better living. In the summer of 1917 Harrison had featured Sarah Tyson Rorer, a pioneer dietician and the most famous cooking teacher of her time. More politically charged speeches might have been delivered by Frank B. Willis, former Progressive governor of Ohio from 1915 to 1917, and Judge Ben B. Lindsey of Colorado, who spent the summer of 1917 speaking out against corporate greed in the manufacture and sale of munitions. Musical acts Harrison booked that summer were the Schumann Quintette; the Royal Dragoons, a military band; the Waikiki Hawaiians, a group of "native" singers; and Metropolitan Opera singer and popular recording artist Elsie Baker. Other entertainers included Glen Wells and Mara Conover Wells in farcical playlets; John Ratto, a "characterist," or impersonator, whose act called "Uncle Sam's Family" featured Ratto in Italian, German and Polish immigrant guises; and Katherine Ridgeway, the "Queen of the Chautauqua Platform," providing dramatic readings from popular plays, novels, and poems.[7]

The chautauqua programs failed to attract soldier patrons in sufficient numbers to pay the expenses of the performers and the cost of transporting and setting up the tents. Harrison and Hanmer thought of the use of chautauqua tents too late to get them into the camps immediately after the chautauqua summer season ended. Transportation problems, a feature of every mobilization effort, and the early onset of a harsh winter disabled the program still further. The venture incurred a debt so large that it depleted funds solicited and initially promised to Marc Klaw so he could book legitimate attractions in the permanent theatres opening in mid–December 1917. The chautauqua debt was finally repaid from theatre admissions when the camp theatres built by the War Department began to attract soldier customers.

Musical Comedy, Tabloid Musical Revues and Burlesque

Hollis Cooley, Klaw's booking agent for Liberty Theatres, announced the availability of time in the as-yet-unfinished camp theatres on December 1, 1917. At that time Klaw had no information about the progress of theatre construction and no money to purchase options on the time of traveling companies. No attractions were booked until January 4, 1918, just six days before the official opening of the first Liberty Theatre at Camp Sherman, Ohio. At this juncture, Cooley had to take what was available and had little opportunity to exercise any judgment of the suitability, by any standard, of an attraction.

The *Report of the Military Entertainment Committee* lists almost all the touring legitimate attractions sent to the camps, most of the concert and specialty performers, most of the musical comedy stock companies, and the most important vaudeville troupes. It also names a few major, war-related motion pictures shown in the camps, and it describes the process by which dramatic directors were assigned to stimulate and guide soldier theatricals. The attention and space given touring shows in the *Report of the Military Entertainment Committee,* the venture's official history, suggests they were the most important kind of entertainment offered in the government theatres. However, analysis of the CTCA's archival records as well as notices in camp and theatrical trade newspapers indicates an anomaly. The presentation of legitimate touring attractions dominated the thinking that went into the design of the camp theatres just as the booking and management of legitimate touring shows dominated the time and attention of entertainment committee chairmen Marc Klaw, Malcolm McBride, and J. Howard Reber. Those shows also attracted the bulk of criticism coming from the camps. However, legitimate touring attractions, mostly musical comedies, made up only about 20 percent of camp shows seen between December 1917 and September 1919. Musical stock companies presenting several shows in a camp over a period of weeks, concert performers, and amateur shows made up another 20 percent. Vaudeville and motion pictures, for which the theatres were not designed and which were managed with the least amount of centralized control from New York and Washington, were featured in the government theatres 60 percent of the time. CTCA managers did not foresee the development of such heavy reliance on vaudeville and motion pictures. In fact, their founding rhetoric suggests they would have preferred that not happen. But it happened. Discussion of the nature of what was actually seen on the stages and movie screens of the camp theatres reveals most emphatically how the CTCA's ideal — government theatres that would counteract the deleterious effects of commercial amusements— was impossibly remote. Their plans, meant to realize that ideal, necessarily came to realization through the channels of commercial production and distribution. The CTCA imagined their Liberty Theatres as a socializing alternative to antisocial amusements, but entertainment market realities co-opted those government stages and screens and turned them into replicas of the stages and screens of the cities and towns adjoining the camps. The Liberty Theatres became commercial theatres built at government expense inside the training camps.

Availability of attractions from commercial producers seems finally to have been the CTCA's basic criterion of selection. Camp shows were in no way carefully selected; they were rather typical of attractions available in theatres in the small towns and cities outside the major theatre centers of the time: New York City, Boston, Philadelphia, Chicago, and San Francisco. Because the CTCA's "chosen" entertainments arrived in the camps so willy-nilly, they provide no evidence of any ideal of a reformed theatre. Instead, they offer a glimpse of the situation confronting every manager-owner of a small-town theatre or movie house in America in 1917-18. Production and distribution practices determined what people in the small cities adjacent to the camps and the soldiers in the camps were able to see, not exhibition practices or market demand. This was the entertainment situation as sociologist John Collier, a founder of the National Board of Film Censorship (later the National Board of Film Review), saw it in 1915, when he argued that producers, distributors and exhibitors, in live theatre as much as in film, should develop new relationships permitting exhibitors greater choice in what they showed their public.[8]

Failing to recognize the aggressiveness and ubiquity of a producer and distributor-controlled market, McBride persisted in imposing irrelevant and debilitating strictures on the camp theatre program. For instance, McBride opposed the policy of booking professional touring companies for a percentage of the gross receipts, believing the system offered producers the chance to exploit the camp theatres for unfair profits. He also joined Lee Hanmer in believing that the CTCA could produce and tour shows less expensively and with better quality control than could commercial producers. Ultimately, the commission had a hand in producing five shows for exclusive camp tours, two musicals, two comedies, and a vaudeville show.

In late April 1918, McBride met with several prominent producers to plead for greater cooperation.[9] Out of this meeting came an offer from Lee Shubert to select five musical comedy successes from among those produced by the Shubert Theatrical Corporation, hire the casts and rehearse them and deliver the complete productions to the War Department. The Shuberts agreed to donate scenery, properties, and costumes from their stock and to keep touring costs to a maximum of $2,000 per week for each show. The productions would tour the Liberty Theatres with the expenses paid by the government. The commission was to reimburse the Shubert Theatrical Corporation for the production expenses, and the CTCA was to pay the company salaries, management salaries, railroad fares, and all advertising costs including the salary for an advance man.[10] This deal essentially allowed the CTCA to become a producer of shows mounted for exclusive camp tours, to assume the financial risks attendant upon touring a show, and to very closely monitor a show's expenses and income. The deal looked a lot better than it turned out to be.

Lee Shubert offered several shows under this agreement, but only two were produced: *Love o' Mike* and *Her Soldier Boy*. Both were recent hits (their runs exceeded 100 performances) in Shubert's Broadway theatres. *Her Soldier Boy*, with a book by Leon Victor and Rida Johnson Young, and music by Emerich Kálmán and Sigmund Romberg, was an adaptation of a Viennese operetta that romanticized the war in telling how a soldier pretends to be his dead buddy so the buddy's family can be spared the bad news. But the buddy isn't dead, as reported, and he shows up in time for his sister's wedding to the pretender. The most famous song from the show was an English music hall hit by George Asaf and Felix Powell, inserted by the producers. "Pack Up Your Troubles in Your Old Kit Bag and Smile, Smile, Smile" remains a strong evocation of the era.

Love o' Mike, with music by Jerome Kern, lyrics by Harry B. Smith, and story by Thomas Sydney (*nom de plume* of Sydney Smith, Harry's son, and Augustus Thomas), was an "intimate" musical, written in the style of Kern's recent successes at New York's tiny Princess Theatre and produced to capitalize on Kern's success with *Very Good, Eddie*. Kern's music was laid on a lighter-than-air story about an English aristocrat (Michael) who throws a house party and charms all the women, thereby driving their beaus into jealous frenzies. The Shubert musicals, while not wildly popular, were choices that promised success on a camp tour. Those tours began in June 1918, but they were not successful. They closed after four weeks of their eight-week tour when the experiment in avoiding standard commercial booking practice was $15,000 in the red.[11] The CTCA booking office reverted to its reliance on commercial attractions that risked the camp tour out of patriotism or for profit. The Shubert shows marked the end of the CTCA's efforts to control costs, quality, and profits by co-opting the function of producing for the camp market.

The staple product of the legitimate theatre was the musical show and it was produced in several varieties: musical comedies built around slight plots involving, mostly, young lovers in contemporary dress; operettas, whose popularity was waning, offering more young love but in fantastic dress and in some far-away middle European court; and musical fantasy and musical review. By a narrow margin, musical shows were the most common legitimate attraction presented in the camps. Touring musicals were booked more heavily in the first six months of the camp theatre venture than in later months. Ultimately Malcolm McBride recognized that they were too expensive for the scale of prices charged in the camp theatres and the booking of full-scale musical shows declined. Still, 27 such shows played engagements lasting from one night in a single camp to several months on tour to many camps. Twenty-two had been produced at one time or another on Broadway and most were of rather recent origin. Camp audiences had a chance to see at least a few performances of many of the most popular musical shows of the time, albeit generally in forms produced for brief stands in small-town theatres. They also had access to touring attractions whose Broadway runs resulted in financial or critical failure, or both.

Soldiers in camp theatres got a taste of the music of America's then most popular composer of musical comedy, hearing in a few camps Jerome Kern's melodies in *Love o' Mike* but also in *Oh! Lady! Lady!*; *Oh, Boy*; *Have a Heart*; and *Very Good, Eddie*. Neither *Love o' Mike* nor *Very Good, Eddie* attracted camp audiences. *Very Good, Eddie*, produced in tabloid form for one-night stands in small towns, closed its unprofitable tour at Camp Upton on June 8, 1918. *Variety* reported that troop movements and the mandatory three-week quarantine of new arrivals kept available camp populations too low to support the show.[12] *Oh, Boy!* (1917), regarded as the best of the Princess Theatre musicals, was a big Broadway and touring success, but the show didn't tour the camps. The road company performing this bustling farce of mistaken identity that featured "Till the Clouds Roll By" at the Wilbur Theatre in Boston did one performance in a Redpath Lyceum tent at Camp Devens, near Boston, on September 30, 1917. The second road company of Kern's *Oh Lady! Lady!*, the last of the Princess musicals, and another resounding hit for Kern, Wodehouse, and Bolton, made occasional camp theatre appearances in April 1919. *Have a Heart* was the most successful of Kern's collaborations with Wodehouse and Bolton. It came to the camps in tabloid form as produced for theatres in small towns in the Midwest. The company played one-night stands and split-weeks in a few camps in March 1918, probably as part of a longer commercial tour.

The equally popular and more prolific Irving Berlin wrote music for *Watch Your Step* and *Stop! Look! Listen!*, musical comedies that played in some camps. *Stop! Look! Listen!* was a backstage comedy about the search for a leading lady that ultimately turns up the chorus girl initially rejected for the role. It played split weeks from mid–November 1918 through the end of March 1919. Soldiers in almost all the larger camp theatres had one or two opportunities to hear two of Berlin's most memorable tunes, "I Love a Piano" and "The Girl on the Magazine Cover." *Watch Your Step* (1914) Berlin's ragtime opus (and his first musical, which some said had no plot) rode the wave of the dance craze then sweeping the nation. Four years after its Broadway opening it was remounted for a national tour beginning September 1, 1918, with lesser lights in the lead roles danced originally by Vernon and Irene Castle. *Watch Your Step* appeared in a few camps along its route.

Most of the 27 legitimate musicals booked into the camps simply dropped in along their commercial tour routes. For instance, *The Better 'Ole*, a musical melodrama, starred Mr. and Mrs. Charles Coburn, who also produced this "extravaganza," as it was billed. It was set in France and it concerned "Old Bill's" dramatic intervention in the efforts of a German saboteur to blow up a bridge under a French regiment. While it was a "war" musical, *The Better 'Ole* did little more than find in the war the villainy necessary to test and prove the mettle of the comic hero. The Coburns took the show to Camp Upton on Long Island during their run in New York, and when they were performing in Philadelphia, they also arranged a performance at nearby Camp Dix, New Jersey.

By 1918, the popularity of Viennese operetta adapted for the American stage had waned from its height a decade earlier when Franz Lehar's *The Merry Widow* (1907) had much of America in a waltzing mood. But these Austro-Hungarian sweets were still produced on Broadway (their origins erased or altered to suit the times) and training camp audiences had a chance to see them. One of the earliest to be booked for the camps was *Flora Bella*. The *faux* Viennese operetta by Cosmo Hamilton toured camps from December 1917 through March 1918, and it was the first touring attraction at the first Liberty Theatre to open. Another such operetta, *The Kiss Burglar* (1918), by Glen MacDonough and Raymond Hubbell, survived for 100 performances on Broadway on the fresh and dainty appeal of Fay Bainter, its star. It then made a national tour, absent Ms. Bainter, that concluded with a three-week Broadway revival starting March 17, 1919. Following that the show played East Coast camps for two weeks in April 1919. Middle-European tonalities echoed through the melodies of Victor Herbert and camp audiences heard them, but in the abbreviated form of the "tabloid" musical. "Tab" versions of Herbert's operettas *The Only Girl* (1914) and *The Princess Pat* (1915) visited some camps in 1918.

Journeyman composer Silvio Hein wrote the songs for a musicalization of Edward Clark's comedy *Coat Tales* in 1917. Some thought *Furs and Frills*, as the musical was called, compared favorably to the intimate concoctions of Kern, Bolton and Wodehouse. However, the show failed to catch the interest of Broadway playgoers and the tour, opening at Camp Merritt, New Jersey, in August 1918, failed as well. Hein was also responsible for songs needed to plump up *The Bride Shop*, a vaudeville that had been performed in variety theatres for four years. The musical comedy that emerged was *Flo Flo* (1917), and it ran 220 performances on Broadway. It involved the amours of a pseudo–Spanish nobleman and their effect on the proprietors of a ladies underwear shop in Paris. It thus offered lots of girls in lingerie and it was deemed to be colorful and light but afflicted with mediocre music and banal dialogue. It was booked for some camps along the route of its national tour beginning in September 1918. Interestingly, the vaudeville upon which *Flo Flo* was based, *The Bride Shop*, continued to be performed on the road and in a few camps.

Earl Carroll, famous in the 1920s for the risqué revues bearing his name, wrote the music and lyrics for *So Long, Letty* (1915). The show was commissioned for Charlotte Greenwood, a loose-limbed, high-kicking show dancer especially beloved across America outside of New York City. California impresario Oliver Morosco produced it (and four other "Letty" shows between 1915 and 1922) first in Los Angeles, then on a long tour that included three months in New York City. This "Letty" show offered Letitia Proudfoot as one of two wives who swap spouses only to find they are no happier. It was still on tour in 1918 and, according to the *Report of the Military Entertainment Committee*, booked for some training camps in 1918. No record of any specific camp dates has appeared, however. Carroll also wrote the book and lyrics for *The Love Mill* (1918). It involved the efforts of a society matron to marry off her three daughters, one of whom is obese, one who is very lean, and one who has no taste for fashionable clothes. Critics found Alfred Francis's music not at all tuneful and Carroll's story and dialogue not at all amusing. The show lost money on its brief run on Broadway, but a tour producer rescued it, trimmed it down, and sent it out on a whistle-stop tour where it ultimately turned a profit. The tour included some camp stops in the late spring of 1918.

Jefferson De Angelis, who had starred in many Broadway musical comedies and produced a few, joined with Howard Lyle to revive Charles Hoyt's *A Trip to Chinatown* (1891). This "Idyll of San Francisco," as it was subtitled, ran for 657 performances and in 1918 this remained the record for long-running musicals. Because De Angelis and Lyle mounted the revival for an exclusive training camp tour, the Hoyt estate waived its royalty and performers worked for their actual expenses. *A Trip to Chinatown* is a farce with music built around the "mistakes of a night" when the guardian of some fun-loving boys allows his charges a chaperoned evening out in San Francisco's Chinatown. However, the guardian flatters himself to believe that a letter accepting her appointment from the lady chaperoning the boys is actually promising an assignation. The comic trouble begins when he tries to keep the date. The special revival played East Coast camps and Camp Jackson, Atlanta, Georgia, in June 1918.

The list of musical comedies routed to the camps included some of the most popular shows of the day, but the list also included works whose Broadway runs had barely surpassed the length that made them marketable as "hits." Moreover, tour producers typically cut production and touring costs to the bone to maintain profitability. Casts seldom or never included the stars or the Broadway supporting players and chorus dancers. Soldier audiences saw instead those desperate enough to endure the hard life of a performer traveling from small city to large town and making stops of one, two, or three nights—the very young or those no longer young enough or trim enough to be cast on Broadway. Settings were simplified, orchestrations scaled down for smaller bands, and costumes quickly became worn and dirty from heavy use and little cleaning. Simple invocation of a half-forgotten title or the name of a famous composer or a hit tune or recitation of the long-run credentials of the Broadway original is not enough to establish the quality of the shows that appeared in the camps. Soldiers saw a semblance of the original, attended to the unraveling of often inane plots, heard echoes of the music, and saw shadows of the fashionable or funny gents and the voluptuous or zany girls who made the piece attractive to Broadway audiences.

Given the prudential bent of the reformers in charge of the camp theatre program, it is surprising to find burlesque shows among those booked for the camps. In 1918 burlesque referred to an entertainment featuring young women displaying as much leg, in flesh-colored tights, as the law would allow. A typical burlesque show involved a few ethnic comics in baggy pants doing knockabout routines accompanied by coarse or suggestive language. Typically they vied for the attentions of an attractive "widow" also pursued by the "wise-guy" or straight man in smart clothing. Frequently a chorus of girls in tights singing and dancing to popular songs, mostly unrelated to the plot, would interrupt the courting. Burlesque was popular and profitable, so much so that *Variety* editorialized that it was the "gleaming beacon" of theatrical business in 1918.[13]

Burlesque managers of the time recognized that profitability lay in the direction of cleaner shows, so they imposed censorship on themselves to keep the courts and the public from doing it. The burlesque circuit managers, producers and theatre owners disallowed "cooch" dancing (bump and grind movement representing the sex act), bare legs, smutty dialogue, and most vulgar jokes and action. As a result burlesque from 1913 to 1920 was the cleanest it had ever been or ever would be again. Striptease, the hallmark of more modern burlesque, did not become common until the mid-1920s.[14]

Despite the temporarily elevated reputation of the highest class of burlesque, "stock" burlesque produced at the same time could be very coarse. Indeed, such shows were surely in the memory of Raymond Fosdick as he reflected on his experience on the Mexican border in 1916. They were surely in Lee Hanmer's fervid imagination of what cheap amusements could do to young minds if wholesome recreation were not offered as a counterbalance. And such shows must have been in Marc Klaw's thoughts as he realized that there were almost as many first-class burlesque shows touring the U.S. as there were legitimate shows. Indeed, the leading burlesque producer of the time, Sam Scribner (a member of Klaw's theatrical advisory committee), headed a single organization that routed 40 burlesque shows through one-week stands in 40 theatres scattered all across the country. However, recourse to burlesque and the featured tab shows after which programs of burlesque were named is only obliquely acknowledged in the *Report of the Military Entertainment Committee*, where their titles are listed, without commentary. Nevertheless 25 burlesque or "girly" shows made their way to the camp stages, nearly equaling the number of legitimate musical comedies that appeared in the camps.

Several musical revues, some termed "girly" shows or burlesques in the theatrical trade press but not in the *Report of the Military Entertainment Committee*, were assembled primarily for the camp circuit and had good success. Probably the most successful of these was *The Mimic World*, also known as *The Junior Mimic World*, a burlesque that included a minstrel show as the first act. Jack Goldberg and Joe Wood produced it and Wood was the featured comic. It played camps from August 1918 through May 1919 while making brief stops at civilian theatres between its camp dates. Girls in the company "paraded" through the camp in trucks each evening before the show. It was exceptionally successful and was sometimes held over in camp for up to 11 days.[15]

CTCA also booked tab shows, abbreviated musical shows, about 45 minutes long, for the camp stages. Sometimes full-length Broadway musicals were condensed to tabloid size, as was done in 1919 with Kern's *Very Good, Eddie*. These brief entertainments included two to four male or female comics or both and a women's chorus. They were produced for the vaudeville stage or the burlesque stage and presented with a few acts of vaudeville to make up an evening's entertainment. They could also be paired with a three- or four-reel motion picture comedy. *The Army Frolic, The Beauty Squad, The Bride Shop, Henpecked Henry, With Love and Kisses, The Queen of the Movies, Tick Tock Girl, Vanity Fair,* and *The Yankee Princess* were tab shows routed off vaudeville and burlesque circuits to the camps. Also included in this class were brief musical shows based on characters from popular newspaper comic strips: *Bringing Up Father, Hans and Fritz,* and *Mutt and Jeff Divorced.*

Three of the tabloids, *With Love and Kisses, The Army Frolic* and *The Beauty Squad*, were produced by members of the Military Entertainment Committee: Moreland Brown, John Travis, and Franklin Sargent. Titles of others were sufficient to raise the eyebrows of anyone passionately committed to the ideals of wholesome entertainment expressed in the language justifying the Liberty Theatres: *Churchill's Girls; The Manhattan Girl Revue; The Martini Girl Revue; Million Dollar Doll(s); The Rialto Girl Revue; Step Lively, Girls;* and *Whirl O' Girls.*

Only in the case of *Step Lively, Girls* did the MEC display overt concern. Produced by burlesque impresario Arthur Pearson, the show had played Sam Scribner's Columbia circuit in 1917-18, appearing in 40 cities in as many weeks. It was a dance show featuring the women's chorus, that is to say it was a girly show. Pearson revived it in 1918 at New York's Columbia Theatre, the flagship of Scribner's circuit, and sought bookings in the army training camps. A board of review of the Military Entertainment Committee saw it at the Columbia in late September 1918 as a step in reassessing the CTCA's adamant refusal to book burlesque in the camps. The ban on burlesque had already failed; a few such shows had played in the camps in the spring and summer of 1918. A very public review of *Step Lively, Girls* opened the way for more bookings and the show was booked for Christmas week at Camps Upton and Merritt. The reviewers asked only that the girls in the beach scene be draped.[16]

Comedies and Melodramas

From the first, the commission wanted to organize its own professional touring companies to play the Liberty Theatres on alternate weeks. The commissioners believed they could better control the quality of their own nonprofit shows and that they would be cheaper than commercial productions.

Marc Klaw at first thought the 16 largest theatres could be served by eight government companies—four legitimate attractions and four vaudeville companies—each of which would play a six-night stand before moving to the next camp. As each company completed the 16-week route, a newly formed company would begin a similar tour. The plan took into account the paucity of touring attractions already on the road and it was attractively neat, but it was never fully realized. Klaw had no start-up operating funds with which to acquire production rights, scenery and costumes and to hire performers to be rehearsed in anticipation of the completion of the camp theatres. Klaw's plan also required a week's stand of each of the eight companies on the camp tour, but it was soon apparent that few of the theatres and few productions could attract such crowds to the camp theatres for six straight evenings.

Nevertheless, commercial producers paid the start-up costs so that three of the anticipated eight companies were organized. *Turn to the Right!*, a comedy by Winchell Smith and John E. Hazzard, became known as Smileage Company No. 1. *Turn to the Right!* was one of the most successful plays on Broadway in the 1916-17 season, launching the 25-year producing career of John Golden, who also produced *Turn to the Right!* for an exclusive camp tour. The first theatrical company owned and operated by the U.S. government (albeit paid from Liberty Theatre proceeds and not from appropriated funds) opened its tour at Camp Dix, New Jersey, on March 4, 1918. Its warm-hearted, genial fun marked it as an entertainment success, but it had hardly a politically or socially aware moment in it. Instead, it presents three ex-convicts who "turn to the right" to save the peach farm of a sweet old woman, the mother of one of the ex-cons. When the convicts expose a dastardly deacon who is trying to steal the farm they also expose the man who framed one of them and sent him to prison. The peach farm is saved, the ex-cons are positioned to marry well, and "Mom's" delicious jam makes them all rich. The plot situations, the setting, the characters and the language of the play suggest it would be suited for a small-town or rural audience. Indeed, it was widely and successfully produced in circuit chautauqua tents and by small-town stock companies after the war until the mid–1920s. The Broadway star, Frank Bacon, headed the touring cast.

Marc Klaw and his partner, Abraham Erlanger, produced the second company and turned it over to the commission on March 25 at Camp Upton on Long Island. *Here Comes the Bride* by Roy Atwell and Max Marcin had been a marginal success in New York, playing only 63 performances beginning September 25, 1917. The producers hired Atwell to repeat his Broadway role on the camp tour and they refined the production during a two-week stand at the Montauk Theatre, Brooklyn, before it went to Camp Upton. Atwell played an impoverished young lawyer who can't afford to marry his beloved, so he agrees to marry another woman, sight unseen, for $100,000 and then to abscond with the money. The jilted woman is determined to have him, but the lovers find a way to evade her at the final curtain. The play offers some fun for viewers who see its absurd situations unfold, driven forward at breakneck speed by emotionally overheated characters chattering in a glib, somewhat sophisticated language. Its tone is distinctly urbane and the play seems aimed to amuse white-collar audiences, few representatives of which would be found among camp audiences.

Both government-owned shows were initially well received, playing one-week (six-night) stands as the Klaw plan envisioned. Such long stands were a rarity on the camp circuit; split weeks were much more common. After completing about half its 16-week tour *Here Comes the Bride* had managed to pay its expenses and generate a slim profit of just over $600 for the producers. Both the government-owned shows completed their tours in June.[17]

The break-even point for *Turn to the Right!* was $1,925 per week, so each theatre in which it played for 70 percent of the box office receipts would have had to gross $2,750 in the six-night stand.[18] Few Liberty Theatres were capable of such a financial feat, so the show probably lost money on its tour.[19] The Klaw and Erlanger production of *Here Comes the Bride* was approximately as expensive as *Turn to the Right!* and *Variety* reported that it came in with a loss of over $5,000 on its 16-week tour.[20] The Liberty Vaudeville Company, the first, and only, government-sponsored vaudeville show, cost its producers about $1,800 per week. The break-even point at 70 percent of the box office receipts would have been about $2,600, well beyond the capacity of most Liberty Theatres most of the time. In fact, *Variety* reported that the Liberty Vaudeville Company cut short its 16-week tour at eight and one-half weeks with a loss of $3,600.[21]

Shortly before he resigned from the commission, Marc Klaw recommended that the CTCA produce no more shows for the camps. Split-week engagements were turning out to be more nearly profitable and that meant twice the number of shows would be needed to fill the camp stages. Klaw argued that the CTCA could not bear so much financial responsibility. Routine quarantining of new trainees for three weeks and the unpredictable movement in and out of the camps of large numbers of soldiers sharply increased the risk of financial loss for the producer of a camp tour. Klaw recommended that the New York booking office continue to fill the theatres on alternate weeks with commercial touring attractions, thus passing the financial risks on to those in business for a profit.[22] Klaw's unstated assumption was that he would write contracts that offered touring companies a very high percentage of the camp theatre's box office receipts. About this Klaw and McBride finally disagreed when Klaw revealed his assumption to McBride. McBride then involved the CTCA in co-producing two Shubert musicals in the belief that tighter controls on expenses was a better expedient than higher gate percentages for the touring group. He was wrong and CTCA productions once again struggled to meet even reduced expenses.

Twenty-nine comedies and melodramas appeared at the government theatres. The musical shows the CTCA booked tended to be more current than the comedies and melodramas, but the "straight" shows were more commonly reproductions of genuine Broadway hits. Among the melodramas playing the camps, only two dramatized the war on the home front. *The Little Teacher*, by Harry James Smith, produced by George M. Cohan and Sam Harris, was fresh from a four-month Broadway run ending in May 1918. It acknowledged the war in Europe in the story of a new schoolteacher in Goshen Hollow, Vermont, who rescues two abused children and earns the town's acceptance. The play ends at a Red Cross sewing bee where the little teacher is offered a job at a shelter for war orphans in France and two lumbermen appear in uniform, on their way to war singing George M. Cohan's "Over There." *Friendly Enemies* by Samuel Shipman and Aaron Hoffman was considered the great American war play of the day. It ran for over a year on Broadway after opening July 22, 1918. In it, the war with Germany precipitates conflict between two German-Americans who have been lifelong friends. But one is pro–American, while the other stands with his home country and disallows as British propaganda the stories of German atrocities. However, the son of the patriot is married to the daughter of the pro–German. The son's troop ship is torpedoed on the way to France and he is reported lost at sea. The shock of this loss reforms the pro–German and everybody is happy when the young man returns, having been rescued. The play's action implied that differing views of the war should be tolerated. It also combined heartbreaking grief with low comedy, provided in New York by two well-known "Dutch" dialect comedians in the lead roles, in a very popular and powerful mix.[23]

One of the most popular melodramas of the day, *The Thirteenth Chair*, by Bayard Veiller, ran on Broadway for 10 months in 1916-1917. It is set in the parlor of the Crosby mansion, where the marriage of an Irish woman, Helen O'Neill, to a proper gentleman, Will Crosby, has just been announced. The after-dinner entertainment is a séance conducted by an old woman, whom Helen recognizes as her mother in disguise. The séance ultimately produces the identity of a person guilty of two murders. Other melodramas were Willard Mack's gangster piece *Kick In* (1914) and Eugene Walter's *The Trail of the Lonesome Pine* (1912) about a Yankee caught up in a blood feud in the Blue Ridge Mountains. Walter's play, based on a popular novel, had only a brief run on Broadway but it was long-lived on tour and in the repertory of stock companies in small-town America. Government agents also booked Max Marcin's *Cheating Cheaters* (1916) about the *femme fatale* leader of a gang of thieves who turns out to be a policewoman.

Romantic and domestic comedy had a small place on the stages of the government theatres. Soldiers were treated to two versions of the Pygmalion legend: Maude Fulton's *The Brat* (1917) has a worldly novelist study the mannerisms of an urchin whom he brings to his lush estate. The streetwise girl uncannily solves everybody's problems. In *Daddy Long-Legs* (1914) by Jean Webster, a wealthy gentleman salvages a teen-aged orphaned girl from a life of drudgery and insists, secretly, that she be educated. When she matures into a beautiful, sophisticated woman, they fall in love and marry. A touring company also brought to the camps *Pollyanna* (1916), Catherine Chisholm Cushing's adaptation of Eleanor H. Porter's famous novel, whose title character has since epitomized inane cheerfulness. These whimsical comedies were the exception, however. Comedies presented in the camps were more typically robust and positive depictions of romantic and domestic strife. Of course, the bedroom was a popular locale for these romps.

The tour of the Avery Hopwood farce *Fair and Warmer* (1915) provided soldiers access to the work of one of the most successful playwrights of the era. Hopwood was the master of producing the risqué moment calibrated to reach precisely to the limit of what was acceptable to sophisticated, urbane audiences in New York. *Fair and Warmer* is a situation comedy featuring two temperamentally mismatched couples. In each couple is a person who loves to go out and a partner who loves a quiet evening at home. The plot begins to congeal when the party pair goes out leaving the homey types at home. As is traditional in bedroom farce, some couple must be caught in "a compromising situation" and that is how the homebodies are discovered, having their own party late at night when their spouses return. Several road companies toured until 1920 and one or more of these visited several camps. Only one camp visit is recorded for *Parlor, Bedroom, and Bath* (1917), by C.W. Bell and Mark Swan, which the press regarded as "naughty," i.e. sexually provocative.

Touring renditions of Ethel Watts Mumford's *Sick-a-Bed* (1918) made occasional camp stops. *Sick-a-Bed* finds a man feigning illness to avoid testifying at his uncle's divorce trial and to avoid his aunt's libidinous pursuit. His hospital room is a rendezvous for quack physicians, conniving lawyers, and gorgeous nurses, one of whom he romances. *Twin Beds* (1914) by Salisbury Field and Margaret Mayo is another bedroom farce in which the life of a young married couple is constantly interrupted by a sex-crazed neighbor. Censors in England asked that the language and situations of *Twin Beds* be less explicit and that the play be given a new title before it could be produced on the London stage, but it appeared in a few camps without revision. Margaret Mayo also doctored Lawrence Rising's farce, *His Bridal Night* (1916). In New York it featured the Dolly Sisters, the Zsa-Zsa and Eva Gabor of their day. One of them (but which one?) is married to the bewildered comic hero, who inadvertently sets off on his honeymoon with the wrong sister. The chance of extramarital sexual relations by "mistake" gave the play its risqué flavor.

Comedies involving gambling and risky adventures brought to the soldiers in training images of American businessmen whose recklessness somehow always paid off. In James Montgomery's *Nothing But the Truth* (1916) a young stockbroker bets his partners $10,000 that he can tell the whole truth and nothing but for 24 hours. He nearly loses his girlfriend and almost ruins his company, but he wins. Frederick Ballard's *Believe Me Xantippe* (1918) features a bold young man who commits a crime then bets he can escape arrest for a year. He wins the bet and the sheriff's daughter. Finally, *It Pays to Advertise* (1914) by Roi Cooper Megrue and Walter Hackett offers the tale of the redemption of the playboy son of a millionaire soap manufacturer. Irked by the disapproval of his father and his fiancé, the playboy forms a rival soap company, invents a cheap soap and devises an advertising campaign to sell it for a dollar a bar. His scheme works too well and his company can't fill the orders that pour in. The father buys him out and the playboy, now blooded for the pursuit of wealth, dedicates himself to business.

Looking at the stage from the auditorium of the training camp theatres, one would never guess there was a war going on. Success in business, the accumulation of status and wealth, and the pursuit of victory in courtship and marriage and embarrassment at being found to have or thought to have an unbridled and blind sexual appetite were persistently the subjects of the comedies seen on the Broadway stage and on the touring routes adjacent to the camps. Contemplating the themes and tones of these plays and examining the general nature of the musical shows sent to the camps presents one with a thicket of ironies. The CTCA built the theatres in the camps to offer soldiers an alternative to the kinds of shows they would find in houses of cheap amusement on the margins of the camps. However, the musicals and comedies actually presented featured dancing girls and leering comics, facile sentiment, ridiculous comic situations and lustful characters just as might have been seen in Des Moines and Rockford, in Alexandria, Louisiana, and Little Rock, Arkansas, in Trenton or Louisville. Conceived as a haven from popular culture and its potentially demoralizing effects, the camp theatres became a haven *for* that culture. Having built the theatres in the camps, the CTCA was faced with the daunting task of filling those stages. And what they found on the entertainment market and brought into the camps was what the soldiers might well have seen had the CTCA permitted commercial businesses to build and supply camp theatres. The CTCA built the theatres in pursuit of the elusive advantage of control of what the soldiers saw. However, the CTCA's advantage from owning its own theatres was little more than the illusion of control.

Response to Touring Musicals, Comedies and Dramas

Beatrice Pollack's bright-eyed impressions of her summer tour of the Liberty Theatres in the Southwest suggests not only the character and quality of the traveling performer's life, but also the quality of the fare offered the soldiers. Miss Pollack appeared in *With Love and Kisses,* a tabloid musical created for the camp theatres by the commission's own Moreland Brown. The tab show included simple ballads from popular operettas such as *Maytime, Leave it to Jane,* and *Mlle. Modiste,* interspersed with comic songs. It featured two comedians, a soubrette, a prima donna, and a character woman and its action occurred in three scenes—a cabaret, a street, and an exterior. All these elements were woven into a flimsy plot affording opportunity for impersonations. Miss Pollack cheerfully recalled the train to Lawton, Oklahoma, the trolley ride to Fort Sill, then the long walk over fields to the theatre at nearby Camp Doniphan. She also remembers that the tour was especially exciting for some of the girls, for they were appearing on the stage for the first time![24] One hopes the performance was spirited; chances are it was unpolished.

Complaints from the camps about the quality of the touring attractions echoed complaints by tour managers about conditions on the Liberty Theatre circuit. Managers found the tour arduous and risky; camp audiences found the shows cheap and unattractive. Early complaints came from Camp Gordon, Georgia, and Camp Dodge, Iowa. Hollis Cooley booked a burlesque called *Million Dollar Doll* for the January 27 grand opening of the camp theatre near Atlanta. The house was full on opening night, but the show failed to draw later in the week. The New York *Clipper,* a widely read entertainment industry newspaper, claimed *Million Dollar Doll,* an example of stock rather than "high-class" burlesque, was a "turkey, with few changes of wardrobe and the 'bit' type of comedy," and suggested that Cooley examine shows more carefully.[25]

Complaints from Camp Dodge, Iowa, led Lee Hanmer to go there to investigate, and he found authorities about to take control of the commission's theatre. The local manager told Hanmer he had repeatedly complained to Marc Klaw about poor shows but to no avail. Camp authorities complained most about three attractions. They thought *Fair and Warmer,* an Avery Hopwood farce from the 1915 Broadway season, a "good show performed by a third class company." *Stop! Look! Listen!,* an Irving Berlin musical comedy that saw 105 performances on Broadway in 1915, was an "inferior show by an inferior company." *Mutt and Jeff Divorced,* a comic strip inspired tabloid musical produced for one-night stands in small towns, was "a bum show by a bum company." Hanmer mollified the complainants by explaining that the head of the booking office (Marc Klaw) had recently resigned and the camps could now expect more cordial and satisfactory service. He then warned Mayer and McBride against sending more cheap shows, suggesting that it would be better to book motion pictures and home talent.[26]

These complaints led McBride to investigate more thoroughly. He wrote to camp commanders in April 1918 to ask them their opinions. Surviving responses that offer any detail indicate that a few shows at the camp theatres were well produced with attractive scenery and costumes and talented, well-rehearsed performers. Most CTCA bookings were perceived to be poor — poor plays and players and little or no scenery. The commanding general of the 87th Division at Camp Pike, Arkansas, reported that the performances at the Liberty Theatre were "amusing and diverting," but the performers were only "medium." He wrote that several four- or five-year old musical comedies had been "dug up and sent to camp," and he concluded that this kind of fare was welcome if nothing better were available, but he added, "better plays with star performers or plays by young talented performers would be the key to even greater success at the Liberty Theatre."[27] R.S. Wallace, a commission district director in Arkansas, saw a tabloid production of *Very Good, Eddie,* a musical comedy from 1915. A company that specialized in shows for one-night stands had produced it. The night Wallace attended about 1,200 soldiers (half the capacity of the theatre at Camp Pike) coolly responded. Wallace reported that the lines were well rendered and the comedy well done, but the singers were poor and the costumes cheap, confirming the widely held opinion of shows produced for one-night stands.[28] From Camp Upton, on Long Island, came the report that *Turn to the Right!* and *Here Comes the Bride* had been well received, but that vaudeville programs that followed were inferior. Both the commandant and the camp theatre manager at Camp Beauregard, near Alexandria, Louisiana, objected to the booking of a burlesque company, but the show played anyway, prompting the commander to put the theatre off limits for a while because of the "evil and corrupt influences of the shows."[29]

Not all reports were so negative. The commander of the embarkation facility at Camp Merritt, New Jersey, reported that the shows were clean and decent and that the performers ranged from "medium" to "splendid." He recommended booking only vaudeville and musical comedies. From Camp Devens, Massachusetts, came the opinion that performances at the Liberty Theatre were "generally commendable." The camp commander at Devens thought high-class motion pictures would be preferable to dramas and musical comedies booked from among those available for tour. And the division's adjutant noted that those at first were not so good. The adjutant mentioned *Turn to the Right!, Fair and Warmer,* and *Here Comes the Bride,* and a special performance given by the women of Filene's Department Store, Boston, as the best shows seen in the camp theatre's first four months.[30] The three shows he mentioned by title, along with *Love o' Mike, Her Soldier Boy,* and *Nothing But the Truth,* were probably the most carefully prepared pieces routed to the camp theatres. *Fair and Warmer,* was one of the longer-running hits of its day, having been produced initially by Klaw and Erlanger associates Selwyn and Company in 1915. *Fair and Warmer* played a long national tour of split weeks and one-night stands before being booked for the camps in September 1918. When it played Camp Dodge, Iowa, in February 1918, the manager of the Liberty Theatre reported a good response from his audience and noted approvingly that the same company had presented *Fair and Warmer* in a theatre in Des Moines where tickets sold for $1.50.

The fare routed to Camp Devens was probably fresher and more carefully crafted than that seen in most of the camps because Camps Devens was in a densely populated urban area near Boston. The close proximity of theatres in the Boston-New York corridor minimized travel costs and this facilitated profitable tours, so tour producers could afford to put more money into better performers and fresher scenery and costumes. Nevertheless, a Boston *American* editorial of April 29, 1918, cited severe criticism of the shows at Camp Devens. The writer complained that the government was sending poor productions to a camp filled with soldiers used to high-quality theatre (contingents drafted from New England trained at Devens), and he suggested that the commission rectify the practice before "the public supporting Smileage feels it has been hoodwinked."[31] The *American* editor's opinion was substantiated a month later when the director of the Boston Smileage campaign warned J. Howard Reber that the program at the Devens theatre had to be improved before Smileage would sell in the Boston area.[32] The complaints from Devens continued into June 1918.[33]

Elsewhere, the *New York Dramatic Mirror* reported complaints of poor shows, especially musical comedies, at Camp Dix, New Jersey, near Philadelphia.[34] A Red Cross executive in New Jersey notified his Washington superiors that volumes of criticism of shows at the Dix theatre were appearing in local papers. Furthermore, the Red Cross man had talked to "Army officers" who considered the Liberty Theatres and Smileage a "huge joke."[35] The Camp Sheridan (Alabama) *Reveille* of May 6, 1918, pleaded for "productions that were not keyed to the lowest order of intelligence," believing that soldiers "were entitled to something worthwhile and not to dramatic puerilities or vaudeville by incompetents." The correspondent complained that camp shows were more boring than shocking, and he suggested that "a rigid censorship of morals had overlooked the grave immorality of taking money under false pretences."[36] He was probably wrong in blaming the poor shows on censorship. There had been talk of censorship but nothing in the record indicates camp shows were actually screened.

The volume of criticism of Liberty Theatre attractions abated after the first five months of operation, although the complaints did not stop altogether. In January 1919, Reber reported unruly audiences and numerous complaints about shows in the Liberty Theatres, but he attributed the trouble to general restlessness and bad morale among soldiers anxious to be discharged.[37] The complaints continued while Reber tried again to rationalize the criticism, explaining that few shows could satisfy the varied tastes and expectations of the Liberty Theatre audiences.[38] But John Prescott, manager of the Camp Taylor theatre, had a different explanation. He grumbled about two shows sent to him in February 1919. *Stop! Look! Listen!*, making its second round of the camps, had a mediocre cast, according to Prescott. He added, "the songs were all old and the chorus neither young nor attractive." The cast of *Nothing But the Truth* (1916), a sprightly farce by James Montgomery making its second tour of the camps, was fair in Prescott's opinion, but the leading man was poor. He concluded that attractions at the Liberty Theatre would have to be as good as those in nearby Louisville if his camp theatre were to attract a soldier audience.[39]

The CTCA can be said to have failed to attract high-quality productions. Indeed, the volume and intensity of criticism suggests that mediocrity was the norm among shows routed to the camps. However, the charge of failure must be mitigated by the very good possibility that there were very few high-quality productions on the routes adjacent to the camps, the pool from which most productions were selected. Mediocrity was probably the norm there as well. Nevertheless, the CTCA made certain strategic errors that increased reliance on the shows typically routed to theatres outside major theatre centers. The first of these was the failure to establish an operating fund to meet booking expenses before the theatres were opened and to subsidize the tours of more expensive attractions.

The commission solicited $72,000 in private loans for a theatre guarantee fund and designated it as working capital for Marc Klaw. Had this money actually gone to Klaw rather than to Harry P. Harrison, Klaw could have used it to underwrite losses incurred as the camp theatres were opening and to subsidize tours to establish a better reputation for the government theatres. As it happened, the shows haphazardly available as the theatres opened failed to attract and build an audience for the camp theatres. Attendance dropped and receipts dropped, and the only expedient was to cut costs. Local operating costs were fixed at a very low rate, so all that remained was to pay less for talent. But cheaper talent meant less satisfied customers and poorer attendance, a condition calling for further cuts in expenses.

Smileage funds were not available because the Smileage campaign started after the theatres opened. Marc Klaw needed working capital weeks or months in advance of theatre openings. Moreover, Smileage finally accounted for only about one-fourth of all camp theatre admissions. About 40 percent of Smileage sold was unredeemed, suggesting that soldiers, even with the price of admission in pocket, were not going to the camp theatre.[40] Klaw's last chance was the $72,000 pledged to the theatres but used instead to pay the debts incurred by Harrison's Liberty Entertainments. Fosdick may have used the theatre guarantee fund appropriately when he redeemed Harrison's failed venture, but it limited the chances of success for the camp theatres.

The low quality of the camp shows alarmed some people, but there is no reason to believe the camp fare was any better or worse than the shows offered to the civilian population on the road throughout the country. Certainly, CTCA bookings avoided the overtly salacious but there is no indication that moralistic censorship impeded the selection of good entertainment. Productions were selected for the camps because they were available and because managers were willing to assume the financial risk of a camp tour. Those who complained that some of the material sent to the camps was keyed to the lowest order of intelligence or that it was dramatically puerile could easily have lodged the same charges against the Broadway stage or the first-class theatres of the major cities. Moreover, in making such charges, these critics would have been in distinguished company, alongside Arthur Hornblow, William Winter, and John Rankin Towse, to name but three of the defenders of elite Victorian taste and detractors of a theatre coming under the domination of the "business man." The comedies, musicals, and dramas sent to the camps were examples of the entertainment products of the time. They were nothing more or less polished than what was available to American theatres generally.

Minstrel, Specialty and Concert Performers

Concert performers, specialty shows such as magic acts, and minstrel shows claimed but a small share of the camp theatre time, but they broadened the range of the types of attractions sent to the camps and they heightened the sense in which the camp stages were replicas of small-town stages all over the country. Francis Ingram, a contralto with the Chicago Grand Opera Company, was said to have appeared before more soldiers in the training camps than any other performer. She presented concerts with motion pictures on three camp tours from August 1918 through January 1919. Violinist Maud Powell appeared in camp theatres for single performances from June 1918 until shortly after the armistice. She gained renown as the first solo instrumentalist to record for the Victor Talking Machine Company's celebrity artist series, and her recordings became worldwide bestsellers. Stage and movie stars Marie Dressler and Nora Bayes also made occasional camp appearances. So did magicians Charles J. Carter and Harry Blackstone. An indoor circus, Perry and Gorman's "Circusland," toured the camps, as did the Rhoda Royal Circus, an equestrian show.

Perhaps the most unusual booking made by the CTCA was for the Isadora Duncan Dancers. The "mother of modern dance" was returning to her dance career in 1918 after recovering from the tragic death by drowning of her two children in 1913. Duncan's athletic and "natural" dance forms made her and her company widely influential. They gave single performances at camps along the eastern seaboard in the summer of 1918, a booking choice Kate Oglebay of the Military Entertainment Committee thought to be emblematic of an inappropriate elitism expressed in the actions of some of her associates.[41]

At the opposite end of the entertainment spectrum, or so it would seem, one finds the minstrel shows that appeared in the camps. Al Fields' Minstrels was the longest-lived such organization still performing in these the very last years that minstrel shows were a part of the American entertainment scene. The troupe performed in their own tent for one night in each of several camps in the Midwest. Reynold's Minstrels appeared in camps in the South and the "Darktown Follies," an all-black minstrel show, played three weeks at the Buffalo Theatre, Camp Upton, Long Island, for African American troops training there.

Motion Pictures

Few motion pictures were presented in the Liberty Theatres prior to July 1918, in spite of the fact that movies were a popular form of entertainment. Although the CTCA supplied a motion picture projector to each theatre, the construction of fireproof projection booths was delayed.[42] Furthermore, Marc Klaw was unable to compel the cooperation of the film industry in providing motion pictures for the camps. Local managers, handpicked by Klaw from the field of legitimate theatre, tended to slight movies and seldom booked or advertised a picture program. Director of Liberty Theatres R.R. Smith frequently reminded them that movies should be given as much effort and attention as legitimate attractions, but the warnings were not heeded.[43]

Initially ignored as an alternative to legitimate attractions and vaudeville, motion pictures rebounded to become the dominant type of attraction by September 1919. After July 1918, use of motion pictures increased to the extent that they were the attraction at Liberty Theatres from one-fourth to one-third of the time in 1918.[44] They were even more prevalent in 1919, and by the time the army took complete control of the theatres September 1, 1919, motion pictures and vaudeville were the only type of shows being seen in the camps remaining open.

In the late winter and early spring of 1918, the YMCA shared with the government theatres the prints of some movies rented for their auditoria and huts. Camp theatre managers also rented films from distributors near the camps. Lee Hanmer was as concerned about the moral content of movies as about what the soldiers might see live on the stage, and he was wary of profiteering by the motion picture industry in the same way he worried about exploitation by theatre businessmen. His fretfulness was heightened by the fact that the CTCA exercised little or no central control over the movies shown in the camps. Needing information about the situation, Hanmer appointed Orrin G. Cocks, a Presbyterian minister and advisory secretary of the National Board of Review of Motion Pictures, to report on their use in and near the camps.

The National Board of Review of Motion Pictures was born in 1909 in a protest of New York City mayor George McClennan's revocation of moving-picture exhibition licenses. Mayor McClennan believed that the new medium degraded the morals of the community and he tried to ban movies by revoking business licenses. The mayor soon relented and allowed movie houses to operate, but theatre owners led by Marcus Loew and film distributors such as Edison, Biograph, Pathe and Gaumont joined John Collier, a sociologist with The People's Institute at Cooper Union, in establishing the National Board of Censorship of Motion Pictures. The group was formed to avert government censorship by endorsing films of merit. In 1916, the group became the National Board of Review of Motion Pictures as a sign of members' rejection of the task of censorship. Beginning in 1916 and continuing until the 1950s, they reviewed and recommended thousands of motion pictures that were labeled "Passed by the National Board of Review."

Cocks, then, was not a government censor, but when he examined the situation he found that the YMCA did not meet camp needs and that the picture houses in towns near camps did not provide what he regarded as quality entertainment. He never said what he meant by quality but it appears that matters other than the morality of film content concerned him. Cocks recommended the CTCA improve the efficiency of the way films were distributed to the theatres, post exchanges, and chaplains in the training camps, but he suggested that the CTCA use the exchanges, or central depositories, of the motion picture manufacturers and distributors rather than to establish its own system. He also called for a set of standards for selecting the "virile type of picture" required for the camps. Cocks proposed that the agents in the New York booking office negotiate with the distributors for discounted rent. Finally, he suggested that the CTCA entrust the National Board of Review to select quality motion pictures for the camps.[45]

Hanmer approved these suggestions and Cocks issued biweekly lists of select films called the *War Service Bulletin*. None of these bulletins has survived but it is most likely that they echoed the content of the National Board's "Weekly Official Bulletin," which had been issued since 1911. Cocks didn't reveal the specific standards to which he held the films he recommended, but he had discussed the standards of the National Board of Censorship of Motion Pictures in an article in *The Survey* in 1914. Cocks explained then that the National Board was especially interested in mitigating the impact of motion pictures on adolescents. "Prolonged love scenes" should be curtailed and film manufacturers should costume actresses modestly, suppress suggestive movement, and exclude images of close dancing. If criminal violence had to be depicted, it should be strongly motivated and punishment for the violence should follow "naturally and fatally." The board opposed any film content that condoned the double standard of morality and it demanded that if prostitutes were represented, the dreary details of their lives should be emphasized. Any representation that aroused fear and hatred of prostitution the board would support. He also noted prohibitions of representations of insanity and of the recreational use of drugs. Finally, he observed that although the board was located in New York it did not accept the standards of "the New York stage or of its complicated, liberal and abnormal life."[46]

Cocks allowed managers to book motion pictures other than those on his lists, but he reserved the right to approve the use of other films. Many exchanges agreed to lower rental rates, and the camp theatre managers continued to rent from nearby distributors whom they paid directly. Cocks cautioned the managers to "study the tastes and desires of your men and choose the pictures best adapted to your camp," and required them to make weekly reports of their use of motion pictures to the Washington and New York offices.[47]

This arrangement proved unsatisfactory for several reasons. R.R. Smith objected to Cocks' list out of the belief that only a very small percentage of pictures with *no* objectionable features would be appealing to the camp audience. Smith also believed the managers could not be trusted to make discriminating judgments of what would be correct or popular in the camps. Furthermore, Smith believed the rental prices arranged between Cocks and the National Association of the Motion Picture Industry were too high. Moreland Brown, who booked motion pictures for the theatres and tents in the National Guard camps, had been able to secure films from the exchanges at one-eighth the rental fee arranged by Cocks. Brown had also found that many of the pictures the distributors were making available to the camps were old re-issues, "stuff that regular exhibitors would not be playing." Brown suggested to Smith that the booking office bypass the National Association of the Motion Picture Industry (NAMPI) with whom Cocks had been working to set film rental prices for the camps, "or have these men in to a meeting in which we go to the mat and see what prices we really can get."[48]

McBride revised motion picture distribution in early May, incorporating several suggestions made by Smith and Brown. McBride's new plan bypassed Cocks and made it clear that availability and cost were higher priorities than moral content and artistic quality. Under the new policy McBride's representatives ignored NAMPI and negotiated rental terms for camp movies with the producers and distributors. The New York booking office then sent theatre managers lists of discounted films, their cost, and the exchange through which they could be obtained.[49] Under the new plan, Cocks was sidelined in favor of Moreland Brown. There is no indication that Cocks' selection lists had any sustained impact on what was shown in the camp theatres. Nevertheless, they had the perhaps unintended but important public relations effect of whitewashing the CTCA's film-selection process. Bristow's claim in *Making Men Moral* that movies shown in the camp theatres were screened by a committee in a paternalistic effort to control soldier access suggests a greater degree of control than Cocks actually had or than was ever actually applied. Cocks probably used National Board of Review selection lists to make up his list of motion pictures suitable for the camps, for there is no indication the camp committee further previewed films on the list he sent to the camps. Thus, in all likelihood, the camp standard was the National Board of Review standard.[50]

The leadership and the mode of operation of the CTCA motion picture program changed again in July 1918, when E.L. Hyman replaced Cocks and Brown. Hyman decentralized booking, a move that demonstrated that Cocks' content controls and the price controls of Brown and McBride were alike impractical and unworkable. CTCA agents in Atlanta and Dallas booked pictures for the camps in the Southeast and the Southwest. Hyman booked them for camps in the New York City area, while other managers, mostly in the Midwest and Northeast, booked their own films. The only form of centralized surveillance was that managers submitted their film rental bills to the New York booking office for payment. Decentralized booking remained a feature of motion picture distribution to the camps throughout 1919.

To Hyman fell the task, or privilege, of writing the history of the Motion Picture Division in the *Report of the Military Entertainment Committee of the War Department*. He named only a few of the films shown in the camps. CTCA files and items in camp and theatrical trade newspapers name a few more. The scarcity of film titles in the historical record is explained in part by how pictures were priced and distributed. Two systems were operating during the war years; one, the "program system," was in decline, and the other, the "star" plan, was in ascendancy. Under the program system, exhibitors such as the Liberty Theatres purchased the right to use a certain number of reels of film per day. The exhibitor paid a flat rental rate per foot of film for a constant supply of two or three reels furnished an agreed-upon number of times per week. The films in a program had titles but they were irrelevant in relations between the exhibitor and the distributor. Distributors shipped "programs," exhibitors showed them, and customers bought tickets for a "grab-bag" of movies. As the public began to discriminate among types of film and the actors in them, distributors began renting "star" attractions. A film allotment to an exhibitor might be several series of seven or eight pictures, each series featuring a particular star. The exhibitor thus rented six Chaplins or six Talmadges.[51] Both systems mitigated against censorship of the sort the CTCA tried to use. Indeed, the way motion pictures were packaged in star sets or program sets surely contributed to the apparent failure of the CTCA's film selection plans and made price and availability the only workable standards of selection.

Hyman's report mentions by title only war-related films conveying patriotic and propagandistic messages, although such films constituted less than 10 percent of all feature-length films produced in the U.S. in 1917 and 1918. But, while war movies were a small portion of all movies made, the war was the subject of about half of the most prestigious and expensive movies, those distributed to the largest urban theatres, promoted in newspaper advertisements, and shown at admission prices comparable to those charged for first-class legitimate theatre. Civilians and soldiers saw far more movies that did not reference the war than movies that did. However, when they went to the best theatres and paid the highest prices about half the time they saw a war movie. Hyman's report emphasizes these big films and leaves entirely out of the account information about the vast majority of films shown in the camps.[52] Craig W. Campbell's filmography and history of motion pictures during the war years names 65 war-related feature films made in 1917 and 125 made in 1918. The Internet Movie Data Base lists over 2,200 feature-length films made in the U.S. in 1917. Since feature-length films (five reels or more) were by 1917 the dominant kind of film made, one can conclude that the 65 war-related films Campbell has identified were a very small percentage of the total number of films made and distributed to the American public. The IMDB lists 1,508 movies made in the U.S.A. in 1918; again, the 125 war-related movies of that year would constitute a very small percentage of the whole output of the U.S. film industry.[53]

Camp theatres showed a few movies made to stimulate military recruitment. *Over the Top* (1918) was based on a best-selling book by actor and author — and soldier — Arthur Guy Empey (who also starred in the movie). Empey (born in 1883) had served in the U.S. Army, rising to the rank of sergeant major, and in the British army as a machine gunner in France. The book and the movie are a chipper, matter-of-fact story of his service in France in 1916, during which he was wounded twice. The movie adds a romantic motive when the hero's sweetheart is abducted by German agents and taken to France and the hero enlists to go to her rescue. *Come On In* (1918), written by John Emerson and Anita Loos for stage stars Ernest Truex and Shirley Mason, was a military farce about a too-earnest young soldier (he enlisted before the draft) and his too-talkative girlfriend who is a Secret Service agent in pursuit of German saboteurs. It played in only a few camps. *The Unbeliever* (1918) takes a bigoted American autocrat into the Marine Corps and to France where his military and war experiences teach him the values of tolerance and brotherhood in a democracy. Finally, *My Own United States* (1918) based on Edward Everett Hale's *The Man without a Country* (1863), is the story of Lt. Philip Nolan, a convicted insurrectionist who vows at his trial that he wishes never to see the United States again. His punishment is the grant of his wish and he spends the remainder of his life at sea, deeply suffering the loss of his ties to his homeland. The movie adaptation of 1918 gave viewers four generations of Philip Nolans who are rebuked by Presidents Jefferson, Jackson, and Lincoln for their lack of loyalty.

Some of the big war films of 1918 were pointedly propagandistic and these were featured in Hyman's report. *My Four Years in Germany* was inspired by a widely read autobiography by James Gerard, American ambassador to Germany just before America's entry into the conflict. The movie represents German leaders as evil manipulators of an otherwise gracious people. In this regard it echoed the Wilson administration's position that we were at war not with the German people, but with a corrupt autocracy. The film is lurid propaganda in which the kaiser and his generals are compared to animals. It pictures the slaughter of refugees and the violent abuse of prisoners of war and it concludes with a title representing the official German position that "America Won't Fight." The title dissolves into newsreel footage of American soldiers marching off to war and fighting their way across France by bayoneting German soldiers. *To Hell With the Kaiser* (1918) is a farcical tale in which the German autocrats are bested by a courageous American girl and several scheming American prisoners of war. It shows the kaiser signing a contract with the devil so he can conquer the world. When he is defeated, a victorious Gen. John J. Pershing banishes him to a desert island where he loses his mind, leaps into the sea, and goes to hell.

The Kaiser, Beast of Berlin (1918), it goes almost without saying, demonstrated the brutality of the German regime. Soldiers witnessed the German kaiser's indifference to a treaty with Belgium, the resistance of the German officer corps to the kaiser's schemes (he's seen gloating over the sinking of the *Lusitania* as the U-boat captain who fired the torpedoes commits suicide), and a massive American army bound for France to bring an end to the war. *The Hun Within* (1918), a vehicle for Dorothy Gish, features the confrontation of a loyal German-American with a son who becomes involved with German saboteurs.

Hyman also reported that all the camp theatres had shown two very widely viewed propaganda films produced by the government's Committee on Public Information (CPI). *Pershing's Crusaders* was the CPI's first feature-length film; *America's Answer* was its second. Both used film shot by the Army Signal Corps in the U.S. and in France interspersed with propagandistic title cards.

Hyman was especially proud of acquiring for the camps the films of D.W. Griffith, the most influential and successful film director of the era. Griffith's films were distributed and marketed outside the conventional program and star plans of the day. Soldiers saw *Intolerance: Love's Struggle Through the Ages* (1916), with a running time of almost three hours, and regarded then and now as complex and occasionally tedious. Its artistic luster served to highlight the rigorous standards the CTCA wanted the public to believe had guided its movie program. Griffith's films released in 1918 focused on linking sentiment and romance with war violence in not-so-subtle emotional appeals for greater American belief in the innocence of the French and British and the evil of the German empire and its war machine. Griffith's *The Great Love* (1918) found romance on the margins of the Great War in the story of an idealistic American who fights for the British, is wounded in France and recuperates in England where he falls in love with the daughter of an Australian minister, played by Lillian Gish. *The Greatest Thing in Life,* story by Lillian Gish and D.W. Griffith, is set in France on the eve of the war. It is a romantic tale of an American girl, played by Gish, who seeks her true love in France. Griffith's *Hearts of the World* (1918) was propaganda solicited by a British government that wanted a film to move the American public toward entering the war. By the time the movie was released, the U.S. was in the war so some of its power was wasted. *Hearts of the World* concerned two American families living in a French village (the Gish sisters play sisters vying for the attentions of a young American man). When the Germans capture the village and brutalize its citizens, the young Americans join the French resistance until the French army actually liberates the town. Griffith's films were immensely popular in civilian theatres. Their appearance on camp screens and their prominence in the 1918 report of the Motion Picture Division of the CTCA's Entertainment Committee aligned the soldiers and their theatres with civilians and theirs.

Hyman's report clearly stresses the propagandistic value of a few of the motion pictures shown in the camps but he also suggested that the soldiers had access to the latest releases by the biggest motion picture stars: Charlie Chaplin, Douglas Fairbanks, William S. Hart, Charles Ray, William Farnum, Elsie Ferguson, Alla Nazimova, Geraldine Farrar, Norma Talmadge and Gloria Swanson. The commission's report also indicates that motion pictures shown in the camps were more or less the same attractions one could see in civilian theatres at about the same time. It makes clear that nothing was done to protect the soldiers from the "evil" influences of commercial entertainment that was not also being done in civilian theatres.

Vaudeville

Vaudeville certainly included comics in baggy pants and big-busted solo singers who belted popular songs from Tin Pan Alley. It also included trained animal acts, magicians, acrobats, impersonators, escape artists, and jugglers. Variety acts in which duets, trios and quartets danced and sang and played a collection of musical instruments were popular. Vaudeville audiences were perhaps less sophisticated and urbane than those in "legitimate" theatres, and they were more varied ethnically and economically. They were, more so than was the audience for drama and musicals, a mass audience.

At the time the CTCA was declining a proposition from E.R. Seamens, representing the Allardt Vaudeville Circuit, a chain of theatres in the Upper Midwest and in Canada, to build and run vaudeville theatres in the training camps, attendance at vaudeville theatres accounted for half of all theatre attendance in the U. S.[54] Why the CTCA should have been so cool toward vaudeville is unclear. Apparently, Raymond Fosdick had seen or heard of smutty vaudeville acts in commercial theatres near the National Guard camps on the Mexican border in 1916. Vaudeville was occasionally criticized in the national press for catering to intellectually lazy audiences with suggestive songs and dirty jokes, but it was more often praised as theatre clean enough for family fun.[55] Also, the CTCA's and the U.S. Army's fear of profiteering and other forms of exploitation kept theatre concessionaires, including vaudeville, out of almost all the camps. When the commission finally brought in a powerful theatre businessman to help plan the theatre program, they got Marc Klaw. Klaw, of course, had included vaudeville magnate Edward Albee on his select advisory committee, but he seems never to have involved Albee in planning the theatres or lining up professional performers to go the camps.

Klaw was a representative of the "legitimate" theatre, and the adjective says a lot about attitudes and business relations. The term "legitimate" is derived in part from the English heritage of the American theatre. It arose in the 18th century when the two most prestigious theatres in London, Covent Garden and Drury Lane, possessors of royal patents, struggled to maintain dominance against "illegitimate" playhouses springing up all over the city. "Legitimate" became in 19th century England an honorific term bestowed on drama to the exclusion of farce, musical comedy, and musical revue. In the U. S., "legitimate" remained an honorific used in the trade press to distinguish theatre that produced plays and musicals from "lower" forms, burlesque and vaudeville, or variety.

Marc Klaw may not have personally felt the moral, ethical lift of the term "legitimate" nor might he have experienced any contempt for the thousands of theatres and managers and performers producing burlesque and vaudeville, but his relations with vaudeville kingpins was poor. He had been involved in 1907 in a failed effort, the United States Amusement Company (USAC), to break the virtual monopoly in vaudeville held by Albee and his partner, B.F. Keith. Klaw and his partner, Abraham Erlanger, put up money to underwrite contracts with leading vaudeville artists; Lee and J.J. Shubert provided 15 theatres (as did Klaw and Erlanger), and William Morris took charge of booking for the USAC. The new company failed in a few months, but it exacted a toll on Keith and Albee. The USAC brought on a season of higher salaries for top performers, and when it failed, Keith and Albee took over the USAC's performer contracts in exchange for a guarantee that the USAC partners would stay out of vaudeville for 10 years.[56] By 1918 the no-compete agreement had expired, but relations between Klaw and the vaudeville tycoons remained cool. Not only had Klaw met resistance from motion picture executives when he tried to involve them in providing entertainment in the training camps, but also he was positioned poorly to appeal to vaudeville's leaders.

Nevertheless, the camp theatres needed vaudeville performers to help fill their time. Accordingly, the first two of many vaudeville troupes assembled especially for the camps opened at Camp Dix, New Jersey, the first week of March 1918. The Military Entertainment Committee, with the cooperation of Keith and Albee's United Booking Office, the leading vaudeville agency of the day, and other vaudeville booking agencies in New York and Chicago, sent out at least 200 vaudeville companies, each including four to seven acts. Each of those acts involved from one to as many as 15 performers. During the summer of 1918, J. Howard Reber depended heavily on volunteer vaudeville performers to fill the bills in camps on the eastern seaboard and in the Upper Midwest. The United Booking Office solicited the volunteers and booked their tours, while the commission paid their expenses.

Vaudeville performers cost less to hire than legitimate actors, vaudeville acts could be moved from camp to camp less expensively than legitimate attractions, and they were reliably appealing to camp populations. Despite the CTCA's heavy reliance on vaudeville, the *Report of the Military Entertainment Committee* lists but 13 vaudeville companies by name, but it notes the existence of an additional 19 troupes put together for exclusive camp tours and 170 vaudeville troupes that played camp dates as a part of longer commercial tours.[57]

Commercial parlance included terms for two ranks of vaudeville: "bigtime" and "smalltime." Bigtime referred to several of the most prestigious vaudeville theatres in New York and one or two theatres in centers such as Chicago, Boston, Philadelphia, and San Francisco, venues that charged top prices, $1 or more, and attracted a higher-class clientele. Bigtime performers got the best salaries and played only two shows per day. Smalltime referred to many theatres in New York, such as those in the Loew's chain, and to hundreds of vaudeville theatres nationwide (there were about 2,000 in total), charging as little as 10 cents per admission and paying performers small salaries to perform from three to 12 times per day.[58] Almost all the performers booked into the camps were smalltime performers, that is, performers not in the front ranks of the business. When bigtime performers such as Eddie Foy gave a performance in the camps, it was noted in the trade press. Otherwise one sees notices about troupes featuring and named after a headliner or simply notices about "vaudeville."

Most of the troupes mentioned in the *Report of the Military Entertainment Committee* were bigtime, but they represent less than 5 percent of the all the troupes sent to the camps. The vast majority of camp vaudeville performers were smalltime. The report doesn't mention Eddie Foy but it acknowledges the Kittie Francis Vaudeville Company, a/k/a Kittie Francis and "World of Girls." Francis was a singer and dancer in bigtime vaudeville as well as in Broadway musicals. She headlined a company that played East Coast camps in July and August 1918. Lew Hearn and Bonita (Hearn's wife) headlined another troupe seen in camp theatres in 1919. Hearn, one of the great comic straight men in vaudeville, had appeared in the revue *Town Topics* on Broadway in 1915 with Will Rogers, Clifton Webb, and Blossom Seeley. Maud Tiffany, a singer who had appeared at the Folies Bergere, a cabaret-restaurant in New York City, led a vaudeville troupe that played one-night stands in East Coast camps in September 1918. Harry Rose and Sam Curtis led another troupe listed in the MEC Report but do not appear on any camp calendar to be found. Rose worked in a style that anticipated that of Jack Benny; Curtis had been part of several successful variety acts, and together they did roughhouse comedy and sang in close harmony. One of the biggest of the bigtime acts in the camps was the Rock and White Revue. William Rock and Francis White were headliners appearing in the Ziegfeld revue in the roof garden of the New Amsterdam Theatre until April 1918, after which they made some camp appearances. Rock had pioneered touring his own band that appeared on stage with him. Willa Holt Wakefield, another bigtime artist, organized a show titled "A Bit o' Broadway" that featured herself, with the support of Princess Whitedeer, Blanche Alfred, the sister act of Lamont and Wright, the Reiff Brothers, an accordionist named Pasquale, and Hip Raymond, a table dancer. The show also included eight chorus girls. Bigtime or not, Malcolm McBride closed Wakefield's show in August 1918 after receiving reports from camp theatre managers that suggestive jokes had crept in and that in the heat of the summer the chorus girls had abandoned their undergarments above the waist, as became evident when they danced.[59] Moreover, for all the CTCA's call for perpetual review of shows sent to the camps, this is one of only two instances of a booking contract being cancelled as a result of some alleged indecency.

Stock Companies

The need to supply shows to isolated camps occasioned the use of professional stock companies, organizations that produced not one play but several that they could perform in rapid rotation, a new show every day for a week, if necessary. "Popular-priced" stock flourished everywhere in the U.S. from about 1885 until 1930, offering a wide variety of plays and musicals, usually in neighborhood theatres in larger cities, for lower and middle-class audiences paying as little as 15 cents to as much as $1 for an admission. Such stock companies either played a season-long residency in one theatre in one city or they moved from city to city for shorter seasons in each locale. Stock companies were well adapted to conditions in the camps and there were more of these organizations operating in 1917 and 1918 than there were touring single-play companies.[60]

Stock companies were a better buy than the single-play companies sent on tour by the New York booking office. They were permanently located in the region of the camp or camps they served, so transportation costs were minimized. Because they were capable of presenting a repertory of plays and musicals, they could adapt quickly to the particular tastes of a camp population. And their repertoire allowed them to change bills frequently if that seemed to be the key to attracting more admissions at the camp theatre box office. Sixteen stock companies played camp dates lasting as long as eight weeks.

Isolated Camp Lewis, Washington, south of Tacoma, hosted the first stock company. The Wilkes Players, a professional organization from Seattle, played an eight-week stand in the summer of 1918 at Camp Lewis, the largest of all the training camps built in World War I. In July, the Orpheum Follies, a musical stock company, opened a four-week stand at Camp Cody, Deming, New Mexico, probably the most remote of the camps, and moved to Camp Travis, San Antonio, Texas, in August for another four-week stand. The 25 members of the Ellsworth Musical Stock Company had a profitable stand at Camp Fremont, Palo Alto, California, from about September 1, 1918, to about October 15, 1918, when the camp theatre closed because of the Spanish influenza epidemic. Volunteers from Los Angeles performed at the theatre at Camp Kearney, San Diego, California, until the manager engaged a stock company that played there until late May 1919.

R.R. Smith, general manager of Liberty Theatres, hired the stock companies and assigned Moreland Brown of the New York booking office to supervise them. The stock companies seemed to adapt well to camp theatre conditions, so Brown recommended that Camp Pike, near Little Rock, Arkansas, and Camp Taylor, near Louisville, Kentucky, be permanently booked with stock companies that could be exchanged periodically. He also recommended that camps Travis, Kearny, Fremont, and Cody continue with stock, and that Camp Dodge, near Des Moines, Iowa, and Camp Sherman, Ohio, book stock companies for one- to two-week stands.

The stock companies were inexpensive, costing the theatres less than the circuit average for talent, which was $830 per week. The Orpheum Follies at Cody and Travis was a 15-member organization with seven principals that cost $667 per week. A 23-member organization at Camp Kearney cost $670 per week. At Fremont, the Ellsworth Company received 60 percent of the box office receipts each week, or about $600, plus $75 per week for production costs, and half their transportation expense, so their cost was surely less than the circuit average. The Leroy Musical Stock Company played a lengthy engagement at Camp Taylor, Kentucky, where the theatre was in an isolated part of the camp and had consistently lost money playing professional touring attractions and vaudeville. Despite being the commission's most expensive stock company ($755 per week or 70 percent of the gross), the Leroy company was the only organization to attract enough patrons at Camp Taylor's Liberty Theatre to pay its way.

R.R. Smith recommended that more stock companies be assigned to the camps, but he was ignored—the use of stock companies decreased in 1919. The regular and rather long-term presence in camp of the women in the companies seems to have created tensions the CTCA sought to avoid. In mid–October J. Howard Reber unexpectedly ordered the discontinuance of the Leroy Musical Stock Company at Camp Taylor, Kentucky. The camp's theatre manager resisted Reber's decision but did not prevail. The flu epidemic in October 1918 closed the theatre at Camp Fremont and ended the visit of the Ellsworth Musical Stock Company, in residence there since August 1. They appeared next at Camp Lewis, Washington, beginning January 11, 1919. The engagement, although financially successful for both company and theatre, was cut short on March 1, 1919, when the commission's district director, Maj. J.W. Harding, voided their contract on the grounds that the company's chorus girls were incompetent and immoral. Harding cited no specific performance incidents, but one or several of the chorus girls had been asked to leave a dance in camp because of the way they were dancing.[61] By and large, the stock companies were successful although the CTCA used them sparingly. Their productions apparently pleased the soldiers and, with a single exception, both the companies and the CTCA profited.

Soldier Shows

McBride's most significant change in the commission's entertainment program was to introduce a program for stimulating soldier shows. The concept of theatre as a recreational *activity* would seem to have been central in an organization built on the principles of social welfare and recreation. Participating rather than spectating was the watchword of the recreation movement, but the idea of theatre as a commercial product dominated the CTCA's idea of how the camp theatres would work. Still, before the Liberty Theatres were built, Lee Hanmer told Marc Klaw that one of the best things the commission could do for the soldiers, aside from furnishing them with entertainment, was to develop the soldier's capacity to produce his own plays and variety shows. Hanmer believed soldier performances would be well attended, and the receipts from them would help defray the expense of other entertainment. He recommended to Klaw the name of Frederick Koch, a pioneer in the introduction of formal instruction in theatrical production techniques in colleges and universities, and a professor at the University of North Dakota. Hanmer thought Koch the kind of man who could be sent to the camps to instruct the men in the rudiments of theatre. Kate Oglebay of the Drama League of America, who had been instrumental in leading the commission to Marc Klaw, was also intensely interested in providing drama instructors for the camps. Oglebay, like McBride, was a Cleveland resident, where her family owned a large lake shipping company. She had trained as an actress, but her major contribution to theatre was as a promoter of art and amateur theatre. She had headed the New York Shakespeare Tercentenary Committee in 1916, and she chaired the Entertainment Committee of the Drama League of America in 1917. One of its purposes was to encourage amateur theatrical talent in the cities near training camps to prepare shows for soldiers. Nothing was heard of Hanmer's proposal until November 21, 1918, when the commission at its regular weekly meeting, tabled it, and there it languished for about six months.[62]

Shortly before Malcolm McBride took over, Hanmer renewed his campaign. Hanmer believed that the dramatic coach in each camp should devote his full time to locating dramatic talent and putting on local talent shows at the theatre and elsewhere, and that the dramatic coach should be on the CTCA's payroll as were song leaders, athletic directors, and theatre managers.[63] McBride approved the idea and asked Hanmer and Oglebay to devise a plan to present to the commission.[64] Six weeks later, when McBride was established in Washington, Hanmer sent him a list of the names of men he was considering as dramatic coaches. Oglebay had suggested most of them from among her acquaintances in the Drama League of America and the rest came from among Hanmer's acquaintances in community recreation.

In early April 1918, when funding became available, McBride established the Department of Dramatic Activities Among the Soldiers and he appointed Franklin Haven Sargent as director. Sargent's experience and training suited him admirably for the task of providing drama coaches to the camps. He had been a teacher of acting and elocution since 1878 and was in 1918 head of America's most prestigious professional acting school, the American Academy of Dramatic Arts in New York City. Sargent, known for his devotion to the production of Greek classical drama in community and college venues, also had ties to Hanmer and the Russell Sage Foundation, having contributed in 1911 to a book critical of commercial theatre in New York City.

On May 16, Sargent assigned the first dramatic director, W.R. Rochester, producer of the Paint and Powder Club of Baltimore, an amateur theatre club, to Camp Meade, Maryland. Sargent appointed dramatic directors who seem to have been knowledgeable and industrious. Some came to the job from well-established theatre careers and several developed such careers after the war. Barrett Clark, who served at Camp Humphreys, Virginia, in the summer of 1918, had been an actor and stage manager with Minnie Maddern Fiske, an actress celebrated not only for the groundbreaking realism of her style, but also for her resistance of the control of Marc Klaw's Theatrical Syndicate. Clark was also a drama critic and editor. His lectures on the chautauqua circuit and books he edited helped popularize French, German, and Spanish drama in the U.S. He later taught at Columbia, Bryn Mawr, and Queens College and became executive director of the Dramatists' Play Service. In this position he enabled playwrights to find an audience outside the professional theatre, in schools, colleges, and community theatres. Harry Neville, who succeeded Sargent as director, after seven months at Camp Grant, Rockford, Illinois, had been a character actor on

Broadway, the career to which he returned after the war and continued for another 25 years. Wade Boteler had been an actor in stock companies and touring shows before the war and his service at Camp Travis, San Antonio, Texas. After the war he went to Hollywood and appeared in over 400 films in the next 24 years. George Brooks, who served at Camp Funston, Junction City, Kansas, and at Camp Devens, Ayer, Massachusetts, had been famous in the role of KoKo in the Gilbert and Sullivan operetta *The Mikado*. Alexander Leftwich, who served at Camp Beauregard, Louisiana, was a Broadway director both before and after his military service, especially renowned for staging such long-running musicals as *Strike Up the Band* and *Girl Crazy*. Not all of Sargent's appointees left such indelible marks in theatre, but these few suggest that Sargent had high recruitment standards and considerable good fortune.

The camp dramatic director idea met some resistance. McBride had written to the commanding general of each National Army cantonment and National Guard camp offering to assign a drama coach as a civilian aide. He pointed out that the British army had had great success with soldier shows and he emphasized the special utility of having the soldiers experienced in providing entertainment for themselves in France, where no commercial attractions would be available.[65] Many camp commanders didn't like the idea, because they thought their troops were too busy with military training to produce plays. By July 1, 1918, only eight directors had been placed. Harry Neville, who later headed the dramatic director office, reported that camp commanders had resisted dramatic directors and did little to support their mission once they were admitted to the camps.[66]

Wary, disbelieving camp commanders were not the only resistance the CTCA encountered. When the commission instructed its dramatic directors to coordinate and direct *all* amateur theatrical activity and to promote it where it did not exist, some YMCA secretaries who ran their own amateur theatre programs resented the interference. Conflict broke out in three camps right away, leading Malcolm McBride to ask the YMCA national organization to order its secretaries to cooperate. Y leaders refused, instead reminding secretaries that the YMCA sanctioned no such camp position as dramatic director and asking their people to continue to organize informal talent nights in their own huts. John Tichenor, YMCA representative on the commission, also argued that the amateur orientation of the YMCA secretary might make him incompatible with the more professionally oriented dramatic director. Tichenor feared the dramatic director might suppress spontaneous, amateur activities because he could see no value in relatively unfinished efforts. Later, the Y leadership told secretaries to cooperate, but they never told them to submit to CTCA supervision.[67] In effect, the YMCA simply affirmed the status quo.

Given the resistance to the CTCA's efforts to place drama coaches in the camps, it is ironic that the theatrical event most closely associated in popular memory with the First World War was a soldier show produced at Camp Upton, Yaphank, Long Island, New York. Irving Berlin's *Yip, Yip Yaphank* was rehearsed and performed at the Liberty Theatre in Camp Upton in July 1918 and then moved to the Century Theatre in New York City for a memorable run starting August 19, 1918. Broadway songwriter Berlin had been drafted in the spring of 1918 and assigned to Camp Upton. His score for *Yip, Yip Yaphank* featured "Oh, How I Hate to Get Up in the Morning" and "Mandy," both popular hits. *Yip, Yip, Yaphank* became something of a legend. It was revived on Broadway in 1942, as *This is the Army*, and it was made into a popular movie in 1943. Berlin tells a version of the story of the creation of *Yip, Yip, Yaphank* in the motion picture *Alexander's Ragtime Band*, for which Berlin wrote the story and the music in 1938. But *Yip, Yip, Yaphank* was not a product of the CTCA's entertainment program. No dramatic director was assigned to Camp Upton at the time the show was being produced. And, unlike shows of lesser renown in other camps, the cast and crew of *Yip, Yip, Yaphank* was made up almost entirely of theatre professionals conscripted out of New York City.[68] *Yip, Yip, Yaphank* lives in history not because of its typicality but because it was a glamorous event in the nation's theatre capital where it was given maximum press exposure.

Moreover, it was not the only soldier show to play an engagement at a New York City theatre. *You Know Me Al!* which ran two and a half weeks at the Lexington Avenue Theatre, was produced and performed by member of the 27th Division from New York, in training at Camp Wadsworth, Spartanburg, South Carolina. Harry Wagstaff Gribble staged the show. He later achieved modest renown as a director [*Johnny Belinda* (1940) and *Anna Lucasta* (1944] and playwright. Soldiers from the Aberdeen Proving Grounds in Maryland presented *Who Stole the Hat* at the Lexington Avenue Theatre in December, and vaudeville headliner Frank Tinney produced and starred in *Attaboy* at Camp Meigs, Washington, D.C., then in New York, Pittsburgh, and Chicago. Neither of these soldier shows was directly the product of the work of a camp dramatic director.

Franklin Sargent assisted the dramatic directors by publishing royalty-free plays for use by the soldiers. In doing so he carried on a program started by Marc Klaw. Just before he resigned, Klaw had formed a Play Bureau comprised of three New York play brokers who were to provide royalty-free scripts to civilian amateurs and soldiers who wanted to produce plays to be presented in the camps.[69] This group established an office in New York City, and a committee appointed by Sargent later supplemented their duties.

Augustus Thomas, director and author of Broadway hits such as *Arizona* (1900) and *The Copperhead* (1918), headed Sargent's Manuscript Division. Thomas was well connected politically. His contributions to Woodrow Wilson's presidential campaign in 1912 netted him an offer to become U.S. ambassador to Belgium, an offer he declined so he could continue to pursue his playwriting career. Another playwright, Austin Strong, assisted Thomas, and together they supervised the publication of service editions of 20 plays for royalty-free use by soldiers.[70]

By November 1918, 25 dramatic directors were at work in the training camps. Sargent's department ultimately provided dramatic directors to a total of 27 camps.[71] From May 16, 1918, to December 31, 1918, the dramatic directors were responsible for 948 performances of plays, musical comedies, and vaudeville and minstrel shows, an average of about two per week in each camp. About one-eighth of these performances were given outside the camps to promote more cordial relations between the camp and a nearby community.[72]

After the armistice, dramatic directors focused their efforts on entertaining convalescents in base hospitals and on establishing a permanent organization to produce camp entertainment in peacetime. By April 30, 1919, just under a year after dramatic directors began to be assigned, the number of performances had grown to 1,631, or an average of 70 performances in each of the 24 camps reporting.[75] In other words, in those camps where directors were assigned, soldier shows of some sort, probably variety shows, filled the Liberty Theatre stage almost a week each month. Dramatic directors and their amateur nights could be said to have been a significant part of camp theatre offerings in most camps. Nevertheless, the Department of Dramatic Activities Among the Soldiers was discontinued in mid–July 1919. Rapid demobilization had ended the need for all but a few dramatic directors and military personnel assumed these posts.

* * *

Camp shows paid their own way in that receipts at the camp box offices covered expenses for talent and general operations and accumulated a tidy profit of about $400,000 by August 31, 1919. Liberty Theatres had access to many forms of theatrical entertainment — legitimate drama and musical comedy, burlesque, vaudeville, minstrels, concert performers, and amateur civilian and soldier shows, as well as movies. But it's important to note that such a wide array of offerings was not at first envisioned by the CTCA. Had they had such foresight they might not have gone through with the camp theatre project, because some of the entertainment forms— vaudeville, burlesque, and movies— had a reputation among the eastern establishment elite that founded the CTCA as potentially injurious to the moral development of young men. Had the founders been able to overcome their reluctance to open the camps to such entertainment, they might well have designed and built smaller, more adaptable theatres. But the theatres they did build, however oversized some of them were, however tardy in arriving in the camps they all were, served to provide some comfort and amusement to millions of soldiers, and they did so as the entertainers themselves raised enough in admissions to pay their way.

13

The Federal Government and the Entertainment Industry

The flow of those live entertainers and movies into the camps was a remarkable spectacle of men and women finding their way through prickly thickets of official resistance. As the war began relations between the federal government and the theatre industry were strained by the weight of heavy taxes. Onerous taxation and licensing fees, a generally depressed economy, and falling attendance had prompted the organization of Broadway producers to ask the actor's union to adopt a combination sharing and salary contract to help productions through periods of low income.[1] In mid–November 1917, the government imposed an admission tax of 10 percent. Box office receipts plummeted as patrons resisted the sudden increase in prices.[2] Following this action, the U.S. Railroad Administration raised fares and terminated group discounts, and the Fuel Administration saved coal by closing theatres on Sunday, Monday, and Tuesday each week. American theatres normally closed Sunday night, and the Fuel Administration eventually withdrew the demand for Monday closing, but theatres had to remain dark on Tuesday evenings through February.

According to the "work or fight" policy of the Selective Service System, theatre industry employees were classified as "non-productive." Musicians and stage and film actors were exempt as long as they worked steadily, a condition many could not meet. Front-of-house and backstage employees, as well as male chorus members, had to enlist or find "productive" employment. The draft hit hard at the entertainment industry's workforce and it decimated the ranks of the touring companies Marc Klaw needed to send to the camps to perform.[3]

In late July, the House Ways and Means Committee stunned the theatre industry with news of a proposal to double the admission tax, from 10 percent to 20 percent, as part of an effort to tax luxuries to raise money for the war. Theatre spokesmen cried foul and pointed to their efforts in behalf of the Liberty Loan, to a policy of reduced admissions for soldiers, and to attractions sent to the camps "at a great cost." They went so far as to warn that soldier entertainments would be ended entirely if admissions were taxed excessively. Despite these arguments, the House passed a tax bill that included a 20 percent tax on theatre and motion picture admissions. Marc Klaw then led a contingent of producers to Washington to plead with the Senate Finance Committee to lower the tax rate. The Senate complied, and the House yielded the point; nevertheless, the war revenue bill of 1919 continued the prevailing 10 percent tax on admissions.[4]

Theatre managers had further cause to complain when theatres in every city in the U.S., except New York City, were closed as health hazards during the influenza epidemic of September and October 1918. Louis R. Reid, managing editor of the *New York Dramatic Mirror,* argued that the closings were evidence of "plain discrimination," and Reid cited the fact that department stores and other public gathering places had not been closed. Reid noted acidly that the "theatre has long been used to this kind of discrimination at the hands of lawmakers in Washington. Whenever it is possible to make the theatrical profession the goat, Washington jumps at the chance." Reid concluded: "Through the dark four years that have passed the theatre has been buffeted by the worst storms it ever encountered. The last year in particular has been a period of uncertainty and difficulty never before approached."[5]

Theatre spokesmen had cause for concern and dismay, especially in view of the success of their fund-raising campaigns throughout the country. During the First Liberty Loan, stage workers collected $3 million in New York City alone, and they added $4 million to the government treasury during the second loan drive. The third drive, under the direction of the Theatrical Allied Interests Committee, collected $33 million in New York City, ranking the theatres there third among businesses supporting bond sales. Keith-Albee vaudeville theatres outside New York City brought in an additional $35 million. Stage workers in the fourth campaign sold bonds valued at $41 million in New York City theatres. The theatres also assisted in enlistment campaigns, Red Cross fund drives, and the United War Work campaigns. By July 1, 1919, the profession had raised $250 million to finance war efforts at home and abroad.[6]

Government actions, some reasonable and necessary, poisoned the atmosphere in which the Commission on Training Camp Activities had to attract volunteer entertainers. Government policies undermined the goodwill of showmen even as the commission's own prejudices alienated them still further. The government's attitudes fused with those of embattled theatre businessmen habituated to cutthroat competition to create a web of circumstances hindering the full utilization of the resources of the theatre. The commission further complicated the situation by choosing Marc Klaw as their only link with the legitimate stage. The Liberty Theatre venture was thus liable to the charge of partisanship in the faction-ridden industry. Klaw was at odds with the Shubert brothers, powerful theatrical producers; with Keith and Albee, leading vaudeville booking agents; and with the NAMPI representatives of the movie industry. Indeed, the vast resources at Lee Shubert's call were not available to the Liberty Theatres until after Klaw's resignation. Klaw's departure also opened the way for improved film booking procedures and prices and it cleared the way for the powerful United Booking Office to endorse a commission appeal for vaudeville volunteers to play the camp stages during the theatrical slack season of the summer of 1918.

The entertainment industry surely could have been better mobilized had they been approached early in the commission's history, given positions of power and status within the commission, and given respect and cooperation as they sought to do the job of entertaining the troops. They, after all, knew best how to do this job. But the commission's handling of Marc Klaw epitomized their idea of the commercial theatre. The key to valuable resources, Klaw was also to be feared for his outspoken manner and distrusted for the taint of venality on him.

14

Demobilization and Army Theatre Since World War I

Few in the United States expected the war to end so suddenly, but with the cessation of hostilities in November 1918, nearly all officers and men in the army became eligible for discharge. Demobilizing as rapidly as possible without disrupting the economy was a legal and political necessity, but few plans for the complex project had been laid. Indeed, planning for demobilization began a month after the armistice. Nevertheless, in its first full month the army released about 650,000 officers and men. Within nine months nearly 3,250,000 had been discharged. Thirty training camps were transformed into demobilization centers and units in the U.S. were shipped around so soldiers could be discharged near their homes, a process mostly completed by February 1919. Units overseas returned as soon as ships were available, processed through European debarkation centers, and entrained to demobilization centers upon their arrival in the U.S.

Malcolm McBride and other commissioners resigned in January 1919, although the commission continued to meet as an advisory and deliberative body until Secretary Baker terminated all commission appointments on June 30, 1919. The commission itself ceased to exist on August 31, 1919, and on September 1, 1919, following the recommendations of the CTCA, the secretary of war transferred its functions, including the provision of camp shows, to the War Plans Division of the General Staff. In a nine-month period in 1919, civilian employees of the CTCA turned over their work to army personnel.[1]

Secretary Baker, anticipating a much larger peacetime army than was finally allowed, promised Fosdick and McBride that the CTCA's valuable work would be carried on.[2] Baker's approval of the commission's effort extended as well to the camp theatres. Earlier he had assured Fosdick that he believed "clean, wholesome entertainment" was "fundamental in supplementing ... physical and military training," and that "this work must be continued and extended."[3] Baker's assurances were borne out in War Department actions. Even as Liberty Theatres in many camps closed due to the rapid demobilization, six new theatres opened.[4] Moreover, in June 1919, the War Department authorized the construction of three new theatres more elaborately appointed than any before.

Baker asked his 3rd assistant secretary, F.R. Keppel, to dismantle the CTCA. Keppel in turn assigned Maj. Jason S. Joy and Maj. James A. Buell to the Commission on Training Camp Activities on January 3, 1919.[5] The day Joy and Buell started to work Malcolm McBride resigned as chairman of the Military Entertainment Committee, leaving his job to J. Howard Reber. Joy and Buell instituted no immediate policy changes. The director of Liberty Theatres in Washington still assigned and supervised theatre managers, both civilian and military, and he approved expenditures for improvements, general upkeep, and the purchase of equipment. The New York Booking Office negotiated all theatrical contracts and paid all film bills. The supervisor of maintenance and construction directed the construction and repair of theatre buildings, a process that continued but at a much slower pace.

Despite the rapid turnover of personnel, the work of the division proceeded rather smoothly but not without a little friction between the civilian administrators and the military officers who succeeded them. A week after Capt. W.P. Wooldridge became director of Liberty Theatres, succeeding Richard R. Smith, Reber complained to McBride that military authorities were interfering with the work of the Military Entertainment Committee by contradicting his orders to officers recently appointed as the commission's district directors. McBride forwarded Reber's complaint to Major Joy and Major Joy explained that McBride's retirement had sent two-thirds of the functions of the Theatre Division to New York. Joy found Reber in New York only two days a week because he was spending most of his time attending to his Philadelphia law practice. The Theatre Division was virtually inoperative the remaining five days. Joy acknowledged that he had usurped Reber's authority, but out of necessity.[6] Reber quickly resigned and Major Joy placed his associate director, Major Buell, in charge of the Military Entertainment Committee.[7] Reber continued to serve as an advisor.

Between March and August 1919, 22 theatres closed; changes in booking practices followed accordingly. During the period of demobilization, decentralization occurred servicewide as the War Department vested broad executive authority in the commanders of nine corps areas established for administration, training, and tactical control of the army. The CTCA followed suit. About April 1, Lt. R.P. Whitfield, assistant director of the Liberty Theatre Division, began to book attractions for theatres in the Washington, D.C., area. In June, Major Joy began closing the New York Booking Office and allowing local managers to negotiate directly with booking agents.[8] Reber and McBride opposed decentralized booking, but Joy was adamant, believing that new conditions in the camps necessitated the change.[9] McBride, Reber, Hanmer, and other civilian volunteers severed all relations with the military by the end of June. On August 31, 1919, the last day of the official existence of the commission, the Liberty Theatre Division consisted of only 12 theatres.

The War Department quickly established an Education and Recreation Branch within the War Plans Division and charged it with responsibility for education, recreation, and morale. In November, a year after the armistice, a Camp Activities Section of the Education and Recreation Branch took over the commission's functions and the Liberty Theatre Division became the Dramatic Sub-section.[10] In the following four months the Camp Activities Section slowly gave up the remnants of the central authority built up by the commission. After January 1920 department commanders decided entertainment policies and requested such help as they needed from the Dramatic Sub-section.[11]

Demobilization brought a rapid rollback of recreational activities, but this fact shouldn't be interpreted as a repudiation of the value of those activities. Army Chief of Staff Peyton C. March recognized recreation as a "military necessity." Gen. Edward L. Munson, the chief of the Morale Branch of the General Staff (of which the Education and Recreation Branch was a part) wrote glowingly of the need for recreational activities of the sort administered by the CTCA. Munson justified recreation as a "safety valve" allowing physical and psychological energy to be released in wholesome, constructive acts, and he lauded all the forms of recreation fostered by CTCA agents: athletics, music, and theatre and motion pictures. He devoted most of his discussion of theatre to urging the value of having soldiers provide theatre for themselves. His book, *The Management of Men: A Handbook on the Systematic Development of Morale and the Control of Human Behavior* (1921), became a blueprint for morale development in the war mobilization two decades later.[12]

The War Department urged Congress to establish a permanent Regular Army of nearly 600,000 and universal military training that would permit the quick expansion of this force as needed. Wilson focused all his waning energy on urging U.S. membership in the League of Nations and gave the War Department scant support for this initiative. Congress and public opinion recoiled against the military and, ultimately, against the

Wilson administration that had led them into and out of a war much more deadly than anybody had imagined it would be. In 200 days of combat, over 50,000 soldiers died and nearly 200,000 were wounded. An appalling 63,000 died of disease, nearly 40,000 of those in training camps in the U. S., most succumbing to influenza. More young Americans died in World War II, in the Korean War and in Vietnam, but over much longer periods of time in each conflict. War-weary hardly describes the conditions on the home front; war-disgusted would be more accurate. The clash of the harsh reality of the fighting against Wilson's idealistic rhetoric in the build-up to war and during the conflict drowned out the few voices that urged continued vigilance and readiness.

By 1920, many political pacesetters in Congress and outside it believed that no major power except Japan posed a significant threat to the U.S. and that only at sea. Senate rejection of the Versailles Treaty and membership in the League of Nations signaled a rising tide of isolationism and an emerging public opinion that the nation needed an army only large enough to defend its borders and possessions and to train civilian volunteers. By 1922, military spending reductions had cut the Regular Army to a force of about 137,000, a number sustained until 1935, when the growing threat of German and Japanese forces urged gradual increases in the size of the U.S. Army.[13]

In the 1920s the World War I training camps were systematically abandoned and their buildings dismantled or sold intact to civilians who moved them and used them as homes, warehouses or farm buildings.[14] Camp Sherman, Ohio, where this account began, was dismantled by 1920. It is now the site for a state prison and the Hopewell National Cultural Historical Park. Camp Upton on Long Island was also dismantled, then rebuilt in 1940. The camp is now the site of the Brookhaven National Laboratory. More permanent theatres built at some Regular Army posts in 1919 and 1920 became motion picture houses when they were used at all.

* * *

Immediately after the European war started again on September 1, 1939, President Roosevelt increased the size of the Regular Army and the National Guard to 227,000 and 235,000, respectively. In the 1930s, continental defense had given way to hemispheric defense. With the lightning-fast German seizure of Denmark and Norway in April 1940 and the precipitous fall of France in May, the United States began accelerating the growth of its military. By September 1940, the War Department plans called for an army of 1.5 million as soon as possible, a goal it reached by mid–1941 mainly through the implementation of the Selective Service and Training Act of September 14, 1940, the first peacetime draft in the nation's history. By January 1, 1942, the United States was at war with the Axis powers. Also for the first time in its history the nation went to war with a large army at the ready and its industrial engines primed for mobilization.[15]

Secretary of War Henry L. Stimson decreed in 1940 that military agencies would conduct all welfare activities on army posts. The experience of 1917–1919 had taught that sectarian welfare groups inside the camps engaged in disabling rivalries. The Wilson administration had been subject to embarrassing charges of discrimination and prejudice when it refused the appeals of some private societies to work in the camps after having allowed several to do so. Impartiality toward all civilian welfare agencies was Stimson's announced aim.[16] None were allowed in the camps.

At the same time the army centralized morale-building services, first in the Morale Division of the Office of the Adjutant General, then, in March 1941, in the Morale Branch of the General Staff. The Morale Branch advised the chief of staff, Gen. George C. Marshall, on welfare and recreation facilities and programs and on the army's relationship with civilian welfare agencies. The Morale Branch was in turn advised by the Joint Army and Navy Committee on Welfare and Recreation. Federal Security Administrator Paul V. McNutt coordinated the efforts of many agencies and organizations to provide leisure-time activities for military personnel and defense workers in communities adjacent to military installations and defense plants, thereby carrying on the work done by the War Camp Community Service in World War I.

The Morale Branch carried on all the recreational programs of the CTCA. Its Welfare and Recreation Division provided liaison with civilian welfare agencies, operated guest houses and clubs in the camps, and provided services to dependents of soldiers. The Recreation Section of this division promoted athletics, amateur dramatics, singing, bands, and dances, while building recreational facilities and monitoring civilian organizations sending professional entertainers to the camps. The Public Relations Division's Radio Section developed camp radio programs and plays and provided broadcast services to forces overseas. The Miscellaneous Division included the Army Motion Picture Service and the Post Exchange Section. Military police coordinated with local police to deal with prostitution. Army recreational services in World War II developed along paths worn during World War I, but it was driven much less by concern about prostitution and the abuse of alcohol than had been the recreation programs in World War I. General Munson's "safety valve" justification for recreation suggested abiding concern about any form of antisocial behavior that tended to undercut efficiency and discipline. Moreover, steps taken to meet the needs of military dependents far exceeded the attention given the families of servicemen and servicewomen in World War I.

By 1943, the Special Service Division of the Army Service Force (ASF) had assumed the functions of the Morale Division of the General Staff. Its

Athletic and Recreation Branch trained theatrical advisors to organize and develop amateur dramatics. It also recruited and trained Mobile Special Service units of five officers and 116 enlisted men for duty close to the front. These were infantry units armed and ready for combat, but they carried motion picture equipment and members were trained to organize amateur theatricals.

The Athletic and Recreation Branch also supervised Camp Shows, Inc., a program of the United Service Organizations. Camp Shows, Inc., coordinated the tours of celebrity performers and professional theatre troupes in the U.S. and overseas.[17] The United Service Organizations (USO), an interfaith agency, was created in 1941 to coordinate recreational services off-post. Its members were the YMCA, the YWCA, National Catholic Community Service, Salvation Army, Jewish Welfare Board, five of the seven "sisters" from World War I, and the national Travelers Aid Society. Early in 1941, entertainment industry professionals helped the USO begin Camp Shows, Inc., to bring live entertainment to soldiers in the U.S. and overseas. By 1944, the USO had established over 3,000 offices and centers throughout the United States and staffed them with volunteers. Between 1941 and 1947, when it was deactivated, USO Camp Shows, Inc., involved over 7,000 "soldiers in greasepaint" performing over 400,000 shows.[18]

Productions sent to the camps were cast and produced by Camp Shows, Inc., from its offices in the St. James Theatre Building and at 8 West 40th Street, New York City. The organization paid union scale salaries to performers as well as transportation for tours that started about December 1, 1941. Eddie Dowling, Pulitzer Prize-winning producer, playwright, songwriter, director, and actor, headed Camp Shows. The USO funded them, providing start-up resources of $800,000. A year later Abe Lastfogel, Broadway producer, succeeded Dowling as president of USO Camp Shows, Inc., and the program's budget had grown to $2.6 million.[19]

All this was a marked change from the situation Marc Klaw encountered when he was engaged by the CTCA in 1917 to mobilize touring theatre companies for the World War I training camps. Also in a clear departure from the experience of World War I, the Federal Works Agency, not a division of the War Department, built recreational facilities, including theatres, for service personnel. The agency used money provided by Congress through the Lanham Act for the construction, maintenance and operation of military recreation centers. Through April 1943 total allocations under the Lanham Act were almost $29 million.[20]

In other respects, however, USO Camp Shows, Inc., replicated the processes of the Liberty Theatre Division of the CTCA. Far more camps needed entertainment services, over 300, and they were divided into two or more circuits, one incorporating large camps and others serving smaller installations. The camps seemed to want "clean shows, funny shows, shows with lots of girls." Dramatic plays were a novelty, however two on the large camp circuit in 1942 played to packed houses. As did the booking office of World War I, Camp Shows drew upon available professionally produced plays and musicals seen on Broadway: *Hit the Deck, Room Service, Arsenic and Old Lace, Flying Colors, Show Time at the Roxy, Shuffle Along, Out of the Frying Pan, Junior Miss, Funzafire, Beachcombers of 1942,* and *Razzle Dazzle*.[21] The first USO Camp Show, *Out of the Frying Pan*, started its tour December 18, 1941.

Accepting the fact that admissions could not pay for the quality entertainment Camp Shows, Inc., wanted to provide, the USO provided a substantial subsidy. Initially, soldiers were charged admission to camps shows: 15 cents in the smaller camps where soldiers saw featured entertainers and vaudeville acts, and 20 cents in the larger camps, where musical comedies, plays and revues dominated. Admissions covered about one-third of production costs, and the USO made up the difference. The USO abolished admission fees in March 1942 and from then on bore entirely the cost of getting a show to every camp at least once every two weeks.[22]

Those charting the course of army theatre in World War II emphasized amateur theatre for and by the soldiers far more explicitly than had been done in World War I. In the summer of 1941, the Citizens Committee for the Army and Navy and the National Theatre Conference proposed a plan to stimulate more soldier theatricals and the army accepted it. Under this plan the National Theatre Conference engaged civilian drama coaches and the Citizens Committee raised the money to pay them, while the Morale Branch assigned them in each of the army's nine corps.[23] In March 1942, the newly organized Special Services Section of the Army Service Force took over the National Theatre Conference program. Professor Barclay Leathem of Case Western Reserve University had organized the NTC effort and remained as a special civilian advisor with Special Services serving in the Sixth Corps area in the U.S. The School for Special Services at Washington and Lee University, Lexington, Virginia, devoted a section to developing theatrical skills of officers and enlisted men assigned to Mobile Special Service units in the army overseas.[24]

While reestablishing programs for bringing professional entertainers into army camps and for providing dramatic directors to develop amateur theatre, the army's World War II programs incorporated significant differences. The army assumed nearly complete responsibility for amateur theatre programs for soldiers, while civilians supplied professional entertainment through Camp Shows, Inc., a well-funded arm of the United Services Organizations. Thus the proven fund-raising prowess of the constituent units of the USO — YMCA, YWCA, Salvation Army, Jewish

Welfare Board and National Catholic Community Service — was marshaled in support of rather than in competition with the program to provide professional entertainment in the camps and overseas. Moreover, army appropriation of theatre for and by soldiers through its Special Services branch meant that amateur theatre was officially an army matter rather than being a civilian imposition as it had been in World War I. These broad organizational adjustments contributed to the greater efficiency with which theatre became a part of Army life in World War II.

However, USO planners were like their CTCA predecessors in seeing an opportunity to address endemic social problems, such as racial and ethnic tensions, gender expectations, and teen delinquency, through war mobilization, and they struggled with how to devise wartime programs that would continue in the postwar years. It is likely they experienced little success in achieving their goals of social transformation through theatrical expression, as little as the CTCA experienced through its Liberty Theatre program.[25] In drawing upon the commercial and educational theatre of the time, the reformers' high idealism encountered the rock solid conventionality of most theatre attractions, artists, and educators. Commercial theatre in the decade of the teens and in the decade of the '40s was not a vehicle for social and political change but an instrument for sustaining the status quo of racism, ethnic tension, and sexism.

Shortly after the end of World War II, Special Services in the army was reassigned to the General Staff as part of the Personnel Section (G-1). The USO was deactivated December 31, 1947, and camp show activities were taken over by Veteran's Hospital Camp Shows, the last of the USO Camp Shows for GIs in Europe having returned to the U.S. in January 1947. However, service to Cold War military installations required the reactivation of the USO on January 1, 1949. The USO could not, however, raise sufficient funds, so it discontinued services about January 1, 1950. The YMCA and the Jewish Welfare Board continued a presence off-post in former USO centers. Their efforts were soon merged in an organization called the Associated Services for the Armed Forces (ASAF).

Following the outbreak of the Korean War on June 25, 1950, ASAF launched a campaign to raise $9.6 million to support expanded programs for service personnel. While deactivated, the USO had retained a corporate identity and it was reactivated in January 1951 to succeed the ASAF as the provider of off-post recreational and welfare services for the armed forces.[26] USO Camp Shows, Inc., was similarly pulled out of mothballs in March 1951 to send entertainment units to Korea and other overseas areas. In May 1951, the first Camp Shows since reactivation left the U.S. By the end of 1951, 33 units involving 226 entertainers had given 1,629 performances. Korean Camp Shows differed from the World War II version in being smaller, only about 10 people, and requiring little support equipment. Troupes went to Korea and Alaska, and also to Labrador, Iceland, Greenland, Trieste, Tripoli, Morocco, the Azores, and Europe, as well as to isolated U.S. bases.

Service unification led in 1951 to the creation of the Armed Forces Professional Entertainment Branch to coordinate all live professional entertainment for the armed forces. The office was under army jurisdiction but it included representatives of the four major services. Camp Shows, Inc., was deactivated in December 1957 due to the lack of funds, by which time it had sent 10,316 performers to entertain 22.8 million service men and women since its founding in 1941.[27] The function of USO Camp Shows, Inc., was continued, however, through USO Shows, an arm of the USO Entertainment Committee, responsible for providing entertainment for forces abroad. USO Shows included professional paid tours; celebrity gratuitous tours, and tours of college theatre companies, arranged through the Overseas Touring Project of the American Educational Theatre Association (AETA).[28]

The U.S. Army Special Services hired civilian employees to stimulate and direct soldier shows, but they also continued to train military personnel to organize soldier shows. Through a program conceived by a former actor, Maj. Thomas R. Ireland, head of the Special Services Entertainment and Recreation Branch, and Paul Baker, Baylor University theatre professor and former special services entertainment officer in Iceland, the army recruited 100 Civilian Actress Technicians — they were called CATS — to teach theatre and direct soldier shows. The first of the CATS went to Europe in 1945 and to Pacific outposts in 1946.[29]

In 1949, the new Department of Defense established the Department of Defense Entertainment Project. Those service personnel involved, mostly army, took a two-month course in acting, singing, dancing, direction, lighting, and set design at Fort Dix, New Jersey. The graduates produced a revue that opened at Fort Dix and then toured other installations until mid–December 1949. They were then assigned as entertainment directors to outfits all over the country, supplementing the CATS.[30] Soldiers specialized in musical variety but also presented revues, musical comedies, and one-act and full-length plays in post theatres and service clubs, and at bivouacs and post hospitals. They also performed off-post to further community relations.[31] Both CATS and the Defense Entertainment Project amply illustrate the army's growing commitment to supporting amateur theatricals produced by and for soldiers.

Speaking to the National Recreation Congress in 1951, Brig. Gen. C.W. Christenberry, chief of Army Special Services, touted planned recreation as important for good morale and efficient performance of duties. He echoed the justification for the World War I programs in suggesting that army programs of the day were designed to assure that "American youth does not deteriorate during his time in service" and "to make the American serviceman a better man for having been in the service." In 1952, the army established its entertainment program as a permanent form of recreational activity throughout the service.[32]

Vietnam War-era army theatre followed the established model: Department of Defense civilian employees and branch service personnel managed amateur theatre at military installations, and the Armed Forces Professional Entertainment Office coordinated attractions offered by USO Shows and by other professionals who applied directly to the military. In 1967 and 1968 dozens of movie and television celebrities played in Vietnam under USO auspices, but declining support for the war undercut the interest of Hollywood celebrities. In 1970, James Sheldon of the Hollywood office of the USO packaged 110 variety shows, few with known personalities in them.[33]

By the early seventies, amateur theatre programs were deeply entrenched as a part of Army life. A summary of Department of Defense recreation facilities indicates the existence of 1,004 theatres with and without stages. The vast majority of these were used mainly for motion pictures, but the number of "theatres" ranked fourth among the types of facilities counted, exceeded only by the number of tennis courts, softball fields and crafts shops.[34]

The army increasingly used civilian employees in Special Services. The Armed Forces Recreation Society, formed in 1949, united professional recreation personnel from all service branches and professionals in agencies and institutions providing services to the armed forces, such as the American Red Cross and the USO. In the early '80s, with the advent of the all-volunteer force, Special Service occupational ratings were discontinued and civilian employees took over the tasks formerly carried out by officers and enlisted personnel, but with military oversight. The Department of the Army consolidated its Morale, Welfare, and Recreation (MWR) programs in the U.S. Army Community and Family Support Center in November 1984. The recreational needs of an all-volunteer army were changing, as more personnel served longer enlistments. In the past two decades an increasing percentage of army personnel have been married, and the needs of their dependents have become more and more important in determining the nature of recreational programs, including amateur theatre.

A growing army that was increasingly professionalized demanded a wider range of recreational services embracing the needs of active duty personnel and their dependents as well as retired personnel and their dependents. In fiscal year 1981, the armed forces spent almost $1 billion on MWR activities, most paid from nonappropriated funds. Managers aimed at ever-higher degrees of self-sufficiency. Profits from post exchanges, user fees, equipment rentals, club memberships and video game machines funded half or more of the cost of the army's MWR programs. Accordingly, patron surveys to anticipate activities that might prove popular and profitable became commonplace.[35] However, heavy and increasing dependence on nonappropriated funds has brought about the commercialization of MWR activities and deflected the unit from its historical mission. Critics of the trend have called for the acceptance of criteria for success that emphasize not bottom-line profitability and fiscal accountability but an ethical accountability to the mission of the Army and the ability of recreation services to support that mission.[36]

Recreation has proven to be a major contributor to the quality of life of both career and short-term personnel and their dependents, and military recreation has become one of the most sophisticated and complex leisure delivery systems in the U.S. A large professional staff provides day care, vacation hotels, game rooms, golf courses, intramural athletics and interservice competition, fitness centers and playgrounds.[37] The 1997 Annual Report of the Morale, Welfare and Recreation services of the Department of the Army claims that the army's entertainment program is the largest single producer of community theatre in the world. In 1943 Camp Shows, Inc., had boasted of being the largest single theatrical producing organization, with the exception of the Federal Theatre, a huge government relief program operating mostly professional theatres in over 40 states from 1936 to 1939. These claims suggest the shift in emphasis away from professional shows and toward theatre of the soldier, by the soldier and for the soldier from the period of World War II to the present. In 1998 the army revived the soldier show, producing the 15th edition of the event that dates back to the first show at Camp Yaphank, Long Island, New York, in 1918. They brought out another servicewide soldier show in 1999, the 16th incarnation. It entertained 130,000 in a six-month tour of 64 locations, including bases in Korea and Alaska. In 1999, Army Entertainment, embracing their amateur theatre program, operated on a budget of $5.4 million, of which 41 percent came from nonappropriated funds. The international tour of the servicewide soldier show continues to this day.[38]

Recreation and theatre professionals in career tracks now deliver vast, expensive and ongoing recreation and theatre programs in an army in a nearly perpetual state of alert and readiness to respond anywhere on the globe to crises deemed to impact upon the national interest. They serve a complex array of constituents, and they are heavily dependent on nonappropriated funds generated within the local military base economy from resale activities and user fees. Theatre programs are no longer justified as a bridge linking the soldier to the civilian life from which he or she was drawn and to which he or she will return, with strengthened moral fiber and heightened patriotism. They are justified as experiences enhancing a soldier's quality of life and thereby supporting the army's capacity to achieve its mission. They help sustain a vast and powerful military culture that emerged in the decades following World War II and that now exists alongside the larger civilian culture of the United States.

15

Amateurs and Professionals: Conscience and Commerce

The War Department's CTCA and its Liberty Theatres were born of idealistic as well as practical concerns for the social and physical wellbeing of conscripted trainees. Dedicated social reformers who believed that skillfully administered social controls could improve the conditions under which conscripted soldiers trained and served established the Commission on Training Camp Activities. Newton Baker and Raymond Fosdick hoped the programs of the Commission on Training Camp Activities, of which the Liberty Theatre came to be the foremost, would ensure that social order as they conceived it would prevail in the camps. The government theatres and other welfare and recreational programs would envelop the conscripted citizen in armor protecting him from what history had proven to be the disorderly effects of military camp life.

Among these reformers were people who thought they saw in commercial amusements powerful inducements to disorder. Commission executives such as Lee Hanmer harbored the view that the business of entertainment was to market commodities for a profit to audiences seeking coarse and destabilizing pleasure. Theatre, movies, and vaudeville could exploit the antisocial and irreligious side of their patrons. A stage show or a movie could be a shabby concoction of smutty jokes, crude physical gags, bawdily suggestive movement, and provocatively immoral situations featuring scantily clad lewd women and effeminate men, peddled for profit by selfish, venal hucksters. Many commercial entertainment products conduced only to bestiality, and this kind of entertainment should be restricted or prohibited in the same way one restricted the use of alcohol and resort to prostitutes.

The founders of the Liberty Theatre project were theatrical amateurs, but not altogether by chance. They wanted entertainment venues inside the camps that provided professionally produced theatre and they wanted those stages shielded from the influence of profiteering entertainment businessmen. The YMCA and War Camp Community Services, with the help of the Drama League of America, were bringing amateur performers into the camps. The CTCA, the YMCA, and the Drama League stood not just outside the commercial theatre but also opposed to its values. CTCA executives had ties to people, like philanthropist Otto Kahn, and organizations, such as the Drama League of America, just beginning to define a noncommercial position for theatre — art theatres, community theatres, school theatres — within the field of cultural production. The CTCA conceptualized its camp theatres as distinctly anticommercial so they must be seen as an element of this emerging position within the field of cultural production.

Fosdick's colleagues in the CTCA were inspired reformers, and they flew at the Liberty Theatre project with prudential and censorious attitudes about the commercial theatre, the institution to which they reluctantly turned as the only establishment that could possibly deliver the program material they needed. Not unexpectedly, the professionals to whom they turned for assistance after much temporizing ran the Liberty Theatres according to the humdrum possibilities of the commercial theatre of the time. Indeed, how could they have done otherwise? Even theatrical management amateurs (though adept businessmen) such as Malcolm McBride and J. Howard Reber, who expelled Marc Klaw and seized control of camp theatre construction, booking and management, made decisions based on commercial ideals: the profitability of the theatres and the sheer amusement potential of the attractions booked into them. Moreover, they adopted theatre management practices characteristic of the time, specifically iron-fisted control of all facets of their program by a central officer.

They believed in the transformational potential of theatre experiences, and this orientation funded their contempt for commercial forms of leisure and recreation. Theatre business was not just venal; it was also subversive. The CTCA's theatre management practices were manifestations of their desire to have professional performers in the camps but without admitting at the same time commercial entertainment's subversive energies. The commission's array of ideals also included the notion that entertainment, far from being an inconsequential frill, was one of the "normalities of life," so they built camp theatres as part of a manifold effort to make the camps more comfortable and hospitable and more like their image of whole, well-run cities. The CTCA seemed to expect a lot of the camp theatres. Assumptions about the function or at least about the potential of the camp theatres suffuse their correspondence and their actions. The government theatres were to be a well-regulated alternative to rowdy and sleazy civilian theatres the commissioners had good reason to believe would spring up on the margins of the training camps. They also seemed to believe a theatre and other in-camp recreational and entertainment venues might help maintain social stability in the camp community and improve the morale of the trainees. A commercially produced play performed on the camp stages was assumed to have recreational value, affording the soldier audience an invigorating break from the tedium of work. It was also thought to have social value as well, for it increased the doughboy's sense of belonging to a group through gathering in a common place and enjoying a common pleasurable experience. Moreover, it was supposed to provide good, clean fun and thereby to function as a wholesome alternative to cheap amusements, saloons and brothels.

The CTCA seemed to have imagined that attending the camp theatre or participating in amateur theatricals had spiritual value. These activities might be good for morale, inducing feelings of enthusiasm and confidence. Camp attractions did not have to contain solemn, moral messages or melodramatically rendered illustrations of the triumph of good over evil to achieve these ends. Shows for soldiers should be lively, gay, colorful, even frivolous, but they should avoid all salaciousness or representation of any criminal activity as anything other than nakedly evil. These ideas were expressive of the emerging view of entertainment as a cultural norm, not a distraction from attention to the stern demands of a life of hard work and flinty piety.

The Liberty Theatre program grew out of contradictory views of entertainment. Given such a tangled ethos, it has not been surprising to find the venture plagued by strategic errors on the part of its planners and executors—errors that suppressed the capacity of the theatres to attract soldier patrons and thereby to achieve the highest aims of the project. In the first place, the need for government-built camp theatres and government-sanctioned attractions was hastily and inaccurately estimated. The YMCA offered free movies and free local talent shows in auditoria, huts, and tents in many locations throughout all the training camps. The Knights of Columbus and the Jewish Welfare Board also offered recreation and entertainment facilities in many camps. The commission itself sponsored programs that competed with the Liberty Theatres for the soldier's leisure time. CTCA song leaders organized singing groups and other musical recreations, while athletic directors assisted morale officers in establishing intramural team sports in all seasons. Camp newspaper advertisements reveal that the camp fringes were entertainment boulevards crowded with restaurants, pool halls, and movie and variety theatres. But the programs of the YMCA and other service organizations, and the CTCA's own leisure time programs, stressed soldier participation. The CTCA initially dedicated the Liberty Theatres to bringing professionally produced shows into the camps, shows that would counterbalance the appeal of commercial attractions in the carnivalesque midways outside the camps. But the commission's initial vision of a captive and grateful audience never materialized. Nor did their worst fears about the sleaziness of businesses on camp borders.

Fundamental decisions about the kind of theatres to be built were based on little else than superficial, *a priori* conceptions of the needs of the men in training. Congress acted on the commission's request for theatre construction funds before military authorities were consulted about the need for theatres in *all* the camps or the kind of building or organization each might need. Similarly, in the first days of the commission's life in the summer of 1917, no professional theatre businessman was consulted for advice on the merit of various kinds of buildings or attractions. When the CTCA finally engaged this professional — theatrical booking mogul Marc Klaw — they allied the camp theatres with a manager who knew very well how to handle the reins of the skittish and weary theatrical touring system of the day. But Klaw and his associates seem to have shared none of the reform zeal of the most highly placed commissioners. Klaw was flattered when asked in this time of national crisis to provide the service the CTCA needed. However, the task of working with CTCA bureaucrats and meeting their needs kept him and those he served in a perpetual state of agitation and disappointment. The two parties in the venture, the War Department's CTCA and the theatre professional, seem never to have reconciled their visions of the purpose of the camp theatre project. Accordingly they worked at cross-purposes, Hanmer and Mayer regarding Klaw as lead-footed and acrimonious; Klaw regarding Hanmer and Mayer as meddlesome and incompetent.

The failure of Congress to appropriate funds with which to initiate the camp shows further handicapped the commission. The disastrous experiment with tent chautauqua during the early winter of 1917 cost Raymond Fosdick the money borrowed to underwrite the expense of securing contracts for attractions prior to the opening of the first theatres in January 1918. Marc Klaw planned an advance ticket sales campaign as early as September 1917, but the plan languished unattended until January 1918, and by then the Smileage money came too late to support a healthy start for the theatres. The attractions used in the first months of operation failed to impress camp authorities and to appeal to soldier audiences. They undermined the reputation of the camp theatre, which became trapped in a steady downward spiral of attendance and income. Too late the commission's booking agents instituted measures to make the camps more attractive to theatrical tour producers who needed only a small profit to stay in business. As a result, other, less expensive forms of entertainment, especially vaudeville and motion pictures, displaced legitimate theatrical productions as the staple of the camp stages. Sharply reducing talent expenses became the key to a watery solvency.

Liberty Theatre executives were inappropriately dedicated to making the camp theatres profitable. They took apparent pride in their ability to cut the cost of talent so that the venture showed a profit. This strategy meshed neatly with others to limit access to better shows that might have attracted the soldiers to the camp theatres. Finally, motivated by their belief in the efficacy of centralized control, officials in Washington and New York appropriated the power to select attractions thereby stripping the local manager of his opportunity to adapt his theatre to local conditions.

At its worst, in the construction of outsized and marginally usable theatre buildings, the Liberty Theatre venture was a waste of the idealistic fervor of its founders and of the public money with which they were entrusted. At its best, in the provision of hundreds of plays, musicals, variety acts, and amateur talent shows, and thousands of motion pictures, it was a qualified success. Nothing about the plays and musicals and the motion pictures and vaudeville shows suggests the entertainment the CTCA brought to the camp differed markedly from that available in the cities and towns near the camps. Its most promising program, indeed its most enduring legacy, was that devised by Lee Hanmer and Kate Oglebay and directed by Franklin Sargent. The assignment of trained drama coaches to 27 camps was the clearest expression of the commission's underlying belief in the recreational value of theatre, but the CTCA's struggles to build theatres and provide professional touring shows overshadowed the accomplishments of this phase of the venture.

Commission records reveal that the theatres were filled to only one-third of their gargantuan capacity on the average. Accordingly, it might be said that the theatres failed to realize their potential, whether it was to arm the trainee with attitudes that would enhance his resistance to the attraction of cheap liquor, cheap amusements, and loose women or simply to distract him momentarily from the low life. The theatres were too large, given the populations they were designed to serve, for the Class A theatres could accommodate from 2,000 to nearly 3,000 for any performance, 5 percent or more of the anticipated population of the largest camps, built for 40,000 trainees. The smaller theatres seated from 1,000 to 1,600, but served smaller camps. The very large capacity of the theatres contributes to an impression that they failed to attract patrons. Nevertheless, the theatres drew over 8.5 million admissions for all kinds of attractions between January 1, 1918, and August 31, 1919. Theatre admissions of $2.4 million paid off a debt of $114,000 run up by the chautauqua tents in the fall of 1917, talent expenses of $1.6 million and operating expenses of $404,000. The War Department used the remaining profit of about $270,000 to subsidize entertainment in the camps remaining open and in the army's permanent installations after September 1, 1919.

Despite emerging from a thicket of twisted motives and stumbling down a crooked path toward initial openings, the camp theatre project gathered momentum in the spring of 1918, having largely abandoned the use of touring comedies and musicals for vaudeville shows and movies. Soldiers went to the theatres in significant numbers, though not to the limits the too-large buildings could have accommodated. More importantly, the CTCA theatres and programs established precedents for morale-building recreational services that the army and the civilian organizations serving it revived in the mobilization for World War II. Shortly after the peace was signed, Secretary of War Baker reconfirmed his belief in the need for entertainment for soldiers. Furthermore, the camp theatre venture had great value as tangible proof, however meager, to millions of soldiers, that their government was capable of humane consideration of individuals drafted into its army.

In 1941 the army vastly enlarged its commitment to camp theatres, but this time the military stressed amateur performances by and for the soldier, while civilian service organizations supplied professional attractions. Since the end of World War II army theatre programs have flourished through continuing reformations to become deeply entrenched features of military culture. As clumsily managed as they were in World War I, the camp theatres indelibly etched an experience in the army's institutional memory, an experience that has called for repetition, but with continually developing strategic differences.

The army's Liberty Theatres embodied a complex idea of theatre, full of internal contradictions and functioning for those who look back on them through the binoculars of history as a moment in the gradual sanctification of entertainment now so typical of the larger civilian culture. They affiliated with fading cultural institutions—a centralized commercial theatre in New York churning out professional touring attractions for a dying road, with vaudeville, and with tent chautauqua. The camp theatres also made heavy use of the products of the new and soon to be culturally dominant entertainment medium, motion pictures. And in the program of amateur theatre, the World War I camps took their own position in the field of limited production, a field now dominated by not-for-profit professional theatre, school and college theatre, and community theatre.

Appendix A: Liberty Theatre Openings and Closings

National Army Cantonments	Opening	Closing
Camp Custer, Battle Creek, Michigan; troops from the upper Midwest, mainly the state of Michigan	20-Jan-18	8-Jul-19
Camp Devens, Ayer, Massachusetts; troops from New England, mainly Massachusetts.	28-Jan-18	
Camp Dix, Wrightstown, New Jersey; troops from the Middle Atlantic region, mainly New York and New Jersey	18-Feb-18	
Camp Dodge, Des Moines, Iowa; troops from the Midwest, mainly Iowa and Minnesota	7-Feb-18	12-Jul-19
Camp Funston, Junction City, Kansas; troops mainly from Kansas, Missouri, and Nebraska	13-May-18	2-Jun-19
Camp Gordon, Atlanta, Georgia; troops mainly from Georgia, New York and Tennessee	27-Jan-18	
Camp Grant, Rockford, Illinois; troops mainly from Illinois and Wisconsin	8-Apr-18	
Camp Jackson, Columbia, South Carolina; troops mainly from South Carolina and North Carolina	5-Feb-18	31-Jul-19
Camp Lee, Petersburg, Virginia; conscripts from Pennsylvania, Virginia, and West Virginia; troops assigned for artillery and engineering training	24-Feb-18	1-Aug-19
Camp Lee, Petersburg, Virginia, Theatre #2; same as above	13-Jan-19	
Camp Lewis, Tacoma, Washington; troops mainly from California and Washington	1-Feb-18	
Camp Meade, Baltimore, Maryland; troops mainly from Maryland and Pennsylvania	18-Feb-18	

Appendix A

National Army Cantonments	Opening	Closing
Camp Meade, Baltimore, Maryland, Franklin Cantonment; same as above	9-Jan-19	1-Mar-19
Camp Pike, Little Rock, Arkansas; troops mainly from Arkansas, Louisiana, Mississippi	13-Feb-18	
Camp Sherman, Chillicothe, Ohio; troops mainly from Ohio	10-Jan-18	16-Jul-19
Camp Taylor, Louisville, Kentucky; troops mainly from Illinois and Kentucky	29-Jan-18	5-Apr-19
Camp Travis, San Antonio, Texas; troops mainly from Texas	19-Jul-18	
Camp Upton, Yaphank, Long Island, New York; troops mainly from New York	19-Mar-18	
Camp Upton, Yaphank, Long Island, New York, Buffalo Auditorium; African American troops mainly from New York.	21-May-18	19-Apr-19

National Guard Camps: National Guardsmen from Many States Were Mobilized at Any One Camp		
Camp Beauregard, Alexandria, Louisiana	25-Mar-18	15-Mar-19
Camp Bowie, Ft. Worth, Texas	31-Mar-18	21-Jul-19
Camp Cody, Deming, New Mexico	13-Apr-18	15-Dec-18
Camp Doniphan, Lawton, Oklahoma	26-Mar-18	1-May-19
Camp Fremont, Palo Alto, California	28-Jul-18	26-Nov-18
Camp Greene, Charlotte, North Carolina (Tent)	25-Apr-18	11-Dec-18
Camp Hancock, Augusta, Georgia	27-Mar-18	20-Mar-19
Camp Kearny, San Diego, California	1-Aug-18	24-May-19
Camp Logan, Houston, Texas	24-Mar-18	1-Mar-19
Camp MacArthur, Waco, Texas	8-Apr-18	17-Feb-19
Camp McClellan, Anniston, Alabama; Post Exchange Building	Unknown	Unknown
Camp Sevier, Greenville, South Carolina; Theatre #1	23-Apr-18	1-Sep-18
Camp Sevier, Greenville, South Carolina; Theatre #2	23-Apr-18	20-Jun-18
Camp Sevier, Greenville, South Carolina; Theatre #2, remodeled	1-Sep-18	15-Feb-19
Camp Shelby, Hattiesburg, Mississippi; Concession Theatre	Unknown	Unknown
Camp Sheridan, Montgomery, Alabama; YMCA Red Triangle Coliseum	Unknown	Unknown
Camp Wadsworth, Spartanburg, South Carolina	6-May-18	1-Apr-19
Camp Wheeler, Macon, Georgia	26-Feb-18	1-Mar-19

Embarkation Camps

Camp Merritt, Tenafly, New Jersey	25-Mar-18	
Camp Mills, Mineola, New York	2-Jan-19	
Camp Stuart, Newport News, Virginia	15-Dec-18	10-Aug-19

Other Stations

Camp Abraham Eustis, Lee Hall, Virginia; Coast Artillery replacement center	22-Feb-19	1923
Camp Knox, West Point, Kentucky; Field Artillery Training Center	15-Jul-18	25-Nov-18
Camp Humphreys, Accotink-Belvoir, Virginia; Engineer replacements training center	4-Dec-18	
Kelly Field, San Antonio, Texas; Tent #1; Army Aviation training field.	5-Jul-18	10-Aug-18
Kelly Field, San Antonio, Texas; Tent #2	19-Jun-18	3-Jul-18
Kelly Field, San Antonio, Texas; Tent #3	11-Jun-18	14-Jul-18

Appendix B: Liberty Theatre Expenses

Week Ending	Talent[1]	Operating Expenses[2]
From first theatre opening to		
March 3, 1918	$67,933	$8,953
March 10, 1918	$17,508	$3,745
March 17, 1918	$27,946	$3,119
March 24, 1918	$22,150	$4,481
March 31, 1918	$24,711	$4,099
April 6, 1918	$23,416	$4,312
April 13, 1918	$22,448	$4,225
April 20, 1918	$23,464	$4,499
April 27, 1918	$26,855	$6,538
May 4, 1918	$23,434	$6,874
May 11, 1918	$27,165	$6,326
May 18, 1918	$22,471	$7,237
May 25, 1918	$20,836	$5,624
June 1, 1918	$17,873	$6,367
June 8, 1918	$18,195	$8,061
June 15, 1918	$15,863	$4,890
June 22, 1918	$13,726	$4,506
June 29, 1918	$17,901	$6,106
July 6, 1918	$16,119	$6,710
July 13, 1918	$11,320	$5,589
July 20, 1918	$10,327	$6,132
July 27, 1918	$12,344	$4,544
August 3, 1918	$15,481	$6,232
August 10, 1918	$16,866	$6,916
August 17, 1918	$18,029	$6,537
August 24, 1918	$16,911	$6,205
August 31, 1918	$13,467	$5,935
September 7, 1918	$19,831	$6,506
September 14, 1918	$24,158	$6,984
September 21, 1918	$19,978	$5,874
September 28, 1918	$14,145	$5,043

Liberty Theatre Expenses

Week Ending	Talent	Operating Expenses
October 5, 1918	$6,078	$1,765
October 12, 1918	$3,846	$1,543
October 19, 1918	$3,811	$1,373
October 26, 1918	$15,803	$2,697
November 2, 1918	$30,349	$6,093
November 9, 1918	$25,858	$4,456
November 16, 1918	$31,691	$4,877
November 23, 1918	$34,959	$5,141
November 30, 1918	$33,391	$6,631
December 7, 1918	$30,698	$6,652
December 14, 1918	$26,695	$5,640
December 21, 1918	$29,713	$5,244
December 28, 1918	$26,375	$6,009
January 4, 1919	$22,804	$4,853
January 11, 1919	$28,309	$5,032
January 18, 1919	$33,597	$5,920
January 25, 1919	$25,697	$4,782
February 1, 1919	$24,812	$4,833
February 8, 1919	$19,998	$4,494
February 15, 1919	$21,763	$5,818
February 22, 1919	$22,869	$5,221
March 1, 1919	$16,228	$4,187
March 8, 1919	$28,084	$5,895
March 15, 1919	$24,907	$4,454
March 22, 1919	$21,229	$4,844
March 29, 1919	$22,149	$5,462
April 5, 1919	$21,939	$5,328
April 12, 1919	$18,581	$4,843
April 19, 1919	$26,938	$6,643
April 26, 1919	$19,970	$3,828
May 3, 1919	$27,553	$6,192
May 10, 1919	$25,918	$5,298
May 17, 1919	$31,850	$4,814
May 24, 1919	$37,517	$7,786
May 31, 1919	$19,850	$4,267
June 7, 1919	$24,003	$5,681
June 14, 1919	$14,571	$3,548
June 21, 1919	$13,288	$3,779
June 28, 1919	$19,807	$6,452
July 5, 1919	$8,807	$3,553
July 12, 1919	$9,190	$4,506
July 19, 1919	$8,826	$3,332
July 26, 1919	$7,751	$3,998
August 2, 1919	$3,643	$2,782
August 9, 1919	$6,295	$3,633
August 16, 1919	$6,336	$3,670
August 23, 1919	$3,863	$2,670
August 30, 1919	$4,704	$4,040
Totals	$1,615,784	$403,728

Appendix C: Gross Receipts and Estimates of Attendance

The *Report of the Military Entertainment Committee* gives total attendance at tents operated by the Commission from September 15, 1917, to June 15, 1918, as 1,809,500 for a weekly average of 5,500 per tent. Red circuit theatres in operation from March 15, 1918, to December 31, 1918, played to 1,244,000 admissions, for a weekly average of 4,000 admissions at each theatre. Blue circuit theatres averaged over 6,000 admissions per week for a total attendance in 1918 of 4,224,000. Total attendance in all categories for the 15½-month period is reported to have been 7,177,500. This estimate is inaccurate, for it is based on grossly wrong reports of the numbers of theatres in operation in a given period. For instance, attendance reported at Red circuit theatres for the period March 15, 1918, to June 15, 1918, is based on the operation of five theatres when 12 Red circuit theatres were open, according to the "Synopsis of Liberty Theatre Receipts" and other documents.[3] During the period January 15, 1918, to March 1, 1918, *The Report of the Military Entertainment Committee* lists only six Blue circuit theatres in operation., In fact, as many as 12 Class A theatres were open. Numbers of theatres and tents operating are consistently too low, and the estimate of total attendance in the report is too low. Accordingly, a new estimate, based on more complete and accurate figures, is offered here.

The new attendance estimate is based on the gross receipts for the theatres as reported in "Synopsis of Liberty Theatre Receipts," a record kept by commission accountants of the financial status of its theatres. The synopsis was brought up to date each week as reports flowed into Washington from the camps, and figures in the synopsis are substantiated by the few reports preserved in the commission's files. The figures for gross receipts have been converted to attendance figures by dividing them by an estimated average single admission price. The average admission price in eight instances where both attendance and gross receipts are recorded is 30 cents.[4] The average admission price used for the estimate of total attendance is 28 cents. The estimated average admission is somewhat lower than the known average because the known average is not fairly representative. It is based primarily on figures from larger theatres where admissions were higher, and it is based on reports from periods when the number of higher-priced entertainments was greatest.[5] Furthermore, the estimated average admission has been adjusted in each report period to reflect an estimate of the deviation of the average for each month from the average for all months. Estimated average admission for the summer months is lower than the grand average because lower-priced attractions, such as movies, were more often featured. The estimated average admission for winter months is somewhat higher than the grand average because of the greater frequency of use of higher-priced attractions. The estimated average admission also reflects the actual average admission for the period when both attendance and gross receipts for all theatres is known.[6]

The ratio of estimated attendance to the capacity of theatres in operation for the period is reported as "% of Capacity." Seating capacities for each theatre are given in *The Report of the Military Entertainment Committee*, p. 55. Terminal dates of operation of each theatre are recorded in Appendix A, while "Synopsis of Liberty Theatre Receipts" indicates those periods when each theatre was not operating, such as during a period of reconstruction, or during the influenza epidemic in October 1918. Given the seating capacity of each theatre and the number of days it operated, one can calculate the total capacity of any theatre for any period of its operation.

Period	Gross Receipts	Estimated Average Admission	Estimate of Attendance (in thousands)	Capacity of Theatres (in thousands)	% of Capacity
1/10/18 to 3/3/18	$98,571	$0.30	325	785	41%
3/4/18 to 3/31/18	$122,587	$0.30	409	796	51%
4/1/18 to 4/12/18	$142,348	$0.29	491	952	52%
4/13/18 to 5/31/18	$147,256	$0.29	566	1550	37%
6/1/18 to 6/29/18	$147,634	$0.26	568	1450	39%
6/30/18 to 7/27/18	$180,842	$0.25	435	1412	31%
7/28/18 to 8/31/18	$159,700	$0.25	639	1863	34%
9/1/18 to 9/28/18	$141,675	$0.27	525	1590	33%
9/29/18 to 10/26/18	$47,275	$0.24	197	684	29%
10/27/18 to 11/30/18	$242,021	$0.28	864	1647	52%
12/1/18 to 12/28/18	$182,496	$0.28	652	1652	39%
12/29/18 to 1/25/19	$167,585	$0.29	578	1787	32%
1/26/19 to 3/1/19	$150,719	$0.30	502	2189	23%

Appendix C

Period	Gross Receipts	Estimated Average Admission	Estimate of Attendance (in thousands)	Capacity of Theatres (in thousands)	% of Capacity
3/2/19 to 3/29/19	$130,257	$0.31	420	1605	26%
3/30/19 to 4/26/19	$113,730	$0.32	355	1365	26%
4/27/19 to 5/31/19	$146,123	$0.31	476	1686	28%
6/1/19 to 6/28/19	$71,684	$0.30	239	1152	21%
6/29/19 to 7/26/19	$46,433	$0.28	166	1024	16%
7/27/19 to 8/30/19	$36,860	$0.28	132	977	14%
Totals	$2,475,796	$0.28	8,539	26,166	33%

Appendix D: Average Weekly Receipts of Liberty Theatres

Based on "Synopsis of Liberty Theatre Receipts," NA, RG 165, Entry 399, Box 192, "Liberty Theatres." Weekly receipts of theaters that increased seating capacity are the average of the combined total receipts.

Camp, Location	Seating Capacity	Weeks Reporting	Weekly Receipts
Camp Beauregard, Alexandria, Louisiana	1,050 1,300	27 14	$665
Camp Bowie, Ft. Worth, Texas	1,050 1,300	23 28	$333
Camp Cody, Deming, New Mexico	1,050 1,300	21	$754
Camp Custer, Battle Creek, Michigan	2,300	75	$1,266
Camp Devens, Ayer, Massachusetts	2,380	80	$1,895
Camp Dix, Wrightstown, New Jersey	2,308	77	$1761
Camp Dodge, Des Moines, Iowa	2,500	74	$1,005
Camp Doniphan, Ft. Sill, Oklahoma	1,050 1,300	24 20	$700
Camp Eustis, Lee Hall, Virginia	1,600	29	$989
Camp Fremont, Palo Alto, California	1,050	17	$1,000
Camp Funston, Ft. Riley, Kansas	3,000	56	$615

Appendix D

Camp, Location	Seating Capacity	Weeks Reporting	Weekly Receipts
Camp Gordon, Atlanta Georgia	2,371	83	$1,375
Camp Grant, Rockford, Illinois	2,493	68	$1,325
Camp Greene, Charlotte, North Carolina	(tent) 1,600	29	$370
Camp Hancock, Augusta, Georgia	1,050 1,300	23 16	$751
Camp Humphreys, Belvoir, Virginia	2,400	39	$924
Camp Jackson, Columbia, South Carolina	2,570	75	$1,700
Camp Kearny, San Diego, California	3,000	27	$1,269
Kelly Field, San Antonio, Texas	(tent) 1,600	6	$254
West Point Artillery Range West Point, Kentucky	(tent) 1,600	2	$204
Camp Las Casas, San Juan, Puerto Rico	3,000	18	$350
Camp Lee, Petersburg, Virginia	2,233	73	$2,144
Camp Lee #2, "Victory" Petersburg, Virginia	1,600	17	$215
Camp Lewis, American Lake, Washington	1,844	78	$1,476
Camp Logan, Houston, Texas	1,050 1,300	23 17	$452
Camp MacArthur Waco, Texas	1,050 1,300	29 11	$537
Camp McClellan, Anniston, Alabama	1,050 1,200	18 22	$558
Camp Meade, Annapolis Junction, Maryland	2,600	72	$2,175
Camp Meade, #2 Franklin Cantonment	1,300	5	$577
Camp Merritt, Tenafly, New Jersey	2,448	71	$2,675
Camp Mills, Mineola, New York	1,600	35	$2,442
Camp Pike, Little Rock, Arkansas	2,200	79	$958
Camp Sevier, Greenville, South Carolina	1,673	16	$757

Average Weekly Receipts of Liberty Theatres

Camp, Location	Seating Capacity	Weeks Reporting	Weekly Receipts
Camp Sherman, Chillicothe, Ohio	2,228	73	$1,393
Camp Stuart, Newport News, Virginia	2,000	34	$1,680
Camp Taylor, Louisville, Kentucky	2,386	47	$871
Camp Travis, San Antonio, Texas	1,942	51	$750
Camp Upton, Yaphank, Long Island	2,380	72	$2,170
Camp Upton, Buffalo Auditorium	2,500	24	$947
Camp Wadsworth, Spartanburg, South Carolina	1,050	46	$631
Camp Wheeler, Macon, Georgia	1,050	33	$844
Average Weekly Receipts of all Theatres Reporting			$1,055

Notes

Introduction

1. Nancy K. Bristow, *Making Men Moral: Social Engineering During the Great War* (New York: New York University Press, 1996).
2. Ronald Schaeffer, *America in the Great War: The Rise of the War Welfare State* (New York: Oxford University Press, 1991).

Chapter 1

1. "Woodrow Wilson's Special Statement," in Edward Frank Allen, *Keeping our Fighters Fit for War and After* (New York: Century, 1918): n.p. See also Jennifer D. Keene, *Doughboys, the Great War, and the Remaking of America* (Baltimore: Johns Hopkins University Press, 2001): 1–34. Keene argues that the "true importance of the Great War in American history ... [is that] the Great War generation shaped the contours of the modern American military and was responsible for the most sweeping piece of social welfare legislation in American history, the GI Bill." Weldon B. Durham outlines efforts to rationalize the camp environment in "Big Brother' and the 'Seven Sisters': Camp Life Reforms in World War I," *Military Affairs* 42 (April 1978): 57–60.
2. See Robert B. Casari, Patricia F. Medert, Luvada D. Kuhn and William H. Nolan, *Chillicothe, Ohio, 1796–1996: Ohio's First Capital* (Chillicothe: Chillicothe Bicentennial Commission, Inc., and the Ross County Historical Society, 1996), and Richard G. Peck, *The Rise and Fall of Camp Sherman* (Chillicothe, OH: Peck Photography and Craftsman Printing, 1972).
3. William Henry Alexander, *A Climatological History of Ohio* (Columbus: The Engineering Experiment Station of the Ohio State University, 1923).
4. Fred D. Baldwin, "The American Enlisted Man in World War I" PhD diss., Princeton University, 1964; Jeffrey Kostic, "War Risk Insurance," q.v., in *The United States in the First World War: An Encyclopedia* (New York: Garland, 1995), p. 776; and M. Lindsay, "Purpose and Scope of War Risk Insurance," *American Academy of Political and Social Sciences. Annals* 79 (September 1918), 52–68, provide details about soldiers' pay.
5. *New York Dramatic Mirror* 76 (May 9, 1916), 16; (May 16, 1916), 8; and (October 21, 1916), 9.
6. George Doran, *The Chronicles of Barabbas* (New York: Rinehart, 1952), p. 198.
7. "Synopses of Liberty Theatre Receipts," in National Archives (hereafter NA), Record Group (hereafter RG) 165, Entry 399, Box 192, "Liberty Theatres."
8. Seating capacities for each theatre are given in the *Report of the Military Entertainment Committee* (Washington, DC: Government Printing Office, 1919), p. 55. Terminal dates of operation of each theatre are recorded in Appendix A, while "Synopsis of Liberty Theatre Receipts" indicates those periods when each theatre was not operating, such as during a period of reconstruction, or during the influenza epidemic in October 1918. Given the seating capacity of each theatre and the number of days it operated, one can calculate the total capacity of any theatre for any period of its operation.
9. "Welfare, Reform, and World War I," *American Quarterly* 19 (Fall 1967): 528. See also Robert H. Zieger, *America's Great War: World War I and the American Experience* (Lanham: Rowman & Littlefield, 2000): 89–91.

10. "The Liberty Theatres," Address by The Honorable Newton D. Baker, Secretary of War, At the Opening of the New Liberty Theatre, Camp Humphreys, Virginia, December 5, 1918. Washington, DC.: War Department Commission on Training Camp Activities, 1918. See also C. H. Cramer, *Newton D. Baker: A Biography* (Cleveland and New York: World, 1961): 104.

11. Raymond B. Fosdick, letter to Weldon Durham, June 13, 1970.

12. *The End of American Innocence: A Study of the First Years of Our Time, 1912–1917* (New York: Knopf, 1959).

13. Kenneth Burke, "Bureaucratization of the Imaginative." in "Dictionary of Pivotal Terms," in *Attitudes Toward History*, rev. 2 ed. (Boston: Beacon Press, 1961): 225–229.

14. Robert Weibe, *The Search for Order: 1877–1920*. (New York: Hill and Wang, 1967), pp. 223 and 288–300.

15. Warren E. Sussman, *Culture as History: The Transformation of American Society in the Twentieth Century* (New York: Pantheon Books, 1984), pp. 86–95.

16. Michael McGerr, *A Fierce Discontent: The Rise and Fall of the Progressive Movement in America, 1870–1920* (New York: The Free Press, 2003), p. xiv and p. 250.

17. Pierre Bourdieu, *The Field of Cultural Production*, edited and introduced by Randal Johnson (New York: Columbia University Press, 1993): 29–141.

18. Thomas Postlewait, "The Hieroglyphic Stage: American Theatre and Society, Post–Civil War to 1945," in *The Cambridge History of American Theatre*, vol. 2: 1870–1945, ed. Don B. Wilmeth and Christopher Bigsby (Cambridge: Cambridge University Press, 1999): 107–195.

19. Bristow, *Making Men Moral*, p. 19. See also Ronald Schaeffer, *America in the Great War: The Rise of the War Welfare State* (New York: Oxford University Press, 1991): 98–107. Schaeffer's assessment of the balance of suppression and the recreation alternative in the CTCA's programs is like Bristow's. Schaeffer makes the point that such success as the CTCA may have had in suppressing alcohol and prostitution derived from the fact that the CTCA's programs meshed with powerful purity and temperance movements in the civilian world. The same could have been said about the link between the CTCA's recreation programs and the civilian recreation and parks movement but wasn't.

20. Baker letter to Fosdick, cited in Raymond B. Fosdick, *Chronicle of a Generation: An Autobiography* (New York, Harper, 1958): 143.

21. Edward Frank Allen, *Keeping our Fighters Fit for War and After* (New York: Century, 1918): 11.

22. Richard Kraus, *Recreation and Leisure in Modern Society* (New York: HarperCollins, 1990), p. 155.

23. Reynold E. Carlson, Theodore R. Deppe, and Janet R. MacLean, *Recreation in American Life*, 2 ed. (Belmont, CA: Wadsworth, 1972), pp. 37–41.

Chapter 2

1. See Bell Irwin Riley, *The Life of Johnny Reb: The Common Soldier in the Confederacy* (Garden City, NY: Doubleday, 1943) and *The Life of Billy Yank: The Common Soldier of the Union* (Garden City, NY: Doubleday, 1952); John Joseph Lenney, *Rankers, The Odyssey of The Enlisted Regular Soldier: America and Britain* (New York: Greenberg, 1950); Jack Coggins, *The Fighting Man: An Illustrated History of the World's Greatest Fighting Forces through the Ages* (Garden City, NY: Doubleday and Co., Inc., 1966); Victor Hicken, *The American Fighting Man* (New York: Macmillan, 1969); Jack D. Foner, *United States Soldier between Two Wars: Army Life and Reforms, 1865–1898* (New York: Humanities Press, 1970); and Edward M. Coffman, *The Old Army: A Portrait of the American Army in Peacetime, 1784–1898* (New York: Oxford University Press, 1986).

2. Jared Brown, *The Theatre in America during the Revolution* (Cambridge: Cambridge University Press, 1995), 22–65, 85–127; Diane B. Malone, "A Survey of Early Military Theatre in America," *Theatre Survey* 16 (1975): 56–64.

3. Linney, p. 41.

4. "Questions of Army Morals," *Nation* 81 (October 26, 1905) : 334.

Chapter 3

1. Haldeen Brady, *Pershing's Mission in Mexico* (El Paso: Texas Western Press, 1966): 21–22, 45, 61.

2. Weldon B. Durham, "Fosdick, Raymond Blaine," q.v., *The United States in the First World War: An Encyclopedia*, ed. Anne Cipriano Venzon (New York: Garland, 1995): 234–35.

3. Typescript copy of letter from Fosdick to Baker, August 10, 1916. Raymond B. Fosdick Papers, Princeton University Library. Dr. M. J. Exner, a physician who visited the camps on the Mexican border, confirmed Fosdick's findings in "Prostitution and its Relation to the Army on the Mexican Border," *Social Hygiene* 3 (April 1917): 206–14.

4. U. S. Congress, House Committee on Military Affairs, *Hearing on Training Camp Activities: Statement of Mr. Raymond B. Fosdick, March 14, 1918*, 65 Congress, 2 Session, p. 8.

5. Raymond B. Fosdick, *Chronicle of a Generation: An Autobiography* (New York: Harper, 1958): 34–135.

6. Russell F. Weigley, *History of the United States Army*. Enlarged ed. (New York: Macmillan, 1984): 340. See also the transcript of Wilson's remarks to a delegation from the American Union Against Militarism (AUAM) on May 8, 1916, in *The Eagle and the Dove: The American Peace Movement and United States Foreign Policy, 1900–1922*. 2 ed., John Whiteclay Chambers II (Syracuse, NY: Syracuse University Press, 1991): 72.

7. Daniel R. Beaver, *Newton D. Baker and the American War Effort, 1917–1919* (Lincoln: University of Nebraska Press, 1966): 1–4.

8. Baker's letter to Wilson, April 2, 1917, is cited in Beaver, p. 220; Baker's regard for Fosdick and the CTCA is discussed on pp. 218–219.

9. Thomas Fleming, *The Illusion of Victory: America in World War I* (New York: Basic Books, 2003): 43–84.

10. "An Invisible Armor," Speech of October 23, 1917, reprinted in *Playground* 11 (January 1918): 479.

11. Mark Thomas Connelly, *The Response to Prostitution in the Progressive Era* (Chapel Hill: University of North Carolina Press, 1980): 6.

12. John F. McClymer, *War and Welfare: Social Engineering in America, 1890–1925* (Westport, CT: Greenwood Press, 1980): 169.

13. John C. Burnham, "The Progressive Era Revolution in American Attitudes toward Sex." *The Journal of American History* 59 (March 1973): 890–97; Connelly, *The Response to Prostitution*, pp. 70–79; Arthur S. Link and Richard L. McCormick, *Progressivism* (Arlington Heights, IL: Harlan Davidson, 1983), 102.

14. Don S. Kirschner, "The Perils of Pleasure: Commercial Recreation, Social Disorder and Moral Reform in the Progressive Era." *American Studies* 21 no. 2 (1980): 28–30.

15. *Popular Amusements*, vol. 8 of *Studies in American Social Conditions* (New York: Association Press, 1915), p. 15.

16. *The Spirit of Youth and the City Streets* (New York: Macmillan, 1909), p. 7.

17. *The Playground* (March 1910): 24.

Chapter 4

1. Beaver, 4–8, 51.

2. John Dickinson, *The Building of an Army* (New York: Century, 1922): 207.

3. Frederick Palmer, *Newton D. Baker,* *America at War,* Vol. I (New York: Dodd, Mead and Co., 1931) : 309–310.

4. *Ibid*, p. 309–310.

5. NA, RG 165, Entry 393, #50047.

6. "Woodrow Wilson's Special Statement," in Edward Frank Allen, *Keeping our Fighters Fit for War and After* (New York: Century, 1918): n.p.

7. McClymer, p. 159.

8. Michael M. Davis, Jr., *The Exploitation of Pleasure: A Study of Commercial Recreations in New York City* (New York: Department of Child Hygiene of the Russell Sage Foundation, 1911).

9. George D. Butler, *Pioneers in Public Recreation* (Minneapolis: Burgess, 1965): 65–74; John M. Glenn, Lillian Brandt, and F. Emerson Andrews, *The Russell Sage Foundation, 1907–1946*. 2 vols. (New York: Russell Sage Foundation, 1947): Vol. I, pp. 249–51.

10. Richard Kraus, *Recreation and Leisure in Modern Society*. 4 ed. (New York: HarperCollins, 1990): 163–164.

11. Arthur P. Young, "War Camp Community Service," q.v., *The United States in the First World War: An Encyclopedia*. ed. Anne Cipriano Venzon (New York: Garland, 1995): 773–74.

12. *The War and Navy Departments Commissions on Training Camp Activities* (Washington, DC: Government Printing Office, 1918), pp. 8–10; *Report of the Secretary of War* in Vol. 1, *War Department Annual Reports, 1918* (Washington, DC: Government Printing Office, 1919), p. 26.

13. Beaver, p. 218; Fred D. Baldwin, "The American Enlisted Man in World War I" (PhD diss., Princeton, 1964): 239.

14. D. Colt Denfeld, "World War I Mobilization Camps," *The Journal of America's Military Past* 29 (Fall-Winter, 2002): 28–54.

15. Baker, "An Invisible Armor," in *Frontiers of Freedom* (New York: Doran, 1918): 467–77; Palmer, I, 307; Weigley, pp. 342–43.

16. Beaver, p. 220.

17. U. S. War Department, *Annual Reports*, 1918, Vol. 1, *Report of the Surgeon General* (Washington, DC: U.S. Government Printing Office, 1919): 431; Baldwin, pp. 87–90, and 125–29; Sue E. Berryman, *Who Serves? The Persistent Myth of the Underclass Army* (Boulder, CO: Westview Press, 1988): 34–36; Robert H. Zieger, *America's Great War: World War I and the American Experience* (Lanham: Rowman & Littlefield, 2000): 86–87. Literacy figures varied widely, in part because several definitions of literacy were in play. The figures published during the war and shortly after probably exaggerated the general level of illiteracy, but, even so, the conclusion still holds that the con-

scripted army had neither the communication skills nor the social sophistication military and civilian planners expected it to have. Moreover, the IQ test administered to soldiers has since been challenged because of apparent ethnic and class biases it projected.

18. Young Men's Christian Association, International Committee, *Service with Fighting Men*, Vol. I (New York: Association Press, 1922): 276–78; 338–42; YMCA, National War Work Council, *Summary of World War Work of the American YMCA* (New York: Association Press, 1920): 205. YMCA entertainment services to the American Expeditionary Force are recounted in pp. 619–636. See also James W. Evans and Gardner I. Harding, *Entertaining the American Army: The American Stage and Lyceum in the World War* (New York: Association Press, 1921): 3–4. Evans and Harding account only for "Y" activities, and their undocumented claims seem highly exaggerated — 20,000 volunteers involved in presenting stage shows, concerts, and lectures in Europe and another 15,000 doing the same in the camps in the US — 87 million admissions in Europe and more than 40 million at home.

19. U. S. War Department, *Commission on Training Camp Activities* (Washington, DC: U.S. Government Printing Office, 1918) : 30–31. Richard F. Knapp, "The Playground and Recreation Association of America in World War I," *Parks and Recreation* 7 (January 1972): 27–31, 110–112.

20. Maurice P. Egan and John B. Kennedy, *Knights of Columbus in Peace and War*, Vol. II (New Haven, CT: Knights of Columbus, 1920): 245–46; 350–63; and *Commission on Training Camp Activities* (1918) : 26–27.

21. U. S. War Department, *Annual Reports, 1917*, Vol. I, *Report of the Secretary of War* (Washington, DC U.S. Government Printing Office, 1918): 36.

22. U. S. War Department, *Report of the Chairman on Training Camp Activities* (Washington, DC: U.S. Government Printing Office, 1918): 11–17. Federal funding, none of it channeled through the CTCA, enabled 23 detention houses to be started, while it provided assistance to nine already in existence. See Mary Macey Dietzler, *Detention Houses and Reformatories as Protective Social Agencies in the Campaign of the United States Government Against Venereal Diseases* (Washington, DC: Government Printing Office, 1922), p. 27. See also Bristow, *Making Men Moral*, pp. 91–136. Bristow dissects the rhetoric of CTCA reformers to reveal overt and covert allegiance to traditional images of womanhood. The repressive impulse she uncovers in Progressivism offers a stark contrast to its more openly avowed support of the liberated "new woman."

23. *Ibid.*, p. 19.

24. NA, RG 165, Entry 393, #4524, Lee Hanmer to Newton D. Baker, August 24, 1917; #14015, Jasper J. Mayer to Commanding General, Camp Pike, Arkansas, December 31, 1917; #16967, Mayer to J F. Lea, Camp Sherman, Ohio, January 29, 1918.

25. *Ibid.*, letter of introduction carried by each theatre manager, e. g., #15374, R. B. Fosdick to Commanding General, Camp Sherman, Ohio, introducing Frank J. Lea, January 7, 1918; #37309, endorsement of General George W. Goethels, Acting Quartermaster General, on R. B. Fosdick letter of May 1, 1918 to Secretary of War forwarding estimates of CTCA requirements for Fiscal Year 1919, May 2, 1918; #18927, Commanding General, Camp Custer, Michigan, to Mayer, January 23, 1918.

26. U. S. War Department, *Report of the Military Entertainment Committee* (Washington, DC U.S. Government Printing Office, 1919), p. 13. Bristow, *Making Men Moral*, lumps together the CTCA's theatres with the buildings and programs of the affiliated organizations, especially the YMCA. However, the purpose and the actual operations of the Liberty Theatres differed markedly from the aim and function of YMCA entertainments. Moreover, the programs of the Liberty Theatres were not "carefully controlled and uplifting" (photo caption, following p. 112).

27. *Ibid.*

28. *Ibid.*, p. 9.

29. NA, RG 165, Entry 393, #17250a, April 2, 1919, a report of activity of the Auxiliary Fund, miscellaneous receipts, and receipts from athletics and the sale of songbooks. Appendix C, "Gross Receipts and Estimates of Attendance," provides an analysis of Liberty Theatre receipts. NA, RG 165, Entry 399, Box 215, "Miscellaneous Civilian Correspondence CTCA," Smileage Report from Accounting Office, the CTCA, for week ending October 6, 1919. Congressional appropriations for CTCA were $500,000 in the Regular Army Act of June 15, 1917, under heading "Military Post Exchanges"; $250,000 in the Urgent Deficiency Act of October 6, 1917; $550,000 in the Urgent Deficiency Act of March 28, 1918; $1,623,000 for Fiscal 1919; $470,000 for Fiscal 1920, by the end of which the CTCA had been absorbed into the War Department General Staff.

30. *Report of the Secretary of War*, Vol. I, Part 1, of *War Department Annual Reports, 1919* (Washington, DC: U.S. Government Printing Office, 1919), p. 33.

31. "The Moral Devastation of War," *Dial* 66 (April 5, 1919): 333–336.

32. *The Building of an Army*, pp. 239–44.

33. "Woodrow Wilson's Special Statement,"

in Edward Frank Allen, *Keeping our Fighters Fit for War and After* (New York: Century, 1918): n.p.

Chapter 5

1. Richard Moody, "The Drama League," q. v., *The Cambridge Guide to American Theatre*, ed. Don B. Wilmeth and Tice L. Miller (Cambridge: Cambridge University Press, 1993) : 51–52; Morris R. Bogard, "Drama League of America," *Dramatics Magazine* 37 (November 1965): 45–48.
2. *Report of the Military Entertainment Committee*, p. 5
3. NA, RG 165, Entry 393, #232, Rachel Crothers to Newton D. Baker, May 8, 1917.
4. *Ibid.*, #251, "Minutes of the Meeting of the CTCA, Saturday, May 12, 1917."
5. *Report of the Military Entertainment Committee*, p. 6.
6. *Ibid.*
7. NA, RG 165, Entry 393, #312 and #7720, Fosdick to Sheppard, May 16, 1917.
8. *Ibid.*, #374, "Minutes of the Meeting of the CTCA, May 19, 1917."
9. The specifics of this resistance are not clear. Fosdick refers to congressional resistance to camp recreational activities and to the resistance of the Army Chief of Staff to placing athletic directors and song leaders in the camps. Fosdick, *Chronicle of a Generation*, pp. 152, 163–64.
10. NA, RG 165, Entry 393, #1206, CTCA announcement of June 8, 1917, circulated through War Department offices.
11. *Ibid.*, #1783.
12. *Ibid.*, #2008, Fosdick to W. A. Starrett of the Council of National Defense, June 28, 1917; #1953, Fosdick to Colonel I. W. Littell of the War Department Cantonment Division, June 28, 1917. See Frederic L. Paxson, *American Democracy and the World War*, Vol. II, *America at War, 1917–1918* (Boston: Houghton Mifflin, 1939): 20, 106–107.

Chapter 6

1. Mary Jane Phillips-Matz, *The Many Lives of Otto Kahn* (New York: Macmillan, 1963).
2. Monroe Lippman, "The History of the Theatrical Syndicate: Its Effect on the Theatre in America," PhD diss., University of Michigan, 1937, provides information about Klaw. See also Lippman's brief biography of Klaw in *Dictionary of American Biography*, XI, Supplements One and Two (New York: Charles Scribner's Sons, 1944, 1958), pp. 363–364; and Charles W. Stein, "Klaw, Marc Alonzo," q.v., *American National Biography* 12 (New York: Oxford University Press, 1999): 785–86.

3. Monroe Lippman, "The First Organized Revolt Against the Theatrical Syndicate," *Quarterly Journal of Speech* 41 (December 1955), 343–351; and "Battle for Bookings: Independents Challenge the Trust," *Tulane Drama Review* 2 (February 1958), 38–45.
4. Peter Davis, "The Syndicate/Shubert War," in *Inventing Times Square: Commerce and Culture at the Crossroads of the World*, ed. William R. Taylor (New York: Russell Sage, 1991): 147–57.
5. *Ibid.* See also Monroe Lippman, "Death of the Salesmen's Monopoly," *Theatre Survey* 1 (1960): 65–81. Foster Hirsch details the battles between the Shuberts and the syndicate in *The Boys from Syracuse: The Shuberts' Theatrical Empire* (Carbondale: Southern Illinois University Press, 1998): 26–32, 44–46, 53–56, 65–67, and 75–58. In 1916, the syndicate passed out of existence as a legal entity. Charles Frohman was dead, and Hayman, Nixon, and Zimmerman had retired, leaving the field to Klaw and Erlanger.
6. Harvey Denkin, "William A. Brady," *The Passing Show* (Newsletter of the Shubert Archive) 5 (Winter 1981): 2–3.
7. Alfred L. Bernheim analyzes business conditions in the theatre in this period in *The Business of the Theatre* (New York: Actors' Equity Association, 1932): 31–109. See also Jack Poggi, *Theatre In America: The Impact of Economic Forces, 1870–1967* (Ithaca, NY: Cornell University Press, 1968): 28–45; "Remedy for Injustice in Booking Conditions," *New York Dramatic Mirror*, February 17, 1917: p. 3; and "Lack of System Causes Tangle in Booking Plays," (Series), *New York Dramatic Mirror*, February 24, 1917, p. 3.
8. *The Art Theatre*, rev. and enlarged ed., first published in 1917 (New York: B. Blom, 1972): 20–31.
9. Arthur Hornblow, *A History of the Theatre in America*, Vol. II. (New York: Lippincott, 1919, reissued by Blom, 1965).
10. John Collier, "The Theatre of Tomorrow," *The Survey* 35 (January 1, 1916), 381–85; and "For a New Drama," *The Survey* 36 (May 6, 1916), 137–41.
11. George M. Mangold, *The Challenge of Saint Louis* (New York: Missionary Education Movement of the United States and Canada, 1917) was one such survey. Its section on commercial recreation sounds a typical note in beginning: "The commercial recreations of this and every other city present a serious social problem" (p. 227). Michael M. Davis, Jr., *The Exploitation of Pleasure: A Study of Commercial Recreations in New York City* (New York: Department of Child Hygiene of the Russell Sage Foundation, 1911) was another. See also Twentieth Century Club, Boston. Drama

Committee, *The Amusement Situation in the City of Boston ... 1909–10*. Boston, n.p., 1910.

12. *New York Times*, June 6, 1914, p. 9; June 7, 1914, p. 5; June 9, 1914, p. 11; August 16, 1915–November 17, 1915.

13. "The War and Broadway," *Theatre Magazine* 17 (April 1918): pp. 203–204.

14. NA, RG 165, Entry 393, #393, Perry to Hanmer, May 21, 1917.

15. *Ibid.*, #394, Perry to Fosdick, May 21, 1917.

16. *Ibid.*, #395, Fosdick to Marc Klaw, May 22, 1917.

17. *Ibid.*, #621, Minutes of the meeting the CTCA, May 26, 1917.

18. *Ibid.*, Crothers to Fosdick, #1783, June 7, 1917.

19. *Ibid.*, #1381, Minutes of the meeting the CTCA, June 9, 1917.

20. *Ibid.*, #2362, Crothers to Fosdick, July 3, 1917.

21. *Ibid.*, #812.

22. *Ibid.*, #770, Hanmer to Fosdick, June 23, 1917.

23. *Ibid.*, #813, Klaw to Fosdick, June 23, 1917.

24. *Ibid.*, #1230 and #29272, Minutes of the Meeting of CTCA, June 28, 1917.

25. See "Edward Lippincott Tilton," *The New International Yearbook*, 1933, p. 583, and *Architectural Forum* 58 (February 1933), 12.

26. NA, RG 165, Entry #393, #3894, Hanmer to Fosdick, August 8, 1917. At $32,500 each construction and equipment of 16 theatres would cost an estimated $520,000.

27. *Ibid.*, #4818, Fosdick to Hanmer, August 15, 1917.

28. *Ibid.*, #4819, Fosdick to Emergency Construction Committee, August 16, 1917.

29. *Ibid.*, #2543, Klaw to Fosdick, August 7, 1917.

30. *Ibid.*, #4345, Fosdick to Baker, Baker to Fosdick, August 16, 1917, and Klaw to Baker, August 23, 1917.

Chapter 7

1. NA, RG 165, Entry 393, #11581.

2. NA, RG 165, Entry 399, "Alphabetical File of Reports," Box 227, "Redpath Lyceum," Hanmer to Harrison, September 8, 1917.

3. *Ibid.*, Entry 393, #4939, Hanmer to Fosdick, September 27, 1917; #11096, C. A. Pepper, Redpath Lyceum Bureau, to Hanmer, October 26, 1917.

4. *Ibid.*, #10877, "Report of Activities of Redpath Chautauqua, October 31, 1917, to November 8, 1917," submitted by Harold Braddock, n.d.

5. *Ibid.*, #29272.

6. *Ibid.*, #17645, Harrison to Hanmer, January 21, 1918; YMCA, International Committee, *Service with Fighting Men*, Vol. I (New York: Association Press, 1922) : 337.

7. NA, RG 165, Entry 399, Box 227, "Redpath Lyceum," Hanmer to McBride, April 12, 1918.

8. *Ibid.*, #30441, February 20, 1918. The CTCA carried the debt incurred by the tents as a debt against the profits of the Liberty Theatres until it was repaid from those profits in January 1919.

9. *Ibid.*, Entry 393, #16712, Harrison to Hanmer, January 19, 1918; Fosdick to Harrison, January 19, 1918.

10. *Ibid.*, #4524, Hanmer to Baker, August 24, 1917; #3838, Minutes of the meeting of the CTCA, August 24, 1917.

11. *Ibid.*, #6068, Mayer to Hanmer, September 8, 1917; #6069; RG 92, Records of the Construction Division, War Department, Decimal File, 1917–1919, Box 2923, File 652 General (j), "Theatres General," memo to Major Wheaton from E. V. Dunstan, advisory architect, August 29, 1917.

12. The CTCA paid equipment costs from allotted funds from the item Military Post Exchanges in later appropriations.

13. RG 165, Entry 393, #7504, Officer in Charge Cantonment Construction to all Camp Constructing Quartermasters, October 13, 1917. In mid–October the CTCA delayed the construction of theatres at Camp Travis, San Antonio, Texas, and Camp Funston, Fort Riley, Kansas, because concession theatres were operating in those camps, thus leaving 14 theatres to be constructed. On November 1, the CTCA lifted the restriction on government theatres at Camp Travis and Camp Funston and on November 13 it authorized a theatre at Camp Merritt, bringing to 17 the number of theatres planned or under construction. Later, the theatre at Camp Travis was again cancelled, reducing the number to 16. They were located in Camp Devens, Camp Custer, Camp Dix, Camp Dodge, Camp Funston, Camp Gordon, Camp Grant, Camp Jackson, Camp Lee, Camp Lewis, Camp Meade, Camp Merritt, Camp Pike, Camp Sherman, Camp Taylor, and Camp Upton. See Appendix A, Liberty Theatre Openings and Closings.

14. *Ibid.*, #7592, Mayer to Tilton, October 26, 1917.

15. *Ibid.*, #7453, Baker to Littell, October 23, 1917; #7592, Mayer to Tilton, October 26, 1917.

16. *Ibid.*, #6788, Tilton to Col. Issac W. Littell, Chief of Cantonment Division, October 15, 1917, copy to CTCA.

17. *Ibid*, #13451, Van Wei to Mayer, November 30, 1917.

18. *Ibid.*, #13014; #13011, and #13578, Fosdick to Constructing Quartermaster, Camp Gordon, Georgia, December 4, 1917, for example.

19. *Ibid.*, #13060, Tilton to Mayer, December 7, 1917; #14267, Clark to Tilton, November 22, 1917, and #15510, War Department to Quartermaster General, December 21, 1917. Law offered 30 sets of noncounterweighted scenery shifting lines and a counterweighted system for raising the act curtain. Clark included as well two tormentor grooves (masking pieces for the side of the stage), rigging for three border lights hanging over the stage, two sets of lines for curtains, and a system for shifting the picture screen, all with steel cable and counterweights.

20. *Report of the Military Entertainment Committee of the War Department*, p. 50.

21. *New York Times*, November 4, 1917, III, 11. A. S. Meloy, *Theatres and Picture Houses* (New York: Architects' Supply and Publishing, 1916) : 4.

22. Meloy, a prominent theatre architect of the period, established a safe minimum for theatre auditorium floors at 80 pounds per square foot. The lowest legally established standard for auditorium floors was 75 pounds per square foot in Seattle, Washington; the highest was 125 pounds per square foot in Boston, New Orleans, Minneapolis, and San Francisco. *Theatres and Picture Houses*, 1916.

23. NA, RG 165, Entry 393, #11752, Maj. R. F. Proctor to Col. Isaac Littell, November 8, 1917, and RG 92, Box 9841, Officer in Charge, Construction Division to Constructing Quartermaster, Camp Jackson, South Carolina, November 14, 1917.

24. NA, RG 92, Box 8982, March 14, 1918. *Ibid.*, RG 165, Entry 393, #13595, E. L. Tilton to Jasper J. Mayer, March 15, 1918. In the absence of detailed plans and specifications for the Class A theatre, Tilton's assertion cannot be substantiated or denied.

25. *Ibid.*, Minnix to Construction Division, March 17, 1918.

26. *Ibid.*, Entry 399, Box 214, "Miscellaneous Civilian Correspondence, CTCA," F. R. Megan to CTCA, October 15, 1918.

27. *Ibid.*, RG 92, Box 8916B; Box 9054.

28. *Ibid.*, RG 165, Entry 393, #15800, George Barton to Jasper Mayer, January 10, 1918.

29. "Report of the Supervisor of Maintenance and Construction," *Report of the Military Entertainment Committee*, pp. 52–53, Dec. 31, 1918. "Expenditures for Liberty Theatres from Appropriation Military Post Exchanges," NA, RG 165, Entry 399, Box 214, "Miscellaneous Civilian Correspondence CTCA," August 31, 1918. RG 92, Construction Division Decimal File Correspondence, File 652-J, as well as Construction Division Completion Reports.

30. Irna Risch, *Quartermaster Support of the Army: A History of the Corps, 1775–1939* (Washington: Quartermaster Historian's Office, Office of the Quartermaster General, 1962) : 607–608.

31. Meloy, p. 4; *Report of the Military Entertainment Committee*, pp. 14, 16; NA, RG 92, Box 9033, Camp Constructing Quartermaster, Camp Sherman, Ohio, to Construction Division, May 15, 1918, describes efforts to improve acoustics in the auditorium.

32. Based on a Seating Chart for the Liberty Theatre, Camp Gordon, Atlanta, Georgia, NA, RG 165, Entry 393, Numbered Correspondence, 1918–1919, #27692, March 7, 1918.

33. *Report of the Military Entertainment Committee*, p. 53.

34. NA, RG 165, Entry 393, #23051, Lee Hanmer and Allen Minnix to Leroy Allen, February 19, 1918.

35. Camps Beauregard and Bowie and Forts Bliss, Cody, Doniphan, Fremont, Greene, Hancock, Johnston, Humphries, Kearney, Logan, MacArthur, McClellan, Sevier, Shelby, Sheridan, Wadsworth, Wheeler.

36. See NA, RG 165, Entry 393, #22500, YMCA Camp Secretary, Camp Sheridan to Harold Braddock, February 5, 1918; RG 92, Box 9029; Box 8969; Box 8916B; RG 165, Entry 393, #21323, February 27, 1918; and *Report of the Military Entertainment Committee*, p. 52.

37. September 7, 1918, "Liberty Theatre Addition, Plan and Elevations," September 7, 1918, in NA, RG 165, Entry 399, Box 212, and "Miscellaneous Civilian Correspondence CTCA," Chief of Construction Division to Malcolm L. McBride, September 14, 1918. See also *New York Dramatic Mirror*, March 9, 1918, p. 4; and NA, RG 165, Entry 399, Box 277. "Redpath Bureaus," R. R. Smith to H. R. Miner, March 12, 1918.

38. NA, RG 92, Box 8969.

39. NA, RG 165, Entry 399, Box 166, "Bulletins (news) Liberty Theatres," R. R. Smith to W. Prentice Sanger and H. Maling, May 21, 1918; Entry 393, #51526, Col. J. S. Joy, Director, CTCA to Commanding General, Camp Upton, August 20, 1919.

40. NA, RG 165, Entry 393, #19870, W. A. Henricks to Hanmer, February 11, 1918; #19870, Alex White, District director, to E. Dana Caulkins, February 13, 1918; #21075, G. A. Nesbitt to E. Caulkins, February 13, 1918; #21241, H. S. Braucher to Fosdick, February 12, 1918; #21266. Nesbitt to Caulkins, February 19, 1918.

41. U. S. Congress, House, 65th Congress,

2nd Session. Committee on Military Affairs, *Hearing on Camp Activities, Statement of Raymond B. Fosdick,* pp. 11-15.

42. NA, RG 165, Entry 399, Box 214, "Misc. Civilian Correspondence, CTCA," A. C. Minnix and W. V. Turley to CTCA, September 27, 1918. Scenery and rigging equipment included in the deal with Traxler was remodeled by the Kansas City Scenic Co. to accommodate a wider proscenium in the rebuilt theatre. Cost to the CTCA was $865.

43. *Ibid.,* Entry 399, Box 211, "Misc. Civilian Correspondence CTCA," War Camp Community Service Representative, San Antonio, Texas, to CTCA, May 15, 1918.

44. NA RG 165, Entry 393, #6165, Copy of Agreement between Camp Travis and Interstate Amusement Co., September 5, 1917; #15508, Adjutant General to Commanding Generals of all National Army and National Guard Camps, September 19, 1917; #34865, R. S. Wallace to W. Prentice Sanger, April 20, 1918; R. S. Wallace to W. Prentice Sanger, May 6, 1918; NA, RG 165, Entry 399, Box 211.

45. NA RG 165, Entry 399, Box 204, "Misc. Civilian Correspondence CTCA," McBride to F. R. Keppell, 3rd assistant secretary of war, July 1, 1918.

46. *Report of the Military Entertainment Committee,* pp. 54-55.

47. As with other Liberty Theatres, the Class C buildings were equipped with motion picture projectors and booths to house them. See NA, RG 165, Entry 399, Box 190, "Kansas City Scenic Company," memo by H. O. Pierce, "Accepted Standard Scenic Equipment for use in Class C theatres," October 31, 1918; *Ibid.,* Zone Supply Officer, St. Louis to Kansas City Scenic Company, January 10, 1919.

48. See NA, RG 165, Entry 399, Box 190, "K. C. Scenic Co.," Smith to K. C. Scenic Co., September 18, 1918.

49. *Report of the Military Entertainment Committee,* pp. 53-54.

50. NA, RG 92, Box 8988; Entry 399, Box 205, "Misc. Correspondence Liberty Theatres," Major Joy to Construction Division, June 26, 1919; U.S. War Department, *Annual Reports, 1918-1919: Report of the Chief of Construction Division,* p. 4056. Theatres of this type were authorized at Fort Sill, Lawton, Oklahoma, in April 1919; at Camp Knox, West Point, Kentucky on May 1, 1919; and at Fortress Monroe, Virginia, on June 15, 1919.

51. U. S. War Department, *Annual Reports, 1918-1919: Report of the Chief of Construction Division,* p. 4056.

52. Fort Barry, California; Fort Strong, Massachusetts; U.S. Troops, Marfa, Texas; March Field, California; Camp Meade, Maryland; Fortress Monroe, Virginia; Fort Morgan, Alabama; Camp Custer, Michigan; Camp Boyd, Fort Bliss, Texas; 82nd Field Artillery, Fort Bliss, Texas; Remount Depot, Fort Bliss, Texas; Camp Devens, Massachusetts; Fort Sam Fordyce, Texas; Camp Furlong, New Mexico; Fort Hancock, New Jersey; Camp Gordon, Georgia; Camp Humphries, Virginia; Camp Jesup, Georgia; Fort Myer, Virginia; Camp S. D. Little, Arizona; Pig Point, Virginia; Ross Field, Arcadia, California; and Camp Stanley, Texas. See NA, RG 165, Entry 393, #55069, Executive Officer, Education and Recreation Branch, War Plans Division, General Staff, to all stations with Liberty Theatres.

53. *Ibid.,* #49516, unsigned TS copy of memo designated "To be incorporated in the Hearing of the Military Affairs Committee of the House in Consideration of the Budget for Military Post Exchanges," undated. Internal evidence indicates commission accountants wrote it about June 1, 1919.

54. George Soule, *Prosperity Decade: From War to Depression,* Vol. VIII of *The Economic History of the United States,* ed. Henry David, et. al. (10 vols.; New York: Harper and Row, Publishers, 1947), p. 171. The *Engineering News Record* index of the combined costs of lumber, steel, cement, and common labor (1926=100) was 44.5 in 1915. It reached 120.8 in 1920.

55. NA, RG 165, Entry 399, Box 206, "Weekly Reports," "Report of Business for Week Ending April 19, 1919," showed a net profit of $533.15 for all theatres; *ibid.,* "Report of Business for Week Ending April 26, 1919," showed a net loss of $4,800.09. Losses continued unstintingly to the last day of the commission's history.

56. "Synopsis of Liberty Theatre Receipts," NA, RG 165, Entry 399, Box 192, "Liberty Theatres."

Chapter 8

1. *New York Times Magazine,* November 4, 1917, p. 4.

2. NA, RG 165, Entry 393, #7832, Klaw to Fosdick, September 19, 1917.

3. NA, RG 165, Entry 393, #5563, Klaw to Fosdick, September 20, 1917. #6368, Klaw to Hanmer, October 4, 1917.

4. The Auxiliary Fund had received $46,469.50 in donations since May 8, 1917, when it was established, but the money was used to pay salaries of CTCA employees prior to their being added to government payrolls on October 17, 1917. By executive order of October 16, 1917, CTCA employees were taken into service of the War and Navy Departments and paid up to $1,800 per year from appropriated

funds. *Ibid.*, #50047, October 16, 1917, and #13486, Fosdick to CTCA commissioner Thomas J. Howells, December 6, 1917.

5. NA, RG 165, Entry 393, 8998, October 25, 1917.

6. *Ibid.*, October 27, 1917.

7. *Ibid.*, #13732, Klaw to Fosdick, December 4, 1917; #20586, Klaw to McBride, February 27, 1918.

8. *Ibid.*, #23585, Klaw to Fosdick, March 6, 1918.

9. *Ibid.*, #12261; #10776.

10. *Ibid.*, #12096, McBride to Fosdick, December 26, 1917; #12096, McBride to Hanmer, December 27, 1917, is substantially the same letter.

11. *Ibid.*, #13011, Mayer to Fosdick, December 4, 1917.

12. *Ibid.*, #12220, December 10, 1917, Klaw to Fosdick.

13. *Ibid.*, #7111, October 19, 1917; #8998, October 25, 1917; #13732, December 14, 1917.

14. *Ibid.*, #13732, Fosdick to Klaw, December 17, 1917.

15. *Ibid.*, #5563, Klaw to Fosdick, September 29, 1917; Fosdick to Klaw, September 22, 1917; #23585, Klaw to Fosdick, March 6, 1918. Klaw's plan is outlined in the *New York Times Magazine*, November 4, 1917, p. 4.

16. *Report of the Military Entertainment Committee*, "Smileage Report of the Military Entertainment Council."

17. *Billboard*, December 8, 1917, p. 21, and December 22, 1917, p. 40.

18. NA, RG 165, Entry 393, #23277, "Preliminary Report of the Smileage Sale to the Chairman of the Military Entertainment Service," March 7, 1918; #9942, Harrison to Hanmer, November 6, 1917, and #10776, Fosdick to Harrison, November 17, 1917.

19. *Ibid.*, #14807, Baker to Fosdick, December 31, 1917.

20. *Ibid.*, #49006, form letter from Braddock to campaign managers, January 12, 1918.

21. Marcus Lee Hansen, *Welfare Campaigns in Iowa* (Iowa City: The State Historical Society of Iowa, 1920): 147–48.

22. NA, RG 165, Entry 393, #22480, Fosdick to Harrison, February 15, 1918; #21891, "Report of the Sale of Smileage," March 6, 1918.

23. NA, RG 165, Entry 393, #38903, "Smileage Report" of December 28, 1918.

24. *Ibid.*, Entry 399, Box 215, "Misc. Civilian Correspondence CTCA," Accounting Office Report Week ending October 6, 1919. Smileage redemption ceased September 30, 1919.

25. *Ibid.*, #48085, F. R. Keppel, third assistant secretary of war, to Newton D. Baker, April 18, 1919.

26. *Ibid.*, Entry 399, Box 215, "Misc. Civilian Correspondence CTCA," "Monthly Smileage Report," September 30, 1919. See also, Appendix C, "Gross Receipts and Estimates of Attendance."

27. *Ibid.*, #4524, Hanmer to Baker, August 24, 1917.

28. *New York Times Magazine*, November 4, 1917, p. 4.

29. *Ibid.*; Entry 393, #16348, Mayer to all Managers, January 16, 1918; #29272, Minutes of Meeting of the CTCA, January 18, 1918.

30. See NA, RG 165, Entry 393, #29243, "Statement of Receipts and Expenditures for the Period ending March 2, 1918," March 14, 1918. Entry 399, Box 208, "Miscellaneous," E. H. Maling, CTCA accountant, to J. S. Lay, American Red Cross, April 18, 1918. Box 242, "Theatre Reports," Accounting Department to Director of the CTCA, February 6, 1919.

31. See Appendix D, "Average Weekly Receipts of Liberty Theatre" for receipts from January 10, 1918, through August 31, 1919. See Appendix B, Liberty Theatre Expenses, for expenses of each week's operations of the entire Liberty Theatre circuit.

32. Harrison, *Culture under Canvas: The Story of Tent Chautauqua* (New York: Hastings House, 1958): 212.

33. "Standard Employee and Salary List for Blue Theatres," no date, but probably before September 1918, NA, RG 165, Entry 399, Box 166, "Bulletins (News) Liberty Theatres"; "Table of Organization Requirements for Liberty Theatres," NA, RG 165, Entry 393, #51925, January 13, 1919; *Report of the Military Entertainment Committee*, pp. 44, 48, and 49.

34. An account of Liberty Theatre income and expenses is found in "Synopsis of Liberty Theatre Receipts," NA, RG 165, Entry 399, Box 192, "Liberty Theatres." Microfilm copy in possession of the author.

35. "The War and Broadway," *Theatre Magazine* 17 (April 1918), pp. 203–204.

Chapter 9

1. NA, RG 165, Entry 393, #11021, Klaw to Edward Coffin, CTCA assistant publicity director, November 1917. The *New York Times Magazine*, November 4, 1917, p. 4, had erroneously credited Klaw with the responsibility for "building and operating the sixteen cantonment theatres."

2. *Ibid.*, #8998, October 27, 1917; #13005, Hanmer to Mayer, November 24, 1917.

3. *Ibid.*, #12184, Klaw to Mayer, November 22, 1917; #12234, Mayer to Klaw, November 24, 1917.

4. *Ibid.*, #13774, December 21, 1917.

5. *Ibid.*, #16061, Klaw to Hanmer.

6. *Ibid.*, #16125, Fosdick to Klaw, January 2, 1918.
7. *Ibid.*, #16914, Klaw to Fosdick, January 4, 1918; Fosdick, Hanmer, and Mayer to Klaw, January 12, 1918.
8. *Ibid.*, #16125, Fosdick to Klaw, January 2, 1918.
9. *Ibid.*, #11309, Mayer to Hanmer, n. d. (probably November 1917); #12226, Klaw to Fosdick, December 6, 1917; #13718, Klaw to Fosdick, December 15, 1917; #10047, Mayer to Klaw, November 13, 1917; #13795, Hanmer to Klaw, November 25, 1917; #16918, Hollis Cooley to Mayer, January 2, 1918.
10. *Ibid.*, #16942, January 12, 1918.
11. *Ibid.*, #16348; #15272, January 20, 1918.
12. *Ibid.*, #16914, Fosdick, Hanmer, and Mayer to Klaw, January 12, 1918.
13. *Ibid.*, #16942, Fosdick to Klaw, January 15, 1918.
14. *Ibid.*, #16958, Klaw to Percy Weadon, Camp Gordon, Georgia, January 28, 1918.
15. *Ibid.*, #18737, Klaw to Charles E. Barton, Camp Meade, Maryland, February 9, 1918.
16. *Ibid.*, #18935, Klaw to Fosdick, February 1, 1918.
17. *Ibid.*, #18935, Klaw to Fosdick, February 2, 1918.

Chapter 10

1. Dickinson, *The Building of an Army*, pp. 284–307, and Phyllis A. Zimmerman, *The Neck of the Bottle: George W. Goethals and the Reorganization of the U.S. Army Supply System, 1917–1918* (College Station: Texas A&M University Press, 1992), pp. 31–43.
2. NA, RG 165, Entry 393, #20586, Klaw to McBride, February 27, 1918. *Variety*, February 15, 1918, p. 1, reported that the CTCA had decided to limit touring companies to 70 percent of the gross each evening, but Klaw continued to write other kinds of contracts.
3. NA, RG 165, Entry 393, #20587, McBride to Klaw, February 28, 1918.
4. *Ibid.*, #20586, February 28, 1918.
5. *Ibid.*, #19009, Hanmer to Klaw, February 18, 1918.
6. *Ibid.*, #20586, March 4, 1918.
7. *Ibid.*, #23585, Klaw to Fosdick, March 6, 1918.
8. *Ibid.*, #28515, McBride to Klaw, March 7, 1919.
9. *Ibid.*, #28513, McBride to Klaw, March 6, 1918.
10. *Ibid.*, #28515.
11. *Ibid.*, #23585, Fosdick to Klaw, March 8, 1918. Klaw wanted a letter of appreciation from Baker, but had received none by May 1918.
12. *Ibid.*, #28513, Klaw to Fosdick, March 9, 1918.
13. *New York Sun* December 17, 1917, p. 4.
14. NA RG 165, Entry 393, #16068, January 11, 1918.
15. *Ibid.*, #16862, January 12, 1918. Jerry Stagg, *The Brothers Shubert,* pp. 126 and 151, confirms Klaw's statement about the editorial policy of the *New York Review.*
16. NA, RG 165, Entry 393, #16862.
17. *Ibid.*, #16918, Cooley to Mayer, January 2, 1918.
18. *Ibid.*, #20586, Klaw to McBride, February 27, 1918.
19. *Ibid.*, #26626, Smith to Cooley, March 12, 1918, enclosing *New York Review* article of March 9, 1918.
20. *Ibid.*, #26371, Fosdick to Klaw, March 9, 1918.
21. Shubert Archives, Contracts Series #1, #342, March 31, 1910. The contract ran for 10 years and was but one of several linking Brady and the Shuberts. Those close to the Shuberts recall that Brady was a buffoon and a drunk manipulated by Lee Shubert. See Foster Hirsch, *The Boys from Syracuse: The Shuberts' Theatrical Empire*, pp. 66 and 114.
22. NA RG 165, Entry 393 #3565, Frederick E. Elliott, executive secretary of the National Association of the Motion Picture Industry, to Fosdick, August 16, 1917.
23. *Ibid.*, #5563, Klaw to Fosdick, September 20, 1917; Fosdick to Klaw, September 22, 1917. Entry 399, Box 216, "Moving Pictures," W. P. McGuire, Jr., executive secretary of the National Board of Review of Motion Pictures, to Hanmer, January 18, 1918.
24. *Ibid.*, Entry 393, #13053, P. A. Powers to Fosdick, December 11, 1917.
25. *Ibid.*, Fosdick to Powers, December 14, 1917. By this time Klaw had assigned Adam Keesler, Jr., to work with Hanmer, thereby removing himself from the process of booking films. *Billboard*, December 1, 1917, p. 4.
26. NA, RG 165, Entry 393, #26363, Klaw to McBride, March 13, 1918. Other materials relevant to the Klaw resignation are: *ibid.*, #20539, Klaw to McBride, March 11, 1918; #26547, Klaw to Fosdick, March 11, 1918; #26362, Klaw to Fosdick, March 11, 1918; Klaw to McBride, March 13, 1918.
27. *Ibid.*, #28537, Klaw to Fosdick, April 10, 1918.

Chapter 11

1. Kate Oglebay, "Recreational Work in Training Camps," *The Drama League Monthly* 3 (October 1917), p. 4.

2. NA, RG 165, Entry 393, #21501, Harrison to Hanmer, February 16, 1918; Entry 399, Box 227, "Redpath Lyceum," Harrison to Hanmer, February 19, 1918.

3. *Variety,* March 15, 1918, p. 12.

4. NA, RG 165, Entry 399, Box 227, "Questionnaires for Male Employees of CTCA." Internal evidence indicates the questionnaires were collected in October 1918.

5. NA, RG 165, Entry 393, #28830.

6. Richard Moody, "The Drama League," q. v., *The Cambridge Guide to American Theatre,* ed. Don B. Wilmeth and Tice L. Miller (Cambridge: Cambridge University Press, 1993), pp. 151–52. Morris R. Bogard, "The Drama League of America: A History and Critical Analysis of its Activities and Achievements," PhD diss. University of Illinois, 1962, pp. 57–59.

7. NA, RG 165, Entry 393, #28830, McBride to Fosdick, March 14, 1918; #28520, McBride to Otto H. Kahn, March 18, 1918; *New York Dramatic Mirror,* June 29, 1918, p. 915.

8. James Cushman was chairman of the Play Review Committee. It included Charles Jehlinger, E. R. Matthews, John C. Travis, A. T. Thornton, Percy W. Darbyshire, and Mrs. Otis Skinner.

9. *Report of the Military Entertainment Committee,* pp. 17–18.

10. *Variety,* December 13, 1918, p. 12.

11. *Cleveland News,* December 9, 1939, in the Kate Oglebay Clipping File, General Reference Division, Cleveland Public Library.

12. NA, RG 165, Entry 399, Box 211, "Misc. Civilian Correspondence CTCA," McBride to Reber, May 27, 1918; Reber to McBride, May 28, 1918.

13. *New York Dramatic Mirror,* June 29, 1918, p. 915.

14. NA, RG 165, Entry 399, Box 193, "Liberty Theatre Managers," January 23, 1918. See also McBride to all Managers, Bulletin #132, August 22, 1918.

15. *Report of the Military Entertainment Committee,* p. 47.

16. NA, RG 165, Entry 393, 20123, R. R. Smith to Byrne C. Marcellus, Galveston, Texas, March 6, 1918; Entry 399, Box 193, "Liberty Theatre Managers," R. R. Smith to all managers, Red Circuit, April 14, 1918; Entry 393, #30123, Reber to McBride, May 21, 1918; Entry 399, Box 165, "Bulletins (Managers)," R. B. Fosdick to Morale Section, War Department General Staff, October 23, 1918; Entry 393, #45885, Howard O. Pierce, acting director of Liberty Theatres, to Col. J. S. Joy, CTCA director, February 10, 1919.

17. *Report of the Military Entertainment Committee,* pp. 13–14.

Chapter 12

1. James R. Schultz, *The Romance of Small-Town Chautauquas* (Columbia: University of Missouri Press, 2002), pp. 1 ff.

2. See Bernheim, pp. 106–108; Victoria Case and Robert Ormond Case, *We Called it Culture: The Story of Chautauqua* (Garden City: Doubleday, 1948), which sketches an anecdotal history of tent chautauqua; and Harry P. Harrison, as told to Karl Detzer, *Culture under Canvas: the Story of Tent Chautauqua* (New York: Hastings House, Publishers, 1958), a richly detailed autobiography by one of the most important tent chautauqua managers.

3. Schultz, pp. 15 ff.

4. See Charlotte Canning, "'The Most American Thing in America': Producing National Identities in Chautauqua, 1904–1932," in *Performing America: Cultural Nationalism in American Theater,* ed. Jeffrey D. Mason and J. Ellen Gainor (Ann Arbor: University of Michigan Press, 1999), pp. 91–105.

5. John E. Tapia, *Circuit Chautauqua: From Rural Education to Popular Entertainment in Early Twentieth Century America* (Jefferson, NC: McFarland Publishers, 1997), pp. 111–124.

6. Lee Hanmer to Maj. Gen. S. D. Sturgia at Camp Pike, Little Rock, Arkansas, September 8, 1917, is an example of letters about circuit chautauqua sent to camp commanders.

7. Tapia, *Circuit Chautauqua,* pp 113–132; 211–212. See also Arthur C. Rieser, *The Chautauqua Moment: Protestants, Progressives and the Culture of Modern Liberalism* (New York: Columbia University Press, 2003).

8. John Collier, "Censorship and the National Board," *The Survey* 35 (October 2, 1915), pp. 9–14.

9. NA, RG 165, Entry 393, #24529, McBride to Fosdick, April 19, 1918.

10. *Ibid.,* Entry 399, Box 205, "Miscellaneous Correspondence," Reber to Lee Shubert, May 1, 1918. Agreements under which other government-sponsored shows operated are not available, but they presumably contained features similar to the Reber-Shubert agreement.

11. *Variety,* June 28, 1918, p. 1.

12. *Ibid,* June 7, 1918, p. 4.

13. *Ibid,* December 13, 1918, p. 11.

14. Anthony Slide, "Burlesque," q.v., *The Encyclopedia of Vaudeville* (Westport, CT: Greenwood Press, 1994): 72–74.

15. *Variety,* September 13, 1918, p. 9.

16. *Ibid,* October 4, 1918, p. 10.

17. NA, RG 165, Entry 393, Box 208, "Misc. Civilian Correspondence CTCA," John Golden to J. Howard Reber, April 18, 1918,

18. NA, RG 165, Entry 399, Box 208, "Misc. Civilian Correspondence CTCA," John E.

Golden to J. H. Reber, April 18, 1918, report of the first seven weeks of the company's tour. Golden produced the show for $3,600 and the average weekly touring expense was about $1,700. Income of another $250 per week was needed to repay Golden for his stake in the production.

19. Camp Merritt exceeded a gross of $2,750 in 36 of its approximately 75 weeks of operation under the CTCA. Camps Lee and Meade exceeded that figure 28 times, and Camp Jackson 13 times. See Appendix D: Average Weekly Receipts of Liberty Theatres.

20. *Variety*, June 28, 1918, p. 1.

21. *Ibid*.

22. NA, RG 165, Entry 393, #20586, Klaw to McBride, February 28, 1918; McBride to Klaw, March 4, 1918.

23. Gerald Bordman, *American Theatre: A Chronicle of Comedy and Drama, 1914–1930* (New York: Oxford University Press, 1995), 82.

24. New York *World*, September 8, 1918, Sec. E, p. 5.

25. New York *Clipper* February 6, 1918, p. 4.

26. NA, RG 165, Entry 393, #27996, Hanmer to J. J. Mayer and Malcolm McBride, March 8, 1918.

27. *Ibid*., Entry 399, Box 202, "Misc. Correspondence," April 18, 1918.

28. *Ibid*., Box 251, "Wallace, Roy Smith," Wallace to W. Prentice Sanger, April 29, 1918.

29. "Ban Put on Beauregard Theatre," *Daily Town Talk*, Alexandria, Louisiana, April 20, 1918, p. 1.

30. *Ibid*., Box 202, "Misc. Correspondence," Adjutant, 76th Division, Camp Devens to McBride, April 12, 1918.

31. *Ibid*., Entry 393, #30204, Typescript copy of Boston *American* editorial.

32. *Ibid*., Entry 399, Box 202, "Misc. Correspondence, Liberty Theatres," Percy J. Burrell to J. Howard Reber, May 24, 1918.

33. *Ibid*., Box 205, "Misc. Correspondence, Liberty Theatres," Reber to Ethel Hinton, Lawrence, Massachusetts, June 7, 1918.

34. *New York Dramatic Mirror*, April 13, 1918, p. 508.

35. NA, RG 165, Entry 393, #2440, J. A. MacArt, director of New Jersey's Second War Fund Committee of the Red Cross to Harvey J. Hill, Advisory Committee, American Red Cross, Washington, April 15, 1918.

36. *Leveille* P. 1.

37. NA, R6 165, Entry 393 #33807a, Reber to Executive Officer, CTCA, January 20, 1919.

38. *Ibid*., Reber to Executive Officer, CTCA, February 24, 1919.

39. *Ibid*., Entry 399, Box 211, "Misc. Civilian Correspondence CTCA," March 1, 1919.

40. *Ibid*., Entry 399, Box 215, "Misc. Civilian Correspondence CTCA," Accounting Office Report Week Ending October 6, 1919.

41. *Cleveland News*, December 9, 1939, in the Kate Oglebay Clipping File, General Reference Division, Cleveland Public Library.

42. Projectors were purchased and the machines and asbestos booths to house them were shipped in December 1917. However, installation was delayed for several weeks. By mid–March 1918, 21 theatres had booths and projectors. See NA, RG 165, Entry 393, #14635, Fosdick to Quartermaster General, December 18, 1917; #16027, Mayer to H. Robert Law, January 11, 1918; Entry 399, Box 223, "Motion Picture Machines," W. G. Smith, general manager, Nicholas Power Co., New York, to R. R. Smith, July 27, 1918; *Report of the Military Entertainment Committee*, p. 39.

43. NA, RG 165, Entry 399, Box 193, "Liberty Theatre Managers," R. R. Smith to All Theatre Managers, September 27, 1918.

44. *Report of the Military Entertainment Committee*, p. 40.

45. NA, RG 165, Entry 399, Box 180, "Films," memo from Cocks to McBride, "The Motion Picture and the War in the United States," n.d.

46. Orrin G. Cocks, "Applying Standards to Motion Picture Films," *The Survey* (June 27, 1914): 337–38.

47. NA, RG 165 Entry 399, Box 166, "Bulletins (News) Liberty Theatres," R. R. Smith to all Managers, March 19, 1918.

48. *Ibid*., Box 210, "Misc. Civilian Correspondence, CTCA," R. R. Smith to J. H. Reber, April 15, 1918; Box 223, "Plans, etc., Camp Dodge," Moreland Brown to R. R. Smith, April 19, 1918.

49. *Ibid*., Box 191, "Letters Unarranged CTCA," Memo of conversation between McBride and Hanmer, May 7, 1918."

50. See *Making Men Moral: Social Engineering During the Great War* (New York: New York University Press, 1996), pp. 36 ff.

51. Howard T. Lewis, *The Motion Picture Industry* (New York: D. Van Nostrand, Inc., 1933), pp. 7–8.

52. *Report of the Military Entertainment Committee*, p. 30. Hyman mentions only 13 titles of films shown in the camps in 1918. Many more, perhaps hundreds, must have been used to fill screens in the camps, but their titles are recorded nowhere.

53. Craig W. Campbell, *Reel America and World War I: A Comprehensive Filmography and History of Motion Pictures in the United States, 1914–1920* (Jefferson, NC: McFarland, 1985). See also Leslie Midkiff DeBauche, *Reel Patriotism: The Movies and World War I* (Madison: University of Wisconsin Press, 1997): 38–48;

and Larry Wayne Ward, *The Motion Picture Goes to War: The U.S. Government Film Effort during World War I* (Ann Arbor, MI: UMI Research Press, 1985): 55–98.

54. John E. Dimeglio, *Vaudeville U.S.A.* (Bowling Green, OH: Bowling Green Popular Press, 1973): p. 11.

55. See, for example, "The Decay of Vaudeville," *American Magazine* 69 (April 1910): 842–48.

56. Dimeglio, pp. 22–23; Shubert Archives, Contracts I, No. 318, Agreement of 27 April 1907 establishing Shubert participation in USAC; *Ibid.*, Box 34, Folder 10, Klaw and Erlanger, Agreement of 6 November 1907, binding Klaw and Erlanger and other USAC partners to get out of vaudeville.

57. *Report of the Military Entertainment Committee*, p. 20.

58. Dimeglio, pp. 19–20.

59. *Variety*, August 30, 1918, p. 5.

60. Weldon B. Durham, "The Revival and Decline of the Stock Company Mode of Organization, 1886–1930," *Theatre History Studies* 6 (1986): 165–167.

61. NA, RG 165, Entry 393, #47542, Charles Salisbury to J. H. Reber, March 12, 1919.

62. *Ibid.*, Box 167, "Curtis Bay Ordnance Plant," Hanmer to Klaw, September 25, 1917.

63. *Ibid.*, #20563, Hanmer to McBride, March 4, 1918.

64. *Ibid.*, Entry 393, #29272; #27957, McBride to Hanmer, January 24, 1918.

65. *Ibid.*, #29999, McBride to Commanding General, Camp Dix, New Jersey, May 23, 1918.

66. *Ibid.*, #33807a, Harry Neville to Major Joy, director of CTCA, March 10, 1919.

67. *Ibid.*, Entry 399, Box 204, "Miscellaneous Correspondence Liberty Theatres," John S. Tichenor to McBride, June 25, 1918; McBride to Tichenor, June 27, 1918, and June 29, 1918; Tichenor to McBride, July 2, 1918; McBride to Tichenor, July 5, 1918; Entry 393, #4818, Tichenor to executive secretary of YMCA, July 9, 1918.

68. Lawrence Bergreen, "Oh! How He Hated to Get up in the Morning," *MHQ: The Quarterly Journal of Military History* 2, no. 4, (1992): 72–80.

69. *Ibid* #20586, Klaw to McBride, February 27, 1918.

70. *Report of the Military Entertainment Committee*, p. 30.

71. *Ibid.*, p. 23; NA, RG 165, Entry 393, #51982, Harry Neville to Maj. A. E. Foote, May 19, 1919.

72. *Report of the Military Entertainment Committee*, p. 35.

73. NA, RG 165, Entry 393, #51892, Neville to Maj. A. E. Foote, May 19, 1919.

74. *Ibid.*, #49725, Fosdick to O'Hara, May 28, 1918; Fosdick, *Chronicle of a Generation*, p. 183.

75. NA, RG 165, Entry 393, #51892, Neville to Maj. A. E. Foote, May 19, 1919. The number of performances in each camp: Pike—130; Jackson—125; Dix—124; Grant—116; Funston—104; Meade—96; Travis—94; Taylor—90; Humphries—85; Gordon—80; Devens—66; Upton, Custer, and Logan—60; Sherman—50; Wadsworth and Merritt—45; MacArthur and Bowie—41; Greenleaf—39; Sevier—37; Wheeler—21; Greene—18; Dodge and Beauregard—17. Number of performances at camps Kearney and Lee was not reported.

Chapter 13

1. *New York Clipper*, November 28, 1917, p. 3.

2. *New York Dramatic Mirror*, December 22, 1917, p. 3.

3. *Ibid.*, June 8, 1918, p. 799; *Billboard*, June 29, 1918, p. 4.

4. *Billboard*, July 27, 1918, p. 115; August 10, 1918, p. 186; August 17, 1918, p. 226; August 24, 1918, p. 259; August 31, 1918, p. 296; September 28, 1918, p. 468; October 5, 1918, p. 504; December 7, 1918, p. 828.

5. *Ibid.*, November 23, 1918, p. 755; December 7, 1918, p. 828; January 4, 1919, p. 4.

6. Walter J. Kingsley, "Keith Vaudeville in the Great War," *New York Dramatic Mirror*, December 28, 1918, p. 957, 970; July 1, 1919, p. 1009.

Chapter 14

1. *Variety*, November 1, 1918, p. 13; *New York Dramatic Mirror*, November 30, 1918, p. 793. NA, RG 165, Entry 393, #50047, McBride, acting chairman of CTCA, to Newton D. Baker, December 6, 1918.

2. *Ibid.*, Baker to McBride, December 7, 1918.

3. *Ibid.*, #13732, Baker to Fosdick, November 30, 1918.

4. The theatres at Camp Fremont, California, and Camp Cody, New Mexico, closed on November 26 and December 15, 1918. There were no closings during January 1919, as the demobilization reached its peak and camps were generally crowded with soldiers. Theatres at Camp Sevier, South Carolina, and Camp MacArthur, Texas, closed February 15 and 17, 1919.

5. NA, RG 165, Entry 393, #50033, Keppel to McBride, December 21, 1918.

6. *Ibid.*, #48798, March 22 and March 25, 1919.

7. *Ibid.* On April 1, 1919, Maj. Earnest E. Wheeler took charge of the New York Booking Office.

8. NA, RG 165, Entry 399, Box 215, "Misc. Correspondence CTCA," Whitfield to Wooldridge, May 10, 1919; Wooldridge to Joy, May 10, 1919; Entry 393, #49952, McBride to Fosdick, June 5, 1919.

9. *Ibid.*, #49952, McBride to Fosdick, June 5, 1919; Joy to McBride, June 19, 1919.

10. *Ibid.*, #54672, Major Wooldridge to Colonel Joy, January 16, 1920.

11. U. S. War Department, *Annual Reports, 1919*, Vol. I, *Report of the Secretary of War* (Washington: U.S. Government Printing Office, 1920), p. 35.

12. Edward L. Munson. *The Management of Men: A Handbook on the Systematic Development of Morale and the Control of Human Behavior* (New York, Holt, 1921): 526–552. General March is quoted on p. 526.

13. Weigley, *History of the United States Army* (1984), 395–420, and *American Military History* (Washington, Office of the Chief of Military History, U.S. Army, 1989), 405–422.

14. D. Colt Denfeld, "World War I Mobilization Camps," *The Journal of America's Military Past* 29 (Fall–Winter 2002), pp. 36–52.

15. Matloff, ed., *American Military History*, pp. 417–422.

16. James Robert Mock and Cedric Larson, "Morale — The Soul of the Army," in *Frontiers of Democracy* 7 (1941): 237–39.

17. "War Recreation Services of Federal and National Agencies," *Recreation* 37 (June 1943): 132–38.

18. http://www.uso.org/about_uso/history.htm accessed September 8, 2001. See also Camp Shows, Inc., New York, *U.S.O. Camp Shows: A Guide to the Foxhole Circuit.* New York: USO-Camp Shows, 1944, and Lynn O'Neal Heberling, "Soldiers in Grease Paint: USO Camp Shows Inc., during World War II," PhD. diss., Kent State University, 1989.

19. *New York Times*, November 7, 1941, 20:3; Irving Spiegel, "Broadway Goes to the Camps," *New York Times*, November 24, 1942, 8, 1:6.

20. "War Recreation Services of Federal and National Agencies," *Recreation* 37 (June 1943): 138.

21. *New York Times*, November 29, 1941, 8, 1:6; November 1, 1942, 1:1–2.

22. U. S. War Department. Bureau of Public Relations. Women's Interests Section. *The Soldier and his Recreation* (Washington, D.C.: U.S. Government Printing Office, 1942): 8; *New York Times*, February 25, 1942, 23:2.

23. *New York Times*, August 13, 1941, 12:6; "Theatre for the Army Camps," *Theatre Arts* 25 (October 1941): 699–700.

24. Louis M. Simon, "Theatre in the Camps," *Theatre Arts* 26 (July 1942): 423–28; "Entertainment for the Armed Forces," *Theatre Arts*, 27(March 1943): 134–36.

25. Gretchen Knapp, "Experimental Social Policy making during World War II: The United Service Organizations (USO) and American War Community Services (AWCS)," *Journal of Policy History* 12 (2000): 321–38.

26. *New York Times*, February 20,1949, 27:3; May 1, 1950, 3:8; January 12, 1951, 30:6; http://www.uso.org/entertainment/nostalgia/photo24.html accessed August 13, 2001, is an account of "Important Dates in USO History."

27. *New York Times*, July 7, 1957, 18:2.

28. C. R. Kase, "AETA Overseas Touring," *Educational Theatre Journal* 11 (December 1959): 291–95. Kase was a professor of theatre in the Department of Speech and Dramatic Art at the University of Delaware and chairman of the AETA Overseas Touring Project in its third year in 1959. Thirteen college theatre programs made overseas tours playing 30 to 40 performances each from January 1958 through September 1959. The USO sponsored nine college shows in 1961–62. See also *New York Times*, May 27, 1961, 21:4.

29. Clayton Going, "They're the CATS," *New York Times Magazine*, May 15, 1949, p. 58.

30. *New York Times*, October 18, 1949, 29:1; November 29, 1949, 2:3.

31. *New York Times*, October 18, 1949, 29:1; A. Scheff, "Fifth Army's Theatre Program," *Theatre Arts* 37 (June 1953): 80.

32. "Recreation and the Personnel of the Armed Forces," *Recreation* 45 (February 1952), 483–86; Scheff, "Fifth Army's Theatre Program," p. 80.

33. "Bad News for the USO," *Newsweek* 79 (January 31, 1972), 54–55.

34. "Armed Forces Recreation," *Parks and Recreation* 6 (August 1971): 67–69.

35. Margaret G. Bierman, "Self-Sufficiency Target of Military Recreation," *Government Product News* 22 (March 1983): 32–34.

36. Pat Harden, "Armed Forces Recreation Services: Our Hallowed Ground raison d'etre," *Parks and Recreation* 29 (December 1994), 24–25.

37. Michael S. Wise, "Military Recreation: Can You Use It?" *Parks and Recreation* 56 (October 1992): 56–59, 87.

38. See Annual Reports of MWR online at http://www.armymwr.com/mwr/annual_report/mwrfy96.pdf ; http://www.armymwr.com/mwr/annual_report/mwrfy97.pdf; http://www.armymwr.com/mwr/planning/mwrfy98.pdf ; and http://www.armymwr.com/mwr/planning/mwrfy99.pdf accessed August 28, 2001.

http://www.armymwr.com/portal/news/display.asp?NEWS_ID=472 accessed March 3, 2005

Appendix

1. RG 165, Entry 399, Box 192, "Liberty Theatres," "Synopsis of Liberty Theatre Receipts," n.d.
2. *Ibid.*, provides no explanation of what expenses are included under "Operating Expenses."
3. NA, RG 165, Entry 399, Box 192, "Liberty Theatres." Other documents include correspondence, memoranda, and reports used to assemble Appendix A.
4. *Ibid.*, Entry 393, #27692, Weadon to Mayer, March 7, 1918, Camp Gordon business from January 27, 1918, to March 2, 1918; Entry 399, Box 205, "Misc. Correspondence," box office statement of Liberty Theatre, Camp Dix, New Jersey, May 8, 1918; Box 166, "Bulletins Director Liberty Theatres," Smith to all managers, December 6, 1918, attendance at 11 theatres for November 1918; Box 214, "Misc. Civilian Correspondence, CTCA," Breinig (Camp Grant) to Smith, February 1, 1919, attendance at Camp Grant in January 1919; Entry 393, #33807a, Smith to Executive Officer, CTCA, February 4, 1919, attendance at all theatres during January 1919; Entry 399, Box 214, "Misc. Civilian Correspondence CTCA," Breinig (Camp Grant) to Capt. Wooldridge, April 1, 1919, attendance at Camp Grant during March 1919; Breinig to Wooldridge, May 1, 1919, attendance at Camp Grant during April 1919; and Entry 393, #51892, Capt. Whitfield to Major Foote, May 19, 1919, attendance at all Liberty Theatres from January 1, 1919, to April 26, 1919.
5. Prices at 22 Liberty Theatres, generally those in the Blue circuit, were 25¢ for general admission, with 750 seats reserved at 50¢. When movies were shown, general admission was 15¢, with 750 seats at 25¢. Prices at the remaining tents and theatres were lower. General admission to one-third of the house at the rear was 15¢, to one-third at the center it was 20¢, and to one-third at the front it was 25¢. When movies were shown, the base rate was 10¢, with one-third of the house sold at 15¢. These prices prevailed until June 17, 1918, when the general admission at the small theatres and at the tents was made 25¢ for any seat in the house. Picture prices remained unchanged. See Appendix B, "Liberty Theatre Expenses."
6. NA, RG 165, Entry 393, #51892, Capt. Whitfield to Major Foote, May 19, 1919, reports attendance and gross receipts for all theatres from January 1, 1919, to April 26, 1919.

Bibliography

Books

Addams, Jane. *The Spirit of Youth and the City Streets.* New York: Macmillan, 1909.
Alexander, William Henry. *A Climatological History of Ohio.* Columbus: Engineering Experiment Station of the Ohio State University, 1923.
Allen, Edward Frank. *Keeping Our Fighters Fit for War and After.* Written with the cooperation of Raymond B. Fosdick, Chairman, Army and Navy Commission on Training Camp Activities. New York: Century, 1918.
The Army Almanac. Washington: U.S. Government Printing Office, 1955.
Baker, Newton D. *Frontiers of Freedom.* New York: Doran, 1918.
Beaver, Daniel R. *Newton D. Baker and the American War Effort, 1917–1919.* Lincoln: University of Nebraska Press, 1966.
Bernheim, Alfred L. *The Business of the Theatre.* New York: Actors' Equity Association, 1932.
Berryman, Sue E. *Who Serves? The Persistent Myth of the Underclass Army.* Boulder, CO: Westview Press, 1988.
Bordman, Gerald. *American Musical Theatre: A Chronicle* 3rd ed. Oxford: Oxford University Press, 2001.
_____. *American Theatre: A Chronicle of Comedy and Drama, 1914–1930.* New York: Oxford University Press, 1995.
Bourdieu, Pierre. *The Field of Cultural Production.* Edited and introduced by Randal Johnson, 29–141. New York: Columbia University Press, 1993.
Brady, Haldeen. *Pershing's Mission in Mexico.* El Paso: Texas Western Press, 1966.
Bristow, Nancy K. *Making Men Moral: Social Engineering during the Great War.* New York: New York University Press, 1996.
Brown, Jared. *The Theatre in America during the Revolution.* Cambridge: Cambridge University Press, 1995.
Burke, Kenneth. "Bureaucratization of the Imaginative" in "Dictionary of Pivotal Terms," in *Attitudes Toward History,* 225–229 Rev. 2nd ed. Boston: Beacon Press, 1961.
Butler, George D. *Pioneers in Public Recreation.* Minneapolis: Burgess, 1965.
Camp Shows, Inc., New York. *U.S.O. Camp Shows: A Guide to the Foxhole Circuit.* New York: USO-Camp Shows, 1944.
Campbell, Craig W. *Reel America and World War I: A Comprehensive Filmography and History of Motion Pictures in the United States, 1914–1920.* Jefferson, NC: McFarland, 1985.
Canning, Charlotte. "'The Most American Thing in America': Producing National Identities in Chautauqua, 1904–1932," in *Performing America: Cultural Nationalism in American Theater,* edited by Jeffrey D. Mason and J. Ellen Gainor, 91–105 Ann Arbor: University of Michigan Press, 1999.

Carlson, Reynold E., Theodore R. Deppe, and Janet R. MacLean. *Recreation in American Life.* 2nd ed. Belmont, CA: Wadsworth, 1972.

Casari, Robert B., Patricia F. Medert, Luvada D. Kuhn, and William H. Nolan. *Chillicothe Ohio, 1796–1996: Ohio's First Capital.* Chillicothe: Chillicothe Bicentennial Commission, Inc., and the Ross County Historical Society, 1996.

Case, Victoria, and Robert Ormond Case. *We Called It Culture: The Story of Chautauqua.* Garden City: Doubleday, 1948.

Chambers, John Whiteclay II, ed. *The Eagle and the Dove: American Peace Movement and United States Foreign Policy, 1900–1922.* 2nd ed. Syracuse, NY: Syracuse UP, 1991.

Cheney, Sheldon. *The Art Theatre.* Rev. and enl. ed., first published 1917. New York: B. Blom, 1972.

Coffman, Edward M. *The Hilt of the Sword.* Madison: University of Wisconsin Press, 1966.

_____. *The Old Army: A Portrait of the American Army in Peacetime, 1784–1898.* New York: Oxford University Press, 1986.

Coggins, Jack. *The Fighting Man: An Illustrated History of the World's Greatest Fighting Forces through the Ages.* Garden City, NY.: Doubleday, 1966.

Connelly, Mark Thomas. *The Response to Prostitution in the Progressive Era.* Chapel Hill: University of North Carolina Press, 1980.

Cramer, C. H. *Newton D. Baker: A Biography.* Cleveland: World, 1961.

Davis, Michael M. Jr. *The Exploitation of Pleasure: A Study of Commercial Recreations in New York City.* New York: Department of Child Hygiene of the Russell Sage Foundation, 1911.

Davis, Peter. "The Syndicate/Shubert War," in *Inventing Times Square: Commerce and Culture at the Crossroads of the World,* edited by William R. Taylor, 147–157 New York: Russell Sage, 1991.

Debauche, Leslie Midkiff. *Reel Patriotism: The Movies and World War I.* Madison: University of Wisconsin Press, 1997.

Dickinson, John. *The Building of an Army.* New York: Century, 1922.

Dietzler, Mary Macey. *Detention Houses and Reformatories as Protective Social Agencies in the Campaign of the United States Government Against Venereal Diseases.* Washington: Government Printing Office, 1922.

Dimeglio, John E. *Vaudeville U.S.A.* Bowling Green, OH: Bowling Green Popular Press, 1973.

Doran, George. *The Chronicles of Barabbas.* New York: Rinehart, 1952.

Durham, Weldon B. "Commission on Training Camp Activities," q.v., *The United States in the First World War: An Encyclopedia,* edited by Anne Cipriano Venzon, 159–161 New York: Garland, 1995.

_____. "Fosdick, Raymond Blaine," q.v., *The United States in the First World War: An Encyclopedia,* edited by Anne Cipriano Venzon, 234–235. New York: Garland, 1995.

Edwards, Richard Henry. *Popular Amusements.* Vol 8 in *Studies in American Social Conditions.* New York: Association Press, 1915.

Egan, Maurice F., and John B. Kennedy. *Knights of Columbus in Peace and War.* 2 vols. New Haven, CT: Knights of Columbus, 1920.

Ekirch, Arthur. *The Civilian and the Military.* New York: Oxford University Press, 1956.

Evans, James W., and Gardner L. Harding. *Entertaining the American Army: The American Stage and Lyceum in the World War.* New York: Association Press, 1921.

Fleming, Thomas. *The Illusion of Victory: America in World War I.* New York: Basic Books, 2003.

Foner, Jack D. *United States Soldier Between Two Wars: Army Life and Reforms, 1865–1898.* New York: Humanities Press, 1970.

Fosdick, Raymond B. *Chronicle of a Generation: An Autobiography.* New York: Harper, 1958.

_____. *Report of the Chairman of Training Camp Activities.* Washington: U.S. Government Printing Office, 1917, 1918, and 1919.

Glenn, John Mark, and others. *Russell Sage Foundation, 1907–1946.* 2 vols. New York: Russell Sage Foundation, 1947.

Hansen, Marcus Lee. *Welfare Work in Iowa.* Iowa City: State Historical Society of Iowa, 1921.

Harrison, Harry P. *Culture Under Canvas: The Story of Tent Chautauqua*. New York: Hastings House, 1958.
Hicken, Victor. *The American Fighting Man*. New York: Macmillan, 1969.
Hirsch, Foster. *The Boys from Syracuse: The Shuberts' Theatrical Empire*. Carbondale: Southern Illinois University Press, 1998.
Hirschfeld, Charles. "The Transformation of American Life," in *World War I: A Turning Point in Modern History*, edited by Jack J. Roth 164–81. New York: Knopf, 1967.
Hornblow, Arthur. *A History of the Theatre in America*. Vol. II. New York: Lippincott, 1919, reissued by Blom, 1965.
Jowett, Garth. *Film: The Democratic Art*. Boston: Little, Brown, 1976.
Keene, Jennifer D. *Doughboys, the Great War, and the Remaking of America*. Baltimore: Johns Hopkins University Press, 2001.
Kennedy, David M. *Over Here: The First World War and American Society*. New York: Oxford University Press, 1980.
Kostic, Jeffrey. "War Risk Insurance," q.v., in *The United States in the First World War: An Encyclopedia*. New York: Garland p. 776.
Kraus, Richard. *Recreation and Leisure in Modern Society*. 4th ed. New York: HarperCollins, 1990.
Lenney, John Joseph. *Rankers: The Odyssey of the Enlisted Regular Soldier of America and Britain*. New York: Greenburg, 1950.
Lewis, Howard T. *The Motion Picture Industry*. New York: D. Van Nostrand, 1933.
Link, Arthur S., and Richard L. McCormick. *Progressivism*. Arlington Heights, IL.: Harlan Davidson, 1983.
Mangold, George M. *The Challenge of Saint Louis*. New York: Missionary Education Movement of the United States and Canada, 1917.
Matloff, Maurice, ed. *American Military History*. Rev. ed. Washington, DC: Office of the Chief of Military History, U.S. Army, 1989.
May, Henry F. *The End of American Innocence: A Study of the First Years of Our Own Time, 1912–1917*. New York: Knopf, 1959.
McClymer, John F. *War and Welfare: Social Engineering in America, 1890–1925*. Westport, CT: Greenwood Press, 1980.
McGerr, Michael. *A Fierce Discontent: The Rise and Fall of the Progressive Movement in America, 1870–1920*. New York: The Free Press, 2003.
Meloy, A. S. *Theatres and Picture Houses*. New York: Architects' Supply and Publishing, 1916.
Moody, Richard. "The Drama League," q. v., *The Cambridge Guide to American Theatre*, ed. Don B. Wilmeth and Tice L. Miller 1151–152. Cambridge: Cambridge University Press, 1993.
Moskos, Charles C. Jr. *The American Enlisted Man: The Rank and File of Today's Military*. New York: Russell Sage Foundation, 1970.
Munson, Edward L. *The Management of Men: A Handbook on the Systematic Development of Morale and the Control of Human Behavior*. New York: Holt, 1921.
Palmer, Frederick. *Newton D. Baker, America at War*. 2 vols. New York: Dodd, Mead and Co., 1931.
Paxson, Frederic Logan. *America at War: 1917–1919*. Vol. II of *American Democracy and the World War*. Boston: Houghton Mifflin, 1936.
Peck, Richard G. *The Rise and Fall of Camp Sherman*. Chillicothe: Peck Photography and Craftsman Printing, 1972.
Phillips-Matz, Mary Jane. *The Many Lives of Otto Kahn*. New York: Macmillan, 1963.
Poggi, Jack. *Theatre in America: The Impact of Economic Forces, 1880–1967*. Ithaca, NY: Cornell University Press, 1968.
Postlewait, Thomas. "The Hieroglyphic Stage: American Theatre and Society, Post–Civil War to 1945," in *The Cambridge History of American Theatre*, vol. 2: 1870–1045, edited by Don B. Wilmeth and Christopher Bigsby. Cambridge: Cambridge University Press, 1999.
Rieser, Arthur C. *The Chautauqua Moment: Protestants, Progressives and the Culture of Modern Liberalism*. New York: Columbia University Press, 2003.

Riley, Bell Irwin. *The Life of Billy Yank: The Common Soldier of the Union.* Garden City, New York: Doubleday and Company, Inc., 1952.
_____. *The Life of Johnny Reb: The Common Soldier of the Confederacy.* Garden City, NY: Doubleday, 1943.
Risch, Erna. *Quartermaster Support of the Army: A History of the Corps, 1775–1939.* Washington, DC: Quartermaster Historian's Office, Office of the Quartermaster General, 1962.
Schaeffer, Ronald. *America in the Great War: The Rise of the War Welfare State.* New York: Oxford University Press, 1991.
Schultz, James R. *The Romance of Small-Town Chautauquas.* Columbia: Univeristy of Missouri Press, 2002.
Sklar, Robert. *Movie-made America: A Cultural History of American Movies.* Rev. ed. New York: Vintage Books, 1994.
Slide, Anthony, ed. *The Encyclopedia of Vaudeville.* Westport, CT: Greenwood Press, 1994.
Soule, George. *Prosperity Decade: From War to Depression, 1917–1929.* Vol. VIII, *The Economic History of the United States,* edited by Ed. Henry David, et. al. New York: Harper and Row, Publishers, 1947.
Stagg, Jerry. *The Brothers Shubert.* New York: Ballantine Books, 1968.
Sussman, Warren E. *Culture as History: The Transformation of American Society in the Twentieth Century.* New York: Pantheon Books, 1984.
Tapia, John E. *Circuit Chautauqua: From Rural Education to Popular Entertainment in Early Twentieth Century America.* Jefferson, NC: McFarland, 1997).
U.S. Army War College. Historical Section. *Order of Battle of the United States Land Forces in the World War.* Washington: U.S. Government Printing Office, 1931.
U.S. Congress. House Committee on Military Affairs. *Hearing on Training Camp Activities: Statement of Mr. Raymond B. Fosdick,* March 14, 1918. Washington: U.S. Government Printing Office, 1918.
U.S. Interstate Commerce Commission. *Statistics of Railways in the United States for the Year Ended December 31, 1918.* Prepared by the Bureau of Statistics. Washington: U.S. Government Printing Office, 1920.
U.S. War Department. *Annual Reports.* Washington: U.S. Government Printing Office, 1918, 1919, and 1920.
_____. Bureau of Public Relations. Women's Interests Section. *The Soldier and his Recreation.* Washington: U.S. Government Printing Office, 1942.
_____. Commission on Training Camp Activities. "Liberty Theatres," address by Newton D. Baker at Camp Humphreys, Virginia, December 5, 1918. Washington: U.S. Government Printing Office, 1918.
_____. *Report of the Military Entertainment Committee.* Washington: U.S. Government Printing Office, 1919.
_____. *War Department Correspondence File, Revised Edition.* Washington: U.S. Government Printing Office, 1918.
Venzon, Anne Cipriano, ed. *The United States in the First World War: An Encyclopedia.* New York: Garland Publishing, 1995.
Ward, Larry Wayne. *The Motion Picture Goes to War: The U.S. Government Film Effort during World War I.* Ann Arbor, MI: UMI Research Press, 1981, 1985.
Weibe, Robert. *The Search for Order, 1877–1920.* New York: Hill and Wang, 1967.
Weigley, Russell F. *History of the United States Army.* New York: Macmillan, 1984.
Wisbey, Herbert A. *Soldiers without Swords: A History of the Salvation Army in the United States.* New York: Macmillan, 1955.
Wittke, Carl. *Tambo and Bones: A History of the American Minstrel Stage.* Durham, NC: Duke University Press, 1930.
Young, Arthur P. "War Camp Community Service," q.v. *The United States in the First World War: An Encyclopedia,* edited by Anne Cipriano Venzon, 773–774 New York: Garland, 1995.
Young Men's Christian Association, International Committee. *Service With Fighting Men.* 2 vols. New York: Association Press, 1922.

_____, National War Work Council. *Summary of World War Work of the American YMCA.* New York: Association Press, 1920.
Zeidman, Irving. *The American Burlesque Show.* New York: Hawthorn Books Publishers, 1967
Zieger, Robert H. *America's Great War: World War I and the American Experience.* Lanham: Rowman & Littlefield, 2000.
Zimmerman, Phyllis A. *The Neck of the Bottle: George W. Goethals and the Reorganization of the U.S. Army Supply System, 1917–1918.* College Station: Texas A&M University Press, 1992.

Periodicals

ARTICLES

"Armed Forces Recreation." *Parks and Recreation* 6 (August 1971): 67–69.
"Bad News for the USO." *Newsweek* 79 (31, 1972): 54–55.
Baldwin, Fred. "The Invisible Armor." *American Quarterly* 16 (Fall 1964): 432–444.
Bergreen, Lawrence. "Oh! How He Hated to Get up in the Morning." *MHQ: The Quarterly Journal of Military History* 2, no. 4, (1992): 72–80.
Bierman, Margaret G. "Self-Sufficiency Target of Military Recreation." *Government Product News* 22 (March 1983): 32–34.
Bogard, Morris R. "Drama League of America." *Dramatics Magazine*, 37 (November 1965): 45–48.
Burnham, John C. "The Progressive Era Revolution in American Attitudes toward Sex." *The Journal of American History* 59 (March 1973): 890–97.
Camfield, Thomas M. "'Will to Win'—The U.S. Army Troop Morale Program of World War I." *Military Affairs.* 41(October 1977): 125–128.
Christenberry, C. W. "Recreation and the Personnel of the Armed Forces." *Recreation* 45 (February 1952): 483–486
Cocks, Orin G. "Applying Standards to Motion Picture Films." *The Survey,* June 27, 1914: 337–38.
Davis, Allen F. "Welfare, Reform, and World War I." *American Quarterly* 19 (Fall 1967): 516–533.
"The Decay of Vaudeville." *American Magazine* 69 (April 1910): 842–48.
DeLay, Ted S. "The Armed Forces Radio Service." *Speech Monographs* 20 (November 1953): 300–5.
Denfeld, D. Colt. "World War I Mobilization Camps." *The Journal of America's Military Past* 29 (Fall–Winter 2002): 28–54.
Denkin, Harvey. "William A. Brady." *The Passing Show* (Newsletter of the Shubert Archive, 5 (Winter 1981): 2–3.
Durham, Weldon B. "'Big Brother' and the 'Seven Sisters': Camp Life Reforms in World War I." *Military Affairs* 42 (April 1978): 57–60.
_____. "The Revival and Decline of the Stock Company Mode of Organization, 1886–1930." *Theatre History Studies* 6 (1986): 165–188.
_____. "The Tightening Rein: Relations between the Federal Government and American Theatre Industry during World War One." *Educational Theatre Journal* 30 (1978): 387–97.
"Edward Lippincott Tilton." *Architectural Forum* 58 (February 1933), 12.
"Edward Lippincott Tilton." *The New International Yearbook* 1933, p. 583.
"Entertainment for the Armed Forces." *Theatre Arts Monthly* 27 (March 1943): 134–196.
Exner, M. J. "Prostitution and Its Relation to the Army on the Mexican Border." *Social Hygiene* 3 (April 1917): 206–14.
Gephart, W. F. "War Risk Insurance Act of the United States." *American Economic Review* 8 (March 1918), 195–202.
Going, Clayton. "They're the CATS." *New York Time Magazine,* May 15, 1949, p. 58.
Harden, Pat. "Armed Forces Recreation Services: Our Hallowed Ground raison d'etre." *Parks and Recreation* 29 (December 1994): 24–25.

Kase, C. R. "AETA Overseas Touring." *Educational Theatre Journal* 11 (December 1959): 291–95.
Kirschner, Don S. "The Perils of Pleasure: Commercial Recreation, Social Disorder and Moral Reform in the Progressive Era." *American Studies* 21, no. 2 (1980): 27–42.
Knapp, Gretchen. "Experimental Social Policy Making during World War II: The United Service Organizations (USO) and American War Community Services (AWCS)." *Journal of Policy History* 12 (2000): 321–38.
Knapp, Richard F. "The Playground and Recreation Association in World War I." *Parks and Recreation* 7 (January 1972): 27–31, 110–112.
Lindsay, M. "Purpose and Scope of War Risk Insurance." American Academy of Political and Social Sciences. *Annals* 79 (September 1918). 52–68.
Lippman, Monroe. "Battle for Bookings: The Independents Challenge the Trust." *Tulane Drama Review* 2 (February 1958): 38–45.
———. "Death of the Salesmen's Monopoly." *Theatre Survey* 1 (1960): 65–81.
———. "The First Organized Revolt Against the Theatrical Syndicate." *The Quarterly Journal of Speech*, 41 (December 1955): 343–351.
Love, Thomas B. "The Social Significance of War Risk Insurance." American Academy of Political and Social Sciences. *Annals* 79 (September 1918): 49–52.
MacKaye, Percy, "The War and Broadway." *Theatre Magazine* 17 (April 1918), 203–204.
Malone, Diane B. "A Survey of Early Military Theatre in America." *Theatre Survey* 16 (1975): 56–64.
Mock, James Robert, and Cedric Larson. "Morale — The Soul of the Army." *Frontiers of Democracy* 7 (1941): 237–239.
Moses, Montrose. "Keeping the Soldier Amused." *Theatre Magazine.* 17 (January 1918), 16.
Moulton, R. H. "Semi-military Buildings in the National Army Cantonments." *Architectural Record.* 44 (July 1918): 21–30.
Oglebay, Kate. "Recreational Work in Training Camps." *The Drama League Monthly* 3 (October 1917): 4, 441.
Scheff, A. "Fifth Army's Theatre Program." *Theatre Arts* 37 (June 1953): 80.
Sharpless, D. R. "To Be of Special Services." *Parks and Recreation* 6 (May 1971): 36–7, 45–52.
Simon, Louis M. "Theatre in the Camps." *Theatre Arts* 26 (July 1942): 423–428.
"Smile and the World Smiles with You." *Theatre Magazine* 17 (May 1918): 280.
Tannenbaum, Frank. "Moral Devastation of War." *Dial* 46 (April 5, 1919): 333–336.
"Theatre for the Army Camps." *Theatre Arts* 25 (October 1941): 699–700
"Typhoon Jane." *Time* 99 (3, 1972): 71.
"War Recreation Services of Federal and National Agencies." *Recreation* 37 (June 1943): 132–38.
Wise, Michael S. "Military Recreation: Can You Use It?" *Parks and Recreation* 56 (October 1992): 56–59, 87.

Camp Newspapers

Camp Beauregard, Louisiana
Camp Custer, Michigan
Camp Devens News, Camp Devens, Massachusetts, September 1917.
Camp Dix, New Jersey
Camp Dix News, Camp Dix, New Jersey, August 1917 — January 1918.
Camp Dix Pictorial Review, Camp Dix, New Jersey, November 1917 — April 1919.
Camp Dodger, Camp Dodge, Iowa, October 1917 — February 1919.
Camp Fremont, California
Camp Funston, Kansas
Camp Gordon, Georgia
Camp Grant, Illinois
Camp Grant Roll-Call Camp Grant, Illinois, August 1918 — October 1919.
Camp Jackson Click, Camp Jackson, South Carolina, October 1918 December 1918.

Camp Meade Herald, Camp Meade, Maryland, September 1917 — December 1918.
Camp Meade, Maryland
Camp Pike Carry-on, Camp Pike, Arkansas, November 1918 — August 1919.
Camp Sheridan Reveille, Camp Sheridan, Montgomery, Alabama.
Camp Sherman News, Camp Sherman, Ohio, November 1917 — July 1919.
Camp Upton, New York
Custer Life, Camp Custer, Michigan, November 1918 — January 1919.
Merritt Dispatch, Camp Merritt, New Jersey, January 1919 — August 1919.
Trench and Camp, YMCA Camp Newspaper

Civilian Newspapers

Billboard, 1918–1919.
New York *Clipper* 1917–1919.
New York Dramatic Mirror, 1917–1919.
New York Times, 1918–2001.
Variety, 1917–1919.

Dissertations

Baldwin, Fred D. "The American Enlisted Man in World War I." PhD. diss., Princeton University, 1964.
Bogard, Morris R. "The Drama League of America: A History and Critical Analysis of its Activities and Achievements." PhD diss, University of Illinois, 1962.
Heberling, Lynn O'Neal. "Soldiers in Grease Paint: USO Camp Shows Inc., during World War II." PhD diss., Kent State University, 1989.
Knapp, Richard F. "Play for America: The National Recreation Association, 1906–1950." PhD diss., Duke University, 1971.
Lippman, Monroe. "The History of the Theatrical Syndicate: Its Effect on the Theatre in America." PhD diss., University of Michigan, 1937.

Online Resources

Hipps, Tim. "Soldier Show set to take 'The Heart of the Soldier' on the road." *http://www.armymwr.com/portal/news/display.asp?NEWS_ID=472* Accessed March 3, 2005
The Internet Broadway Database. *www.ibdb.com* Accessed 2001–2005.
The Internet Movie Database. *www.imbd.com*. Accessed 2001–2005.
1996 Annual Report, Morale, Welfare and Recreation Service of the Department of the Army. *http://www.armymwr.com/mwr/annual_report/mwrfy96.pdf* Accessed August 28, 2001.
1997 Annual Report, Morale, Welfare and Recreation Service of the Department of the Army. *http://www.armymwr.com/mwr/annual_report/mwrfy97.pdf* Accessed August 28, 2001.
1998 Annual Report, Morale, Welfare and Recreation Service of the Department of the Army. *http://www.armymwr.com/mwr/planning/mwrfy98.pdf* Accessed August 28, 2001.
1999 Annual Report, Morale, Welfare and Recreation Service of the Department of the Army. *http://www.armymwr.com/mwr/planning/mwrfy99.pdf* Accessed August 28, 2001.

Unpublished Sources

National Archives

Fosdick, Raymond B. "Report of the Chairman of Training Camp Activities," 1921, (manuscript 1921).
Record Group 92: Office of the Quartermaster General, Classified Files, 1915–1922; General Correspondence, 1917–1922; Construction Division Completion Reports.
Record Group 94: Records of the Adjutant General's Office.

Record Group 165: Records of the War Department General Staff, contains Records of Discontinued Divisions, Branches, Sections, and Boards, 1888–1924, which includes Records of the Commission on Training Camp Activities. See Entry 393, Numbered Correspondence, 1918–1919; Entry 394, Correspondence with Civilians and Civilian Agencies; Entry 395, Reports Relating to Training Camp Activities; Entry 396, Miscellaneous Correspondence, 1917; Entry 399, Reports, 1918–1919; Entry 400, Miscellaneous Correspondence, Dramatics Department, 1918; and, Entry 402, Bulletins of the Department of Dramatic Activities.

Unpublished Materials in the U.S. Army Military History Research Collection, Carlisle Barracks, Pennsylvania

Private Papers

Cleveland Public Library, Clipping Files.
Correspondence (1900 to 1970)
Legal and Financial Records (1900 to 1979)
Press and Publicity Material (1900–)
Raymond B. Fosdick Papers, Seeley G. Mudd Manuscript Library. Princeton University.
Shubert Archives. The Shubert Theatrical Corporation purchased the assets of the Klaw and Erlanger Exchange in the mid–1920s, thereby acquiring such correspondence, legal and financial records, contracts, manuscripts and music as the exchange had acquired and saved. These papers have been integrated into the Special Collections of the Shubert Archive, including:

Index

Aberdeen Proving Ground, Aberdeen, Maryland 153
Addams, Jane 35
admission tax 157
Agar, John G. 39
Al Fields' Minstrels 138
Albee, E.F. 62, 84, 145–146, 158
alcohol, abuse of 24, 27, 28, 34
Allardt Circuit (vaudeville) 50, 145
American Library Association 11, 43, 90
American Red Cross 39, 90, 168
American theatre as a cultural institution 2–3
America's Answer 144
Anderson, F. Richard 63, 84, 96
Armed Forces Professional Entertainment Branch 167–168
Armed Forces Recreation Society 168
The Army Frolic 127
Army Sanitary Corps 44
art theatres 3
Attaboy 153
Atwell, Roy 128

Bacon, Frank 128
Baker, Elsie 118
Baker, Newton D. 17, 21, 28, 29–30, 32–33, 36–42, 50, 66, 69, 88, 89, 101, 106, 111, 159–160, 171, 176
Baker, Paul 167
Ballard, Frederick 132
Bayes, Nora 51, 138
The Beauty Squad 127
The Beaux' Stratagem 23
Belasco, David 84
Believe Me, Xantippe 132
Belmont, August, Jr. 85
Berlin, Irving 84, 123, 153
Bell, C.W. 131

Better Business Bureaus of the War Camp Community Service 42
The Better 'Ole 123
A Bit o' Broadway 148
Blackstone, Harry 138
Boteler, Wade 152
Bourdieu, Pierre 19
Braddock, Harold 67, 90–92
Bradford, Col. William 24
Brady, William A. 57, 105–106
The Brat 131
Braucher, H.S. 86
The Bride Shop 124
Bringing Up Father 127
Bristow, Nancy K. 1, 20–21, 141
British Army, Revolutionary War, theatre 23–24
Brooks, George 152
Brown, Moreland 127, 133, 140–141
Bryan, William Jennings 117
Buell, Maj. James A. 160
Buffalo Auditorium, Camp Upton, Yaphank, Long Island, New York 77, 178, 187
Bureau of Social Hygiene 30
bureaucratization of the imaginative 18, 111, 115, 120, 171–176
Burke, Kenneth 18

Camp Beauregard, Alexandria, Louisiana 76, 80, 134, 152, 178, 185
Camp Bowie, Fort Worth, Texas 76, 79, 80, 178, 185
Camp Cody, Deming, New Mexico 75, 76, 80, 149, 178, 185
Camp Custer, Battle Creek, Michigan 67, 70, 74, 177, 185
Camp Devens, Ayer, Massachusetts 63, 67, 70, 74, 122, 135, 152, 177, 185
Camp Dix, Wrightstown, New Jersey 74, 123, 128, 135, 146, 177, 185

213

214 Index

Camp Dodge, Des Moines, Iowa 74, 133, 135, 149, 177, 185
Camp Doniphan, Fort Sill, Oklahoma 76, 133, 178, 185
Camp Eustis, Lee Hall, Virginia 40, 80, 81, 82, 179, 185
Camp Franklin, Baltimore, Maryland 178, 186
Camp Fremont, Palo Alto, California 76, 149, 178, 185
Camp Funston, Fort Riley, Kansas 74, 152, 177, 185
Camp Gordon, Atlanta, Georgia 74, 133, 177, 186
Camp Grant, Rockford, Illinois 67, 71, 74, 91, 151, 177, 186
Camp Greene, Charlotte, North Carolina 80, 178, 186
Camp Hancock, Augusta, Georgia 76, 80, 178, 186
Camp Humphreys, Belvoir, Virginia 17, 40, 74, 151, 179, 186
Camp Jackson, Columbia, South Carolina 74, 125, 177, 186
Camp Kearny, San Diego, California 74, 149, 178, 186
Camp Knox, West Point, Kentucky 40, 80, 179, 186
Camp Las Casas, San Juan, Puerto Rico 80, 186
Camp Lee, Petersburg, Virginia 73, 74, 80, 177, 186
Camp Lewis, Tacoma, Washington 74, 148–149, 150, 177, 186
Camp Logan, Houston, Texas 76, 80, 178, 186
Camp MacArthur, Waco, Texas 76, 80, 178, 186
Camp McClellan, Anniston, Alabama 77, 80, 178, 186
Camp Meade, Baltimore, Maryland 72–74, 151, 177, 186
Camp Meigs, Washington, D.C. 153
Camp Merritt, Tenafly, New Jersey 40, 72–75, 124, 127, 134, 179, 186
Camp Mills, Mineola, New York 40, 179, 186
Camp Pike, Little Rock, Arkansas 70, 74, 134, 149, 178, 186
Camp Sevier, Greenville, South Carolina 77–78, 178, 186
Camp Shelby, Hattiesburg, Mississippi 178
Camp Sheridan, Montgomery, Alabama 135, 178
Camp Sherman, Chillicothe, Ohio 10–12, 67, 70, 74, 119, 149, 162, 178, 187
Camp Shows, Inc. 164–167
Camp Stuart, Newport News, Virginia 40, 74, 75. 179, 187
Camp Taylor, Louisville, Kentucky 70, 74, 109, 136, 149, 178, 187
Camp Travis, San Antonio, Texas 78–79, 149, 152, 178, 187
Camp Upton, Yaphank, Long Island, New York 73–74, 77, 123, 127, 128, 153, 162, 178, 187
Camp Wadsworth, Spartanburg, South Carolina 76, 153, 178, 187
Camp Wheeler, Macon, Georgia 76, 178, 187
Campbell, Craig W. 142
Candler, Asa G. 90
canteen checks 93
Cantonment Division (later Construction Division) Office of the Quartermaster General 5, 52, 68–70, 72–73
Cantor, Eddie 4
Carroll, Earl 124
Carter, Charles J. (magician) 138
Cato 24
Chapin, R.C. 80
Cheating Cheaters 130
Cheney, Sheldon 58
Christenberry, Brig. Gen. C.W. 167
Churchill's Girls 127
Civilian Actress Technicians (CATS) 167
Clark, Barrett 151
Clayton Antitrust Act 17
Clipper (New York) entertainment (trade newspaper) 133
Coburn, Mr. and Mrs. Charles 123
Cocks, Orrin G. 139–141
Cohan, George M. 51, 84, 130
Collier, John 59, 120, 139
Columbia Amusement Company 12, 84, 126, 127
Come On In 143
commercial entertainment and recreation 34–35, 48–51, 171
Commission on Training Camp Activities (CTCA): achievement of 2, 16, 47, 154–155, 160, 161, 175–176; Athletic Division 38, 44; criticism of 46, 133–137; demobilization 159–162; Department of Camp Music 44, 46; financial affairs 46, 51–53, 62, 76, 85–95, 175–176; Law Enforcement Division 2, 37, 43–44; legacies 4–5, 21, 160, 161, 162–170, 175, 176; Liberty Theatre Division 44, 74, 108–115, 161; Military Entertainment Committee 76, 98–115, 127, 146, 160; purpose of 3, 21, 28, 32, 36–47, 50, 58, 117, 171; relations with Congress 51, 53, 85, 101; relations with entertainment industry 17–18, 37, 38, 53, 58–61, 84–88, 94–115, 140–41, 156–158, 171–175; relations with military 53, 66, 70, 87–88, 134, 152; Social Hygiene Division 44; strategies of 1, 19, 22, 28. 35, 36–47, 48–51, 53–54, 66–68, 82, 87, 101–115, 127–130, 172–175; theatrical producer 121–122, 128–130
Committee on Military Affairs, U.S. House of Representatives 78

Committee on Public Information 144
common soldier, social reputation of 23, 27–28
Concert performers, booking of 137–138
Connolly, Mark Thomas 33
Continental Army, Revolutionary War 24
Continental Congress 24
Conwell, Russell 117
Cooley, Hollis 103, 105, 110, 119, 133
cost-plus construction contracts 53, 73
Couzens, James 87, 90, 109
Cox, George B. 104
Crothers, Rachel 50–52, 61–62
Curtis, Sam 147
Cushing, Catherine Chisholm 131

Daddy Long-Legs 131
Darktown Follies 138
Davis, Allen F. 16
De Angelis, Jefferson 124–125
de Lisser, Horace 86
Demobilization, World War I 83, 154, 159–162
Department of Defense Entertainment Project 167
Department of Dramatic Activities Among the Soldiers 151, 154
DePuy, Clifford 90
Dickinson, John 46–47
Dirks, Rudolph 12
District Directors, CTCA 43
Donnelly, Dorothy 12
Dowling, Eddie 164
draftees: characteristics of 40–41, 117; pay of 13
Drama League of America 48–49, 54, 108, 110, 112, 150–151, 172
Drama League of New York 48–49, 54, 112
Dramatic Sub-section, Camp Activities Section, Education and Recreation Branch, Morale Branch, General Staff 161
Dressler, Marie 51, 138
Duncan, Isadora Dancers 112, 138
DuPuy, Clifford 90

Eagan, John J. 98, 108
Edwards, Richard Henry 34–35
Ellsworth Musical Stock Company 149–150
Emergency Construction Committee of the Council of National Defense 52, 65–65, 68
Emerson, John 143
Empey, Arthur Guy 143
entertainment: in Civil War camps 25–26; in frontier posts 24, 26–27
entertainment industry: relations with the federal government 156–158
Erlanger, Abraham 55, 84, 128, 146

Fair and Warmer 131, 133, 134
Federal Reserve Act 17

Federal Trade Commission 17
Federal Works Agency 164
Field, Salisbury 131
field of large-scale cultural production 19–20
field of restricted production 19–20, 48–49, 176
Fields' Minstrels 138
Finance Committee, United States Senate 157
Fiske, Harrison Grey 58
Flo, Flo 124
Flora Bella 12, 14, 123
Fort Myers, Virginia, officer training camp 51–52
Fosdick, Harry Emerson 30
Fosdick, Raymond B. 17, 30–32, 36–44, 51–52, 58–59, 61–62, 64–65, 70, 78, 85–89, 96–101, 105–108, 111, 126, 137, 145, 159, 171, 172, 174
Foy, Eddie 147
Francis, Kittie Vaudeville Revue 147
Friendly Enemies 130
Frohman, Charles 55
Frohman, Daniel 61, 108
Fulton, Maude 131
Furs and Frills 124

Gatti-Cazazza, Guilio 84
Gerard, James 143
Gibson, Charles Dana 85
Gish, Dorothy 144
Gish, Lillian 144
Goldberg, Jack 126
Golden, John 84, 128
Great Lakes Naval Training Camp 51
The Great Love 144
The Greatest Thing in Life 144
Gribble, Harry Wagstaff 153
Griffith, D.W. 144
Guggenheim, Daniel 85

Hackett, Walter 132
Hamilton, Cosmo 14, 123
Hammerstein, Arthur 84
Hanmer, Lee 37–38, 48–50, 53–54, 62–68, 84–88, 96–100, 102, 104, 106, 108, 119, 120, 126, 133, 139–140, 150–151, 161, 171, 174, 175
Hans und Fritz 12, 127
Harding, Maj. J.W. 150
Harris, Sam 51, 61, 84
Harrison, Harry P. 66–68, 86–92, 95, 108–109, 116–119, 136, 137
Have a Heart 122
Hayman, Alfred 56
Hazzard, John E. 128
Hearn, Lew and Bonita 147
Hearts of the World 144
Hein, Silvio 124
Henpecked Henry 127
Henry Street Settlement, New York City 30

Her Soldier Boy 121, 135
Herbert, Victor 123–124
Here Comes the Bride 102, 128–129, 134
Hill, Gus 12
His Bridal Night 131
Hoblitzelle, Karl 78–79
Hoffman, Aaron 130
Hopkins, Arthur 84
Hopwood, Avery 131
Hornblow, Arthur 58, 137
Hostess Houses of the YWCA 43
Hubbell, Raymond 123
The Hun Within 144
Hyman, E.L. 141–145

Ingram, Francis 137
International Association of Rotary Clubs 90
Interstate Amusement Company 78–79
Intolerance: Love's Struggle Through the Ages 144
Ireland, Maj. Thomas R. 167
isolationism, post-WWI 162
It Pays to Advertise 132

Janis, Elsie 51–52
Jewish Welfare Board 11, 42, 164, 166
Joint Army and Navy Committee on Welfare and Recreation 163
Joy, Maj. Jason S. 160
Julliard, August D. 85

Kahn, Otto 54, 61, 90, 172
Kaiser, The Beast of Berlin 144
Kálmán, Emerich 121
Keating-Owen Act 17
Keith, Benjamin Franklin 62, 146, 158
Keith-Albee theatres 157
Kelly Field, San Antonio, Texas 75, 80, 179, 186
Keppel, F.R. 160
Kern, Jerome 121–122
Kick In 130
The Kiss Burglar 123
Klaw, Joseph 84, 102–103
Klaw, Marc 39, 54–65, 84–90, 94–95, 101–110, 119, 126, 127, 129, 133, 136, 138, 145–146, 150, 153, 156–158, 164, 174
Klaw and Erlanger Exchange 56, 62, 86, 102, 104–107, 110
Knights of Columbus 11, 42, 173
Koch, Frederick 150

Lanham Act 164
Lastfogel, Abe 164
Law, H. Robert 70
Lea, Frank 13, 15
League of Nations 161, 162
Leathem, Barclay 165
Lee, Joseph 38
Leftwich, Alexander 152

legitimate theatre vs. vaudeville 146
The Leroy Musical Stock Company 149
Liberty Entertainments 68, 137
Liberty Loans 157
Liberty Theatre, Camp Sherman, Ohio 11–16, 119; attractions, censorship of 110–113, 120, 140–141, 148, 149–150; criticism of 133–137; managers, appointment and supervision of 97–100, 109–110, 114–115; Manuscript Division 154; operations, financing 15, 45, 53, 62, 84–95; Publicity Department 109, 113; responsibilities of 92–93, 111, 113–115
Liberty Theatres: architecture 69–77, 119; attendance 16, 76, 79, 82–83, 92–93, 175, 182–184; box office receipts 15, 16, 46, 76, 79, 82, 92–94, 175–176, 182–184, 185–187; burlesque shows in 12, 125–127; construction of 63–65, 69–77, 80–81, 96–97, 175; cost of 63–64, 69–77, 80–82; expenses for talent 180–181; functionality 70–77; local operating expenses 92–94, 180–181; motion pictures in 105–106, 120, 138–145; Play Review Committee 110–113, 127; professional touring attractions in 16, 49, 62, 119–137; purposes of 45, 95, 100, 117, 120, 173; soldier shows in 22, 119, 150–154; stock companies 119–120, 148–150; success of 93–95, 114, 160; types of attractions 45, 111, 119–120; vaudeville bookings 120
The Liberty Vaudeville, Company 129
Lillard, W.L. 84
Lindsey, Judge Ben B. 118
Littell, Col. I.W. 52, 69
The Little Teacher 130
Loew, Marcus 139
Loos, Anita 143
The Love Mill 124
Love o' Mike 121, 122, 135
Lyle, Howard 124–125

MacDonough, Glen 123
Mack, Willard 130
MacKaye, Percy 58–60, 94
MacKaye, Steele 26
The Manhattan Girl Revue 127
March, Gen. Peyton C. 161
Marcin, Max 128, 130
Marshall, Gen. George C. 163
The Martini Girl Revue 127
Mason, Shirley 143
May, Henry F. 17
Mayer, Jasper J. 39. 64–65, 69–70, 84, 87–88, 95–101, 105, 108, 109, 134, 174
Mayo, Margaret 131
McBride, Malcolm 38, 50, 79, 87, 101–115, 119–121, 129, 134, 141, 148, 150–152, 159–161, 172
McGeer, Michael 18
McNutt, Paul V. 163
Megrue, Roi Cooper 132

melodrama, moral concerns about 111
Meloy, A.S. 74
Mercedes (mind-reader) 91
The Merchant of Venice 26
Mexican border hostilities, 1916 29, 37, 59
Military Affairs Committee, U.S. Senate 51
military camp life 2
Military Entertainment Committee CTCA *see* Commission on Training Camp Activities, Military Entertainment Committee)
Military Entertainment Council Smileage Fund 90
Million Dollar Doll(s) 127, 133
The Mimic World aka *The Junior Mimic World* 126
Ministerial Union of San Antonio 79
Minnix, Allen C. 73
minstrel shows, booking of 138
mobilization: World War I 1, 2, 9–10, 40, 101; World War II 162–163
Montgomery, James 132, 136
Morale Branch, General Staff; World War II; Welfare and Recreation Division; Recreation Section 81, 163
Morale Division, Office of the Adjutant General 163
Morale Division, War Department General Staff 163
Morale, Welfare, and Recreation (MWR), U.S. Army Community and Family Support Center 22, 168–169
Morosco, Oliver 124
Morris, William 146
Motion Picture Division Military Entertainment Committee 145
motion pictures, camp bookings of 138–145
Mott, John R. 38
Mumford, Ethel Watts 131
Munson, Gen. Edward L. 160, 163
Murdoch, James E. 26
musicals, camp bookings of 119–125
Mutt and Jeff Divorced 127, 133
My Four Years in Germany 143
My Own United States 143

National Army camps 9
National Association of the Motion Picture Industry (NAMPI) 106, 140–141, 158
National Board of Review of Motion Pictures 37, 139–141
National Catholic Community Service 164, 166
National Guard camps 9
National Theatre Conference 165
Neill, Charles P. 39, 64
Neville, Harry 151, 152
New York Dramatic Mirror 58, 113, 135, 157
New York Morning Telegraph 105
New York Review 104–106

Nicholls, Samuel J. (U.S. Rep., South Carolina) 78
Nirdlinger-Nixon, Fred 56
noncommercial theatre 3, 58–59
Nothing But the Truth 132, 135, 136

Oglebay, Kate 22, 54, 108–109, 112, 138, 150–151, 175
Oh, Boy 122
Oh! Lady! Lady! 122
The Only Girl 124
The Orpheum Follies 149
Over the Top 143
Over There (song by George M. Cohan) 51
Over There Theatre League 42
Overseas Touring Project American Educational Theatre Association (AETA) 5, 167

Pack Up Your Troubles in Your Old Kit Bag and Smile, Smile, Smile (song by George Asaf and Felix Powell) 121
Parlor, Bedroom, and Bath 131
Pearson, Arthur 127
Pennsylvania Chautauqua Circuit 67, 117
Perry, Clarence A. 48–50, 61
Perry and Gorman's "Circusland" 138
Pershing, John J. 29
Pershing's Crusaders 144
Pierce, Howard O. 109
Pierce, Gen. Palmer E. 39
Pierson, Paul 67, 117
Plattsburg camps 40–41
Playground and Recreation Association of America 37–38, 42, 86
Pollack, Beatrice 133
Pollyanna 131
Powell, Maud 137
Powers, P.A. 106
Prescott, John 136
The Princess Pat 124
privately owned theatres in camps 50–51, 66, 77–79
Producers and Distributors War Camp Motion Pictures Committee 106
Production and distribution practices: burlesque theatres 125–127; legitimate theatres 120; motion pictures 120, 142; vaudeville theatres 147

The Queen of the Movies 127

Ratto, John 118
Raycroft, Joseph 38
Reber, J. Howard 108–115, 119, 135–136, 146, 149, 160–161, 172
recreation movement 21–22, 35, 37–38
Redpath Lyceum Bureau 66–68, 88, 109, 116–119
reform process 4
Regular Army 9, 161, 162

Reid, Louis R. 157
Report of the Military Entertainment Committee of the War Department 5, 92, 114, 119, 126, 127, 141, 147, 182, 183
Reynold's Minstrels 138
Rhoda Royal Circus 138
The Rialto Girl Revue 127
Richard III 26
Ridgeway, Katherine 118
Rising, Lawrence 131
Rochester, W.R. 151
Rock, William 148
Rock and White Revue 148
Rockefeller, John D., Jr. 30
Romberg, Sigmund 121
Rorer, Sarah Tyson 118
Rose, Harry 147
Rotary International 90
Royal Dragoons 118
Russell Sage Foundation 37, 48, 59, 85, 151

Salvation Army 11, 43, 164
San Jose State University 5
Sanger, W. Prentice 39
Sargent, Franklin Haven 108, 127, 151–153, 175
Savage, Henry W. 84
Schaeffer, Ronald 2
Schumann Quintet 118
Scribner, Sam 84, 126, 127
Seamens, E.R. 50–51
sectarian welfare agencies, war work of 2, 10, 41–43, 68
Selective Service System 156
Sheldon, James 168
Sheppard, Senator Morris 51
Shipman, Samuel 130
Shubert, Jacob J. 56, 146
Shubert, Lee 56, 60, 84, 105, 107, 121–122, 146
Shubert, Sam S. 56
Shubert Archives 6
Shubert Theatre Corporation 56–57, 60–62, 104–107, 121–122, 146
Shubert-Theatrical Syndicate relations 56–57, 84, 104–107, 146
Sick-a-Bed 131
Smileage 46, 75, 86, 89–93, 95, 135, 136, 137, 174
Smith, Harry B. 121
Smith, Harry James 130
Smith, Richard R. 109–110, 138, 140, 141, 160
Smith, Winchell 84, 128
So Long, Letty 124
soldier pastimes: Civil War 25–26; frontier 24–25, 26–28; Revolutionary War 23–24
soldier shows 150–154
Special Service Division, Army Service Force (ASF) 22, 163–168
Square Deal Associations, War Camp Community Service 42

Stage Women's War Relief 49–52, 54, 61, 89
Starrett, W.A. 52, 64
Step Lively, Girls 127
Stimson, Henry L. 163
stock companies, camp booking of 148–150
Stop! Look! Listen! 123, 133, 136
Strong, Austin 154
Sussman, Warren 18
Swan, Mark 131
Sydney, Thomas (Sidney Smith and Augustus Thomas) 121
symbolic goods 19

tab shows 126–127
Tannenbaum, Frank 46
temperance 33–34
tent chautauqua 66–68, 116–119
theatre closings, influenza epidemic 157
theatrical booking 2, 55–57
theatrical business conditions 3, 62, 65
theatrical production practices 2
theatrical reforms 19–20
Theatrical Syndicate aka Theatrical Trust 56–57
theatrical touring 3, 55–57
The Thirteenth Chair 130
Thomas, Augustus 108, 121, 154
Tichenor, John S. 152
Tick Tock Girl 127
ticket prices 182–183
Tiffany, Maud 147
Tilton, Edward Lippincott 63–66, 68–77, 96
Tinney, Frank 153
To Hell with the Kaiser 143
Towse, John Rankin 137
The Trail of the Lonesome Pine 130
training camps, abandonment and dismantling of 162
Travelers Aid Society 164
Travis, Dehull N. 109, 113
Travis, John 127
Traxler, D.B. 78
A Trip to Chinatown 124–125
Truex, Earnest 143
Turn to the Right! 128–129, 134
Twin Beds 131

The Unbeliever 143
United Booking Office 62, 84, 146, 158
United Manager's Protective Association 54, 59–61
United Service Organizations, Inc. (USO) 4, 22, 164–167, 168
United States Amusement Company 146
U.S. Army Community and Family Support Center, U.S. Department of Defense 22, 168
United States Fuel Administration 156
United States Railroad Administration 156
United War Work Campaign 39, 157

Index

University of Oregon 5
USO Shows 167

Vanity Fair 127
Variety (entertainment trade newspaper) 113, 122, 125, 129
vaudeville, camp bookings of 145–148
Vawter, Keith 116
Veiller, Bayard 130
Very Good Eddie 121, 122, 126, 134
Veterans' Hospital Camp Shows 166
Victor, Leon 121
Villa, Francisco 29
Volstead Act 39
volunteerism 36, 41–43

Wadsworth, Eliot 39
Waikiki Hawaiians 118
Wakefield, Willa Holt 148
Wald, Lillian 30
Wallace, R.S. 134
Walter, Eugene 130
Walter Reed Army Hospital, Washington, D.C. 93
War Camp Community Services (WCCS) 38, 42, 163, 172
War Camp Motion Picture Committee 106
War Plans Division, General Staff, U.S. Army 159
Watch Your Step 123
Ways and Means Committee, U.S. House of Representatives 156
Webster, Jean 131
Weibe, Robert 18

Welfare and Recreation Division Morale Branch, War Department, General Staff 163
Welfare League of the 367th Infantry Camp Upton, Yaphank, Long Island, New York 77
Wells, Glen and Mara Conover Wells 118
Whirl o' Girls 127
White, Francis 148
Whitfield, Lieutenant R.P. 161
Who Stole the Hat 153
The Wilkes Players 148
Willis, Frank B. 118
Wilson, Woodrow 28, 29, 30, 32, 36, 47, 117, 161–162, 163
Winter, William 58, 137
With Love and Kisses 127, 133
Wood, Joe 126
Woods, Al 84
Wooldridge, Capt. W.P. 160
Woolworth, F.W. 90
World Film Corporation 106

The Yankee Princess 127
Yip, Yip Yaphank 153
YMCA Triangle Entertainments 68
You Know Me Al! 153
Young, Rida Johnson 121
Young Men's Christian Association (YMCA) 2, 11, 21, 35, 38, 42, 49, 67–68, 77, 139, 152, 164, 165, 172, 173
Young Women's Christian Association (YWCA) 21, 38, 43, 164, 165

Zimmerman, Fred 56

www.ingramcontent.com/pod-product-compliance
Lightning Source LLC
Chambersburg PA
CBHW032053300426
44116CB00007B/724